Alice, The Enigma

A Biography of Queen Victoria's Daughter,
Princess Alice, Grand Duchess of Hesse-and-by-
Rhine

Christina Croft

A Hilliard & Croft Book

Acknowledgement

I would like to thank Her Majesty, Queen Elizabeth II, for her kind permission to quote from Queen Victoria's online journals.

Contents

Who's Who..7

Prologue...11

Chapter 1 – To Whom Much Is Given...............13

Chapter 2 - What a joyous childhood we had!.........32

Chapter 3 – A Vain Little Thing.......................48

Chapter 4 – Our Little Riots...........................57

Chapter 5 – The Real Separation from Childhood...68

Chapter 6 – A Very dear Companion.................76

Chapter 7 – Her Future is Still Undecided...........86

Chapter 8 – A Very Dear Good Fellow..............101

Chapter 9 – Everything Has Changed...............109

Chapter 10 – A Strange Sort of Presentiment.......121

Chapter 11 – Mute Distracted Despair..............129

Chapter 12 – Strength of Mind & Self-Sacrifice...138

Chapter 13 - A Love Which Increases Daily.......147

Chapter 14 – How Wonderfully We Are Made....165

Chapter 15 – She Should Accommodate Herself To My Habits...178

Chapter 16 – The Uncertainty of Life...............189

Chapter 17 – This Too Horrid War.................200

Chapter 18 – This Mad, Wicked Folly of Women's Rights...210

Chapter 19 – To Love One's Grief.................218

Chapter 20 – How Far From Well I Am............230

Chapter 21 – Dear Papa!............................241

Epilogue..247

Who's Who

AFFIE (Alfred) (1844-1900) Alice's younger brother

ALBERT (1819-1861) Prince of Saxe-Coburg & Gotha; Prince Consort; Alice's father

ALICE, (1843-1878) Princess of Great Britain, Grand Duchess of Hesse-and-by-Rhine; Queen Victoria's second daughter

ALIX (1872-1918) Alice's fourth daughter

ANNA (1843-1865) Princess of Hesse; Alice's sister-in-law

ARTHUR (1850-1942) Duke of Connaught and Strathearn; Alice's younger brother

BEATRICE (1857-1944) Alice's youngest sister

BERTIE (Albert Edward) (1841-1910) Prince of Wales; Alice's eldest brother

CHARLES (1809-1877) Prince of Hesse; Alice's father-in-law

EDWARD (1776-1820) Duke of Kent; Queen Victoria's father

ELIZABETH (1815-1885) Princess of Hesse; Alice's mother-in-law

ELLA (Elizabeth) (1864-1918) Alice's second daughter

ERNEST AUGUSTUS (1771-1851) King of Hanover; Alice's great-uncle and godfather

ERNEST II (1818-1893) Duke of Saxe-Coburg & Gotha; Alice's uncle and godfather; Prince Albert's brother

ERNIE (Ernst Ludwig) (1868-1937) Alice's eldest son

FEODORE (Feo) (1807-1872) Princess of Hohenlohe-Langenburg; Alice's aunt and godmother; Queen Victoria's half-sister

FRITTIE (Frederick Wilhelm) (1870-1873) Alice's second son

FRITZ (Frederick Wilhelm) (1831-1888) Crown Prince of Prussia; Vicky's husband

HENRY (1838-1900) Prince of Hesse; Alice's brother-in-law

HILDYARD, Sarah (Tilla), Governess to Alice and her siblings

IRÈNE (1866-1953) Alice's third daughter

LENCHEN (Helena) (1846-1923) Alice's younger sister

LEOPOLD (1790-1865) King of the Belgians; Alice's great-uncle

LEOPOLD (1853-1884) Duke of Albany; Alice's youngest brother

LOUIS (1837-1892) Alice's husband; Prince and later Grand Duke of Hesse-Darmstadt

LOUISE (1800-1831) Duchess of Coburg; Prince Albert's mother

LOUISE (1848-1939) Alice's younger sister

LUDWIG III (1806-1877) Grand Duke of Hesse

LYTTELTON, Sarah (1787-1870) Governess to Alice and her siblings

MAY (Mary) (1874-1878) Alice's youngest daughter

SOPHIE MATILDA (1773-1844) Duchess of Gloucester; Alice's great-aunt and godmother

STRAUSS, David (1808-1874) German theologian and writer

VICKY (1841-1901) Princess of Great Britain/Crown Princess of Prussia; Alice's elder sister

VICTORIA (1786-1861) Duchess of Kent; Alice's grandmother

VICTORIA (1819-1901), Queen of Great Britain; Alice's mother

VICTORIA (1863-1850) Alice's eldest daughter

WILHELM I (1797-1888) Crown Prince, later King of Prussia/German Emperor; Fritz's father

WILLIAM (1840-1879) Prince of Orange; Heir Apparent to the throne of the Netherlands

WILLIAM (1845-1900) Prince of Hesse; Alice's brother-in-law

WILLY (Wilhelm II) (1859-1941) Prince of Prussia; Alice's nephew; Vicky's eldest son

Prologue

Of all Queen Victoria's nine children, none was more intriguing than her second daughter, Alice. The contradictions in her personality are so striking that, while she has often been overshadowed by her more illustrious brother, King Edward VII, and her brilliant sister, the German Empress Frederick, she remains to this day an enigma, the depths of whose character are virtually impossible to penetrate.

Renowned for her cheerfulness and sense of humour, she was nonetheless prone to melancholy and virtually driven to the point of despair by the tragedies in her public as well as her personal life. A dedicated philanthropist, who devoted herself to the service of the poor, she was simultaneously attracted to beautiful jewellery and earned her mother's censure for her love of 'fine society'. Unorthodox, yet profoundly spiritual, she, who wrote of her resignation to the will of God in the most heartrending circumstances, was accused by the Prussian Queen of atheism, and was not ashamed to be associated with one of the most controversial theologians of the age. She loved her children deeply and was devoted to her husband, yet her marriage became increasingly unsatisfying and, as she told the Queen, being a wife and mother did not come naturally to her.

Unconventional and unafraid of involving herself in taboo causes, she was ever conscious of the privileges and responsibilities of her royal status; and, while inspiring devotion in the people whom she selflessly served, she was criticised, too, by those closest to her for her outspokenness and inability to endure a lack of commitment in others.

At the age of eighteen, during her mother's overwhelming grief at the death of Prince Albert, Alice put aside her own sorrow to assume all the duties of the monarch, but, while the country applauded her diligence, the stress of her repressed grief would affect her to the end of her life. For Alice was, first and foremost, her father's daughter. He alone had, she believed, understood the most profound aspects of her character, and she created of him a model of perfection to which she would always aspire. The greatest tragedy of her life was not so much his demise as the fact that he had created so perfect and happy a childhood for her that nothing that came afterwards could ever quite live up to her high expectations.

By the time of her premature death at the age of only thirty-five, Alice had lived through two wars, had lost two of her children, and had exhausted herself in her devotion to duty to the extent that she suffered from disillusionment almost to the point of despair. Nonetheless, in the final tragic weeks of her life, she met unimaginable grief with courage and serenity, and her last words demonstrated her ultimate redemption and the beautiful restoration of all she had loved and lost.

Chapter 1 –
To Whom Much Is Given

Scents of jasmine and magnolia drifted from the terrace and mingled with the salty sea air in the warmth of a summer's afternoon. In front of a wooden cabin, a posse of little children busied themselves with wheelbarrows and spades, each tending a separate garden plot while their father looked on and smiled. Amid the abundance of flowers, carrot-tops sprouted through the soil. Now they were ready to harvest and present to Prince Albert, who would examine them studiously before taking several coins from his pocket to purchase the fruit of his children's labour.

Ten-year-old Alice proudly gathered her offerings and eagerly anticipated her father's approval. Few things in life brought her greater pleasure than winning his smile, and, nowhere captured his essence more completely than here in the gardens of 'dear Osborne' – the house he had designed as a private home for his family. This was the place to which Alice's heart would forever return, for although her destiny lay overseas, Osborne, with its memories of 'dear Papa' would forever be home.

Prince Albert studied the home-grown offerings and, after checking the certificates issued by the Head Gardener, he murmured a few compliments and handed over the payment at the market-rate. Even as Alice took the coins, she knew that this was more a reward for her industry than for the quality of her produce. Prince Albert of Saxe-Coburg Gotha, consort to one of the most prestigious monarchs in an era of monarchical glories, had little need of his children's vegetables but he gained great satisfaction from knowing that they had learned the most important lesson of all: with privilege comes responsibility, and, for all the advantages of their station, the children of Queen Victoria must recognise their duty to live useful and independent lives. It was a lesson which his second daughter, Alice, would take to heart and, from her earliest years to the end of her short life, she would strive to live up to his ideal of a dutiful princess.

No one would ever have a greater influence upon Alice than her father, in whom she found not only a model worthy of imitation, but also an empathetic soul who, alone in the world, seemed to understand the depths of her sensitivity. From him, she would acquire a determined self-sacrifice, and in him she would find the inspiration to raise her own children in the same loving and happy atmosphere which he had created for her.

Unlike the majority of princes of the age, Prince Albert undertook the responsibilities of parenthood with great diligence. While many of his contemporaries were content to consign the welfare of their offspring to the nannies whom their wives had appointed, Prince Albert paid close attention to every detail of his children's upbringing, devoting himself to creating a healthy environment in which they could nurture their talents; and planning the best possible education to prepare them for their future roles as altruistic servants and leaders of their people. Above all, he wished to cultivate simplicity so that, whatever their futures might be, they would never become so proud of their exalted position that they would forget the Gospel line, which formed the foundation of his own life:

> '*For unto whomsoever much is given, of him shall be much required: and to whom men have committed much, of him they will ask the more.*'

Apart from his genuine love of his family and his deep-rooted spiritual beliefs, two motives spurred Prince Albert in his quest to perfect his children's upbringing. His own childhood memories were far from idyllic, for, although as the second son of the Duke of Saxe-Coburg-Gotha he grew up in the picturesque beauty of Schloss Rosenau, his early years were marred by an event which

14

would affect him for the rest of his life. With great fondness he always remembered his loving mother, Louise of Saxe-Coburg-Altenburg, whom he resembled both in looks and in character. Seventeen years younger than her husband, she delighted in joining Albert and his elder brother, Ernest, in their games, but there was no doubt at all that Albert was her favourite, and he, in return, adored her.

Unfortunately for Albert, this domestic idyll was soon to be shattered. While he was still a small infant, his rakish father regularly neglected his wife to spend more and more time with his mistresses. Abandoned and lonely, Louise sought comfort with an army officer, the Duke's stable master, Count Alexander von Hanstein, but when her unfaithful husband, with the double-standards of the age, discovered the liaison, he was incensed and seized the opportunity for a separation. Louise was banished from Coburg and was never permitted to see her children again. In time, she married her lover but their happiness was short-lived. In 1831 she died of cancer at the age of only thirty.

For five-year-old Albert, his mother's sudden departure was inexplicable. In vain he waited for her return but, as time passed and it was clear that she was not coming home, he learned to hide his feelings and suppressed his distress by devoting himself wholeheartedly to duty, study and the acquisition of knowledge:

> "From his earliest years he seems never to have flinched from labour, and he had amassed vast treasures of exact knowledge, which he did not for a moment exhibit for ostentation..."[1]

Nonetheless, he never forgot his mother and even though, when his father remarried Albert developed a close bond with his stepmother, this early childhood experience left him with a tendency towards melancholy, an extreme work-ethic and a sense of the transient nature of life. Years later, according to Queen Victoria, he:

15

"…spoke with much tenderness and sorrow of his poor mother and was deeply affected in reading, after his marriage, the accounts of her sad and painful illness. One of the first gifts he made to the Queen was a little pin he had received from her when a little child."[2]

His sad experience left him, too, with a horror of infidelity and the determination to ensure that his own children would be raised in a more stable family.

A second, more practical, consideration inspired his scrupulous plans for his children's upbringing: the absolute necessity of restoring the tarnished image of a monarchy which had sunk into disrepute during the reigns of his wife's predecessors.

By the time of Queen Victoria's accession, the intermittent madness of her grandfather, George III, and the wayward behaviour of her Hanoverian uncles had caused immense damage to the reputation of the Royal Family. The Queen's 'wicked uncles' – the sons of King George III – were too preoccupied with their creditors and pleasure-seeking to pay a great deal of attention to their duties, and the numerous cartoons and caricatures which featured in periodicals of the era, demonstrated the extent to which the public viewed them with disdain.

The eldest of these sons, the Prince Regent who succeeded as King George IV, was infamous for his gluttonous excesses and his very public dislike of his wife, Caroline of Brunswick, whom he had married solely to secure a government grant to settle his numerous debts, and whom he so despised that he even refused her access to Westminster Abbey for his coronation.

Miraculously, considering their mutual antipathy, George and Caroline managed to produce an heir – a daughter named Charlotte on whom the future of the ruling House of Hanover depended. When, following her marriage to the dashing Prince Leopold of Saxe-Coburg-

Saalfeld, Charlotte became pregnant, the succession seemed secure, but her untimely death in childbirth at the age of only twenty-one shattered such hopes and, since her father was now long-estranged from his wife, sparked an unseemly race among her uncles to produce a legitimate heir.

George III's second son, Frederick, Duke of York, whose inadequacies as a soldier were celebrated in the popular rhyme, *The Grand Old Duke of York,* was unhappily married and predeceased his elder brother, dying without legitimate issue.

The third son, the Duke of Clarence and St. Andrews, who eventually succeeded as King William IV, had enjoyed an unspectacular career in the Royal Navy, and, although he had fathered at least ten illegitimate children, he, too, had failed to produce a legitimate heir.

The fourth son, Edward, Duke of Kent, had had an equally unimpressive military career. In his role as Governor of Gibraltar, he had imposed such harsh discipline on the troops that he had provoked a mutiny. Although he developed a keen interest in freedom of worship and the improvement of working conditions for the poor, he, like his brothers, squandered a fortune in gambling and other excesses and preferred to maintain a mistress than to marry. Eventually, following the death of Princess Charlotte, the fifty-year-old Edward decided to do his duty (and to receive a settlement of his debts) by finding a wife. Discarding his long-time lover (who retired briefly to a French convent before marrying a South American prince), he married Victoire of Saxe-Coburg-Saalfeld, sister of the widowed Prince Leopold.

Nine months later, the future Queen Victoria, was born but Edward had little time to enjoy the delights of fatherhood. When his daughter was only eight months old, he took her to the seaside in Devon where he caught a chill which developed into a fatal pneumonia. Though too young at the time of his death to have any recollections of him, Queen Victoria was later assured by those who knew him that he was the best of the sons of King George III.

The fifth son, Ernest Augustus, Duke of Cumberland, who would inherit the throne of Hanover[a], enjoyed the worst reputation of all. He had fallen in love with a twice-married woman, Frederica of Mecklenburg-Strelitz, whose second husband died so unexpectedly that it was rumoured that she had poisoned him in order to marry Ernest. Such was her unpopularity that even Ernest's mother, Queen Charlotte, refused to receive her at court, while Ernest himself became the victim of increasingly lurid tales. Slanderous stories about him abounded: it was said that in a fit of anger he had slit his valet's throat; that he had struck an innocent woman; that he had driven Lord Graves to commit suicide by conducting an affair with his wife; and even that he had conducted an incestuous liaison with sister, who bore him a child. Although the majority of the stories were fictitious, the fact that such tales circulated at all demonstrates the extent of his unpopularity.

Queen Victoria's favourite uncle, Augustus, Duke of Sussex, married three times (twice to the same lady) but, since he repeatedly failed to obtain the King's approval, his marriages contravened the Royal Marriages Act and were deemed invalid. They did, however, lead to his most memorable achievement: the popularising of municipal cemeteries. Knowing that his wife would not be permitted to rest beside him in the hallowed Royal Vaults, Augustus requested that they should be buried together in Kensal Green Cemetery, thereby starting a new fashion in interments.

[a] Since the reign of George III the Kings of Great Britain and Ireland were also Kings of Hanover. As Salic Law prevented a female from inheriting the throne, Ernest, as the eldest surviving son of George III, became King of Hanover on Queen Victoria's accession in 1837.

With so much scandal in the family, it was unsurprising that, by the time Queen Victoria ascended the throne, the monarchy was viewed with contempt, and, were it not for the wise and calming influence of Prince Albert, that tawdry image might well have continued to deteriorate.

Following the death of the Duke of Kent, his widow, a foreigner in a strange land, turned for support to her late husband's equerry, John Conroy, whom she appointed as her chief advisor and the comptroller of her household. An ambitious and self-seeking man, Conroy soon ruled every aspect of her life, including the upbringing of her daughter, Victoria. Such was the Duchess's dependence upon him that it was rumoured that they were lovers. Whether or not the stories had any foundation, Conroy recognised the possibility of Victoria coming to the throne before her eighteenth birthday, in which case a regent would be required. The most obvious candidate for the role was her mother, and Conroy realised that by controlling the Duchess he would, in effect, control the Queen and the country. He therefore devised the 'Kensington System', ostensibly to prepare Victoria for her future role, but in reality to break her spirit and make her malleable to his wishes.

The system involved isolating the young princess and imposing a series of stringent rules to protect her from any outside influence, including that of her extended family. With only her dolls and her dogs as playmates, her days were governed by such a minutia of rules that, even as she approached her eighteenth birthday, she was not permitted to mix with her contemporaries, to be alone or even to sleep in her own bedroom. Unsurprisingly, Victoria grew to despise Conroy and resented her mother for allowing him such authority. This resentment was fuelled by her possessive governess, Louise Lehzen, who also despised Conroy and attempted to protect her young charge from some of his more excessive demands.

Ultimately, Conroy's scheming came to nothing. His plans were scuppered when Victoria reached her eighteenth birthday just one month before the death of her uncle and predecessor, William IV. Now, requiring no regent, and free to make her own decisions, she took her revenge, dismissing Conroy from her service and allocating her mother a separate household in a few remote rooms in Buckingham Palace. As the Duchess refused to be parted from Conroy, Victoria maintained minimum contact with her.

Throughout her life, Queen Victoria was fiercely loyal to those whom she loved, and Lehzen was no exception. At the time of her accession, the former governess was her closest confidante but the young Queen recognised, too, the need for a strong male advisor to guide her through the early years of her reign. Within days of her accession, she found such a man in the fifty-two-year-old Whig Prime Minister, William Lamb, Lord Melbourne.

Melbourne's life had been dogged by scandal. His wife, the histrionic Lady Caroline Lamb, is best remembered for her widely publicised affair with the poet, Lord Byron, while Melbourne himself had been the victim of blackmail following a purported liaison with the married poetess, Caroline Norton. Renowned for his numerous affairs with aristocratic ladies, he was even alleged to have enticed orphan girls into his home with the promise of improving their lot while actually engaging them in his sado-masochistic pleasures.

Notwithstanding his sexual proclivities, to eighteen-year-old Victoria, Melbourne was something of a cross between a father figure and a mythical knight dedicated to her service and protection. Such was her devotion to him that they spent up to five or six hours a day together until rumours began to circulate that she intended to marry him. Matters came to a head when Melbourne was voted out of office. The Queen refused to abide by the customary practice of replacing the outgoing politicians' wives and daughters, who served as Ladies of the Bedchamber, with the wives and daughters of the incoming government ministers. Her intransigence demonstrated such a lack of political impartiality that the Tory leader, Robert Peel, declared he was unable to form a government under such circumstance, and to Victoria's delight, Melbourne was reinstated. While the Queen rejoiced, her reputation had been seriously compromised and her popularity plummeted still further when a second scandal compounded the 'Bedchamber Affair'.

In 1839, it came to the Queen Victoria's attention that her mother's lady-in-waiting, Flora Hastings, was suffering from a painful abdominal swelling but refused to be examined by the royal physician. Rumours spread that the unmarried lady must be pregnant, and the Queen, encouraged by Lehzen and Melbourne, soon deduced that the detested Conroy must be the child's father. As the gossip spread, the unfortunate Lady Flora was coerced into permitting a medical examination as the only means of clearing her name. When she eventually consented to the humiliating procedure it was discovered that, far from being pregnant, she was suffering from a cancerous and ultimately fatal tumour of the liver. Her death two months later provoked outrage, as her mother, brother and Conroy united in creating a press campaign to discredit the Queen and her physician for attempting to destroy the innocent woman's reputation. The effect was startling. When the Queen attended Ascot that year, she was openly hissed and booed amid cries of 'Mrs Melbourne,' and for a while it appeared that her reputation had sunk even lower than that of her predecessors.

Fortunately, both for Britain and for the Queen, her uncle, King Leopold of the Belgians, had a plan to take his petulant niece in hand. What better means could there be of distracting the passionate young woman from the aging roué, Melbourne, than presenting her with a younger, more handsome and eminently more suitable man?

In fact, King Leopold and his mother, the Dowager Duchess of Coburg, had an ideal suitor in mind – the Queen's first cousin, King Leopold's nephew, Prince Albert of Saxe-Coburg-Gotha. Since Albert's early childhood, King Leopold and his comptroller, Baron Stockmar, had been carefully grooming him for such a role:

> "...the Prince used to relate that when he was a child of three years old, his nurse always told him that he should marry the Queen, and that when he first thought of marrying at all, he always thought of her."[3]

Prior to the Queen's accession, Albert and his elder brother had been dispatched to England in the hope that he would attract Victoria's attention and, though the initial meeting gave little inkling of the romance which was to follow, Albert created a good impression:

> "He was most amiable, natural, unaffected, and merry – full of interest in everything – playing on the piano with the princess, his cousin; drawing; in short, constantly occupied. He always paid the greatest attention to all he saw, and the Queen remembers well how intently he listened to the sermon preached in St. Paul's...on the occasion of the service attended by the children of the different charity schools. It is indeed rare to see a prince, not yet seventeen years of age, bestowing such earnest attention on a sermon."[4]

Shortly after Queen Victoria's coronation, Albert was sent again to further his cause, but by now Victoria was under Melbourne's sway and had no intention of sacrificing her new-found freedom to anyone, least of all a rather studious and serious-minded husband. Although the meeting appeared to be inauspicious, the Queen agreed to correspond with Albert, and three years later when he returned to England, his persistence paid off. This time Victoria was struck by the improvement in his appearance, his handsomeness, his 'sweet' smile and the intelligent expression in his warm, blue eyes. Now there were no excuses or doubts and the Queen acted with the impulsiveness that would characterise so much of her life. As protocol demanded, she proposed, and Albert dutifully accepted.

The wedding took place on February 10th 1840 in the Chapel Royal of St James' Palace, and the following morning the Queen recorded in her diary that her wedding night had brought her 'bliss beyond belief.' To Melbourne, too, she wrote in uninhibited detail of what had passed between her and Albert, informing him of the 'bewildering and gratifying experience.'

Her delight in married life, however, did not extend to a willingness to share her authority. The novelty of queenship had not yet waned and she was reluctant to permit her husband even the slightest participation in affairs of state. As she worked through her papers, the highly-intelligent Albert was reduced to standing beside her desk and blotting her signature. His life wasn't made any easier by the ubiquitous former governess, Lehzen, who, reluctant to share her charge's confidence, had opposed the marriage and, resenting Albert's presence, sought every opportunity to discredit him and to drive a wedge between him and Victoria.

Notwithstanding Victoria's stubbornness and Lehzen's meddling, Albert's brilliant intellect could not remain inactive for long. Denied any meaningful role in official business, he set about reorganising the running of the extremely disorderly palaces and creating order out of the chaos of the numerous departments responsible for their upkeep. At the same time, his tact and diplomacy not only helped heal the rift between Victoria and her mother, but also, as Melbourne's influence declined, eased the animosity between the Queen and Robert Peel's Tories.

It was not, though, until the birth of his children that Albert's talents truly began to shine. Much as Queen Victoria took pleasure in the physicality of her marriage, the 'unecstatic' consequences annoyed and revolted her, making her increasingly dependent upon Albert as her pregnancies progressed.

Nine months after the wedding, on 21st November 1840, Princess Victoria Adelaide Mary Louisa (Vicky) was born. The Queen, relieved to have survived the ordeal, cheerfully announced that, 'the next one will be a prince', and, despite Albert's distress at the pain his wife had suffered, mother and child at once became the chief object of his devotion. Throughout the Queen's convalescence, he carried her to and from her bed, waited upon her and read aloud from her favourite novels. With even greater solicitude, he cared for the baby, maintaining frequent correspondence with Uncle Leopold's advisor, the physician, Baron Stockmar, to seek his advice in all matters relating to her health and wellbeing.

This concern for his daughter soon led Prince Albert into an even more virulent conflict with the former governess. In her typically presumptive manner, Lehzen had taken it upon herself to appoint staff and oversee the running of the nursery, where she spent an inordinate amount of time gossiping and, to Albert's intense annoyance, dandling the baby.

"The nursery gives me more trouble than the government of a kingdom would do," Albert wrote in exasperation to Stockmar, but, far from supporting him, Queen Victoria sided with Lehzen and responded so petulantly to his complaints that he frequently locked himself in his room, refusing to respond to her frantic hammering on the door until she ceased her imperious tantrums.

The simmering antipathy between Prince Albert and Lehzen reached a climax when Vicky fell ill. As days passed with no improvement, the Prince became convinced that the unhealthy heat of a constantly blazing fire was contributing to her failure to thrive. Both Lehzen and James Clark – the doctor whom she had appointed – refused to accept the seriousness of her condition and, when the Queen failed to heed Albert's warnings, an angry argument ensued, culminating in Albert's declaration that, if the child died, it would be Victoria's fault. At last, the Queen gave way. Vicky recovered and Lehzen was gently relieved of her duties and packed off to Germany with a generous pension. Although she and the Queen maintained a correspondence to the end of her life, Lehzen's hold over Victoria had finally been broken; relations between the Queen and her mother improved and Albert's genius could finally shine.

Now, with undivided loyalties, Queen Victoria came to realise the extent of her husband's abilities. A gifted musician and painter, whose compositions were admired by Felix Mendelssohn, and whose paintings were so impressive that members of the Royal Academy declared he could have made a career as an artist, his appetite for learning was insatiable. Eager to understand the latest technological advances, he invited the foremost scientists and engineers to give lectures at the palace and made a point of studying the workings of industrial machinery.

His political acumen was so astute that when Queen Victoria gave him a golden key to her despatch boxes, allowing him access to official papers, his advice became crucial to her, and even the most unsympathetic ministers couldn't fail to recognise his wisdom.

"Lord Melbourne has formed the highest opinion of the judgement, the temper, and the discretion of His Royal Highness," the former Prime Minister wrote to the Queen, shortly before his retirement, "and it gives him the greatest comfort and satisfaction to know that Your Majesty is in a position in which she enjoys the inestimable advantage of such counsel and assistance. Lord Melbourne is convinced that Your Majesty cannot do better than to have recourse to this when it is needed, and to rest on it with confidence."[5]

A man of great social conscience, Prince Albert was passionately concerned about working and housing conditions. He regularly visited factories and mines, and wrote numerous epistles and memoranda to parliament, offering suggestions for improving the lot of the poor. No subject touching the lives of the Queen's subjects was beyond his consideration: one moment he was writing to Robert Peel pressing him to ban duelling in the army, the next he was speaking as Chancellor of Oxford University, urging greater tolerance towards the re-establishment of Roman Catholic dioceses in England.

So dependent was the Queen upon his judgement that she had no qualms in urging her ministers have him declared king – a request which, much to her annoyance, was refused, due partly to the xenophobes in parliament who viewed the Prince simply as 'a German'. Eventually, after fifteen years of marriage, the Queen had to settle for bestowing upon him the title 'Prince Consort'.

To her chagrin, not everyone shared the Queen's high regard for Prince Albert. From the moment he arrived in England, he had been subjected to harsh and unjust criticism from politicians, 'society', the press, and consequently a large section of the public who considered him as a mere foreigner who did not fit their image of an English prince.

"That he did not dress in quite the orthodox English fashion; that he did not sit on horseback in the orthodox English way; that he did not shake hands in the orthodox English manner etc. etc. all this even those…who knew and esteemed him could not quite get over. One heard them say, "He is an excellent, clever, able fellow but look at the cut of his coat, or look at the way he shakes hands.'"[6]

Officials objected to his suggestions for the reorganisation of many disorderly institutions; politicians objected to his voicing an opinion; and the press objected to his Germanic influence over the Queen. The perceived interference of 'a German' was so irksome that any assistance he offered was viewed as meddling; his willingness to speak out again injustice was viewed as dictatorial; his lack of interest in pleasure-seeking was seen as dull; and his marital fidelity was viewed as prudery.

Even to this day, the myth is perpetuated that he was an arrogant and humourless 'German', with megalomaniac tendencies. Those who actually knew him – his family, servants, tenants and the local people of Balmoral and Osborne – saw an entirely different image, as indeed did several ministers whose prejudices were deflated when they met him.

Lord Greville wrote that he had not met the Prince prior to a visit to Balmoral but from the moment of their first meeting, he was:

> "…struck with him. I saw at once…that he is very intelligent and highly-cultivated, and moreover he has a thoughtful mind and thinks about subjects that are worth thinking about. He seemed very much at his ease, very gay, pleasant, without the least stiffness or air of dignity."[7]

Such relentless criticism was deeply wounding to the Prince, and, unsurprisingly, the more he was lampooned, libelled and criticised, the more determined the Queen became to publicise and extol his qualities. Throughout her life she appeared to be constantly battling to ensure that posterity would remember him and hold him in the same high esteem in which she venerated him.

Disregarding the hostility, Prince Albert continued to apply himself to numerous projects from the Chancellorship of universities to the Presidency of the Society of Arts, and from supporting the Royal Horticultural Society to encouraging qualifications for tradesmen, but, effective as he was in the social and political arena, he did not allow his many commitments to distract from the care of his children. As Queen Victoria had predicted, 'the next one' *was* a prince: Albert Edward, known in the family as Bertie, and, from the moment he was born, his young parents were faced with the daunting task of raising a future king.

Having little personal experience of small children, they sought advice from Albert's trusted mentor, Baron Stockmar, who, insisting that 'a man's education begins the first day of his life', immediately set to work devising a 'thoroughly moral and thoroughly English' plan for the education and formation of the royal offspring. Stockmar's overriding principle was the necessity of preserving the children's innocence by preventing them from being tainted by the outside world. This, to Albert and Victoria, seemed particularly important in Bertie's case to ensure that he did not err along the path of the wayward Hanoverian uncles. The Royal Family must present an ideal of domestic harmony, and the children must be paradigms of morality to set a fine example to the rest of the country. For this reason, Albert decided that his children should be educated at home and, though tutors would be carefully selected to instruct them in various wide-ranging subjects, he would take overall charge of their education.

For Vicky, the plan worked perfectly. Having inherited her father's brilliant intellect, she relished the hours spent in study, and delighted in impressing Prince Albert, who was thrilled by her achievements. By the age of three, she could read and write and was already fluent in English, French and German, leading her proud father to state, "I hold her to be exceptionally gifted even to the point of genius."[8]

Sadly, the same could not be said of Bertie. With little aptitude for book-learning, study bored him and he found the isolation from his peers frustrating. While his parents despaired of his lack of intellect and his failure to apply himself to his lessons, he rebelled against the oppressive regime with rages and tantrums, culminating in his being *occasionally* beaten and, more often, banished to his room.

> "The systematic idleness, laziness – disregard of everything is enough to break one's heart, and fills me with indignation,"[9] wrote the Queen as Bertie approached adulthood.

In an attempt to understand the children's behaviour, a prominent phrenologist, George Combe, was invited to examine their skulls in order to diagnose any innate character flaws which might be remedied through appropriate education. Unfortunately for Bertie, Combe concluded that his intellectual organs were only 'moderately well developed', which prompted still more intensive programmes of study.

Much has been made of the supposed cruelty of such a stringent regime but in the nineteenth century it was common practice to beat unruly children; and, even if the attempt to mould Bertie into an ideal prince was both fruitless and futile, his parents genuinely had his best interests at heart. They might have mistakenly sought to turn him into someone he could never be, but they did so with the highest intentions, believing it would benefit him and the country. Having been self-effacing enough to seek guidance from Stockmar, they believed – initially at least – that it was important to implement his instructions, which, though they might appear astounding today, were viewed at the time as the most appropriate and beneficial methods of child-rearing.

By the time of the birth of their third child, Alice, however, Queen Victoria and Prince Albert had gained confidence in their own abilities as parents and relied less on Stockmar and more on their experience and intuition. They recognised the importance of creating a loving environment for their children, and, unlike many of their contemporaries, realised that this could be best achieved by spending time with them.

> "The greatest maxim of all," wrote the Queen, "is that the children should be brought up as simply as possible; that (not interfering with their lessons) they should be as much as possible with their parents."[10]

True to her word, the Queen bathed her own babies, and, when organising her suite at Windsor, specifically arranged for the schoolroom to be adjacent to her audience chamber and sitting room so that she could be close to them. Despite her alleged dislike of babies, her diary entries and letters reveal the pleasure she took in her growing family and her enjoyment of spending time with the children.

So it was that Queen Victoria's second daughter, Alice, was born into a more stable family than her elder siblings had been. The disputes which had led to many stormy scenes in the early months of her parents' marriage had given way to a delightful contentment; Lehzen was gone; Melbourne had retired from politics; and Prince Albert was beginning to employ his gifts to the full. By now, Queen Victoria had formed a close bond with her mother, who often accompanied the Royal Family on their travels; and she had come to admire and adore her devoted husband, whose brilliance she relied upon in everything. Unsurprisingly, therefore, as Alice's letters would later reveal, she could not have hoped for a more idyllic childhood.

Chapter 2
What a joyous childhood we had!

Princess Alice, 'a pretty and large baby', was born in Windsor Castle at four o'clock on a lovely spring morning, 25th April 1843. Although it was a relatively easy birth, the Queen, as was customary, did not appear in public for over a fortnight following her confinement but during her recuperation she found time to write excitedly to her uncle, King Leopold of the Belgians:

> "Our little baby, who I really am proud of, for she is so very forward for her age, is to be called Alice, an old English name, and the other names are to be Maud (another old English name and the same as Matilda) and Mary, as she was born on Aunt Gloucester's[a] birthday."[11]

What the Queen did not mention was that, with Prince Albert's agreement, 'Alice' was chosen partly as a kindness to Lord Melbourne who had once mentioned that this was his favourite name.

In spite of a few grumbles from various ministers that the child was not male (the spare to the heir), Prince Albert was delighted by the new addition to his family and set about using her christening to ameliorate the relationship between the Queen and her unpleasant uncle, Ernest, King of Hanover.

Prior to the Queen's accession, cantankerous Uncle Ernest made no secret of the fact that he considered a mere girl unfit to inherit the throne, and it was widely rumoured that he intended to lead a coup against – or even murder – his niece in order to proclaim himself king. Naturally, Ernest denied the allegations but he relished any excuse to denigrate the young Queen and, the death of his brother, Augustus, Duke of Sussex, four days before

---

[a] HRH Princess Sophia Matilda of Gloucester, a cousin of Queen Victoria's father.

Alice was born, provided him with a perfect opportunity for criticism. Queen Victoria had been particularly fond of Uncle Augustus and readily acquiesced to his request to be interred in Kensal Green Cemetery rather than the family vault at Windsor. Uncle Ernest complained bitterly that such a thing was unheard of in royal circles, and – amusingly, considering his own reputation – claimed that by agreeing to such a request, the Queen was demeaning the monarchy. The dispute was compounded by a disagreement about a collection of jewels left by his late mother, Queen Caroline, which, Uncle Ernest believed were rightfully his as the next male heir. Queen Victoria, on the other hand, insisted that they belonged to the Crown and irked him immensely by wearing them in his presence.

Ever eager to heal disputes, Prince Albert sought to placate Uncle Ernest by inviting him to act as Alice's godfather. Somewhat grudgingly, he accepted, but, as the small congregation gathered in the private chapel of Buckingham Palace on 2nd June 1843, he showed his contempt by arriving 'just in time to be too late'.

Fortunately, the other godparents – Albert's elder brother, Ernest of Coburg (represented at the ceremony by the Grand Duke of Mecklenburg-Strelitz), the Duchess of Gloucester, and the Queen's half-sister, Feodore[b] (represented by her mother, the Duchess of Kent) – were far more accommodating and, as the Queen told the King of the Belgians:

> "Our christening went off very brilliantly...; nothing could be more anständig [respectable], and little Alice behaved extremely well. The déjeuner was served in the Gallery...and there

---

[b] Queen Victoria's mother was a widow at the time of her marriage to the Duke of Kent and had two children – Karl, Prince of Leiningen, and Feodore, Princess of Hohenlohe-Langenburg. Although they were a good deal older than the Queen, she was fond of both of them, particularly Feodore.

being a profusion of flowers on the table, etc., had a beautiful effect...Pussy [Vicky] and Bertie (as we call the boy)...appeared after the déjeuner... and I wish you could have seen them; they behaved so beautifully before that great number of people, and I must say looked very dear, all in white, and very distingués; they were much admired."[12]

After such a cheerful welcome, baby Alice could now begin the serious business of growing up as a member of one of the most privileged families in the world.

Surrounded by beauty, attended constantly, and doted upon by her family, the world was a thrilling place to the infant Alice. As yet uninhibited by her elder siblings, and blissfully unaware of her family's status and responsibilities, she thrived, becoming so podgy that her mother spoke of her as 'good, fat Alice', while her doting father nicknamed her 'Fatima'. She was a quick and lively child, and it was not long before the Superintendent of the nursery, Lady Lyttelton, reported that she was beginning to show 'forwardness' and "clasps her fat hands so beautifully when asked to say, 'Up so high!'"[13]

Making little distinction between servants and kings, Alice was undaunted by the stream of foreign royalties passing through the palace in the first eighteen months of her life. Her great uncle, King Leopold of the Belgians, was a regular visitor; and in the early summer of 1844, the unassuming King Frederick Augustus II of Saxony – who was to die a decade later when a horse stepped on his head – arrived, to be followed the next day by Tsar Nicholas I of Russia.

Queen Victoria had anticipated the Tsar's visit more with trepidation than with excitement. Her mistrust of Russians would not fully develop until the Crimean

War but already her natural reticence left her anxious about entertaining so powerful an autocrat, particularly one who, in her opinion, came from one of the most opulent and decadent courts in the world.

To the Queen's relief, the Tsar was far more congenial than she had expected. For a man of such wealth, his simplicity was astounding – he asked that no bed be prepared for him as he always travelled with a 'long leather bag stuffed with hay from the stables', which served as a mattress; he was extremely civil and courteous to members of the household; he paid kindly attention to the royal children; and, most importantly to the Queen, he spoke highly of Prince Albert – 'Nowhere will you find a handsomer young man; he has such an air of nobility and goodness,'[14] he told one member of the household; and in conversation with Robert Peel,

> "…The Emperor spoke with extraordinary warmth and praised Prince Albert with tears in his eyes. He said that he knew that people considered him as playing a part, but that really he was a thoroughly honest man."[15]

There could be no better way to win the Queen's heart than to esteem her husband, and, although she considered the expression in the Tsar's eyes quite formidable, she wrote in wonder to the King of the Belgians that:

> "He is very easy to get on with. Really, it seems like a dream when I think that we breakfast and walk out with this greatest of all earthly Potentates…"[16]

Fourteen-month-old Alice shared none of her mother's awe. The mighty autocrat was simply another adult whom she approached, holding out her 'fat hands' until her picked her up in his arms and allowed her to kiss him 'de son propre accord.'[17]

35

For his part, the Tsar was enchanted by Alice and her siblings, commenting to Lady Lyttelton that he was,

"...very much pleased with the royal children, especially their footing with their parents, and the affection and care shown to them."[18]

Not long after the Tsar's departure, the Prince of Prussia arrived; and in the autumn the aged King Louis Philippe was warmly received by the public as the first French King to undertake a State Visit to Britain. Queen Victoria so enjoyed his company – not least because of his high regard for Prince Albert – that she would soon be preparing for a return visit to France.

Shy herself, Queen Victoria was relieved that her children were so comfortable in the presence of illustrious visitors but she and Prince Albert were keen to prevent their confidence from escalating into arrogance. Most of the time, the children were kept away from the business of the court, to the extent that many members of the household claimed never to have seen them; and their parents did their utmost to create as normal a family life as was possible for people in their position. Hanoverian extravagance was replaced by a modest frugality; the children's meals were plain ('only a bit of roast beef and perhaps a plain pudding', according to one of their nursery maids): no new baby linen was bought for Alice when there were perfectly adequate hand-me-downs from Vicky and Bertie; and even amid the grandeur of Windsor and Buckingham Palace, the children were expected to show deference to their elders, whether they were the doctors who came to attend them, or the lowliest members of the household. On one occasion, when Vicky dropped a handkerchief, which she had been coquettishly waving through a carriage window, Queen Victoria stopped the footman who stooped to pick it up, and insisted that Vicky should retrieve it herself.

It was clear to Prince Albert, however, that if he were to raise his children simply, he would need to find a more homely setting than the ancient, rambling Windsor Castle or the very conspicuous and overcrowded Buckingham Palace. Moreover, the heart of London was hardly the healthiest place in which to raise children. At the height of the Industrial Revolution, the air was thick with the smog of the burgeoning factories, which pumped their waste into the Thames where it combined with the outfall of slaughterhouses and public sewage to create a flowing cesspit. It was estimated that over four hundred thousand tonnes of sewage flowed into the Thames each day, and the stench became so intolerable that in the 'Great Stink' of 1858, Parliament had to be suspended. Predictably, throughout the 1840s and 1850s, the insanitary conditions and lack of clean water led to frequent cholera and typhoid epidemics; infant mortality rates were rising rapidly; and the average life expectancy for an upper class man was forty-seven years old and for a tradesman only twenty-seven.

More accustomed to the clean air of Schloss Rosenau, Prince Albert went in search of a healthier environment for his children, and shortly before Alice's first birthday, his quest took him to the Isle of Wight where Lady Isabella Blatchford had recently offered her property, Osborne House, for sale. Instantly enraptured by the view across the Solent, which reminded him of the Bay of Naples, he recognised the estate's potential and was eager to share his discovery with the Queen. A few months later, she accompanied him back to the island and was equally enchanted by the prospect of owning an island retreat, far enough from London to provide privacy from the public gaze but close enough to facilitate contact with her ministers.

The sale was eventually finalised and, in the spring of 1845, Queen Victoria wrote delightedly to Lord Melbourne that it was:

> "...impossible to imagine a prettier spot – valleys and woods which would be beautiful anywhere; but all this near the sea (the woods grow into the sea) is quite perfection; we have a charming beach quite to ourselves. The sea was so blue and calm...and then we can walk about anywhere by ourselves without being mobbed."[19]

It soon became clear that, while the eight-hundred-acre estate was beautiful, the house was inadequate for the needs of the royal suite. Various ideas were mooted about renovating and extending the original building but eventually it was decided that it would be less expensive to demolish the old house and replace it with an entirely new structure.

At once, Prince Albert's imaginative instincts came to the fore as, working closely with the architect Thomas Cubitt, he set about creating an Italianesque mansion which would not only meet all the requirements of his growing family but would also be self-sufficient and provide work for the local population. Unlike Buckingham Palace and Windsor Castle, this was to be a private family home where as much care went into the design of the nurseries as into the relatively few State Rooms. The estate, much of which had been neglected, could be transformed into profitable farmland alongside beautiful Italian-style gardens, leading down to the private beach where the royal children could benefit from the healthy sea air and learn to swim. Prince Albert personally oversaw the plans, taking care to ensure that the labourers were released from the site in late summer to bring in the harvest, with the promise that work would be available if they wished to return afterwards.

Little by little, the house took shape and, in September 1846, three-year-old Alice and her siblings made the crossing to the Isle of Wight to spend their first night in their new home.

"Everything in the house is quite new, and the dining-room looked very handsome." Lady Lyttelton wrote. "The windows, lighted by the brilliant lamps in the room, must have been seen far out at sea. After dinner we rose to drink the Queen's and Prince's health as a house-warming and after it the Prince said very naturally and simply, but seriously, 'We have a hymn' (he called it a psalm) in Germany for such occasions. It begins...' and then he quoted two lines in German which I could not quote right, meaning a prayer to 'bless our going out and coming in'. It was dry and quaint, being Luther's; but we all perceived that he was feeling it. And truly entering a new house, a new palace, is a solemn thing to do."[20]

The Queen and Prince Albert's love affair with Osborne reached its zenith on summer evenings when Albert delighted in imitating the nightingales and waiting for them to respond. In so romantic an atmosphere, he had a special lock fitted to his and Victoria's bedroom door, which could only be opened from the inside. In the mornings the royal couple would take breakfast on the terrace amid the magnolias and jasmine.

Even once the house was completed, there was still plenty of work to do on the estate, and Alice enjoyed helping her father as he joined the workmen in their labours.

"I, partly forester, partly builder, partly farmer and partly gardener, expect to be a good deal on my legs and in the open air,"[21] he wrote cheerfully before one visit to the island.

One afternoon each summer, a garden party was held in the grounds for the workers of the estate and the crew of the royal yachts. Luncheon was served in marquees, after which there was country dancing to the accompaniment of military bands, and the royal children joined the labourers in noisy games of blind-man's-buff, leapfrog, cricket, dunking-oranges, three-legged races and all kinds of other lively fun. The festivities continued until the evening, when the workers departed and the children returned to their nursery.

> "This rural retreat," wrote Lady Canning, "...perfectly enchants the Queen and Prince, and you never saw anything so happy as they are with the five babies playing about them."[22]

For the children, this was a magical holiday home where they learned to ride and swim, and where there were woods to explore and beaches on which to gather shells, stones, fossils and leaves which were stored in their own museum alongside souvenirs of their travels. Years later, one of Queen Victoria's granddaughters described her memories of Osborne:

> "It meant summer holidays, it meant the sea and the seashore, it meant wonderful shells to be found when the tide was low – shells of every colour and shape. It meant glorious bathing when the tide was high, and drives in the big 'wagonette,' as we called our brake, through the sweet-smelling woods, past hedges full of honeysuckle...It also meant the beautiful terraces in front of Osborne House where the big magnolias grew against the walls, those giant magnolias which had a lemon-like fragrance and in which you could bury your whole face...There was also jasmine on those terraces, and jasmine has always filled me with a sort of ecstasy."[23]

A particularly enchanting feature of Osborne was the Swiss Cottage, imported in pieces from Germany by Prince Albert in 1853. Hidden in the grounds of the main house, the little Alpine villa was intended not only as a playhouse but also as a place where the children could develop independence by choosing their own occupations and learning the practical skills of cooking and gardening. In an age of revolutions, when monarchies could be ousted overnight, Prince Albert had the foresight to prepare his children to adapt to whatever circumstances they might face in the future. Equipped with child-sized ovens and utensils, the kitchen became a workroom in which Vicky and Alice pickled fruits, prepared the vegetables which they had grown in their own little gardens, and made meals to be distributed to the tenants and the poor, or, on special occasions, to be served to their parents and other guests. Here, too, they could sew and paint, creating gifts for one another and for members of the household, while their brothers practised stone masonry and woodwork in their carpenters' shop.

Alongside the Swiss Cottage, the Victoria Fort and Albert Barracks were built by Alice's boisterous brothers under their father's supervision, and provided not only a training ground for their future military careers but also a place in which they could charge around wildly, often accompanied by an extremely energetic Alice whose agility outdid their own. Indoors, the nurseries were filled with dolls, skittles, rattles, picture books, model trains, rocking horses and other toys, including a mechanical life-sized lion, which could swallow a toy soldier.

Shortly after the completion of Osborne, the Royal Family acquired an even more remote estate: Balmoral Castle on the banks of the River Dee. By the time of four-year old Alice's first visit to Scotland in 1847, her mother's love of the Highlands already bordered on obsession. Thanks largely to the writer, Sir Walter Scott, the Queen's initial visit to Scotland several years earlier had been marked by a great display of Celtic 'traditions' – several of which had actually been invented for the occasion. Queen Victoria was enchanted not only by the gathering of the clans hailing her as their chief, but also by the lack of ostentation which seemed so prevalent in London. The place, she remarked was 'more natural and marked by honesty & simplicity which always distinguishes the inhabitants of mountainous countries' and, when she was told that the 15th Century Balmoral Castle was for sale, she and Prince Albert were overjoyed.

"Now I can breathe! Now I am happy!" the Prince exclaimed whenever he was in the countryside, and, if Osborne reminded him of the Bay of Naples, Balmoral reminded him of the mountains of Thuringia.

Once again, though, it was clear that the house was unsuitable for the royal suite, so Prince Albert set to work on creating a new design. As at Osborne, he used the construction to provide employment for local people, ensuring that their wages were above the typically low rates paid in the Highlands, and putting a great deal of effort into creating comfortable accommodation and amenities for the tenants and labourers. Deeply concerned by the insanitary design of slum dwellings, Prince Albert insisted that there were sufficient windows to provide fresh air; and when a scarlet fever epidemic struck the district, Queen Victoria provided new iron beds for every household. Discovering that the nearest school was inaccessible to many of the local children, the Queen and Prince arranged for other schools to be built, alongside providing a library for the use of their tenants. The outcome of the plans impressed not only the residents and local people but also the numerous philanthropists who came to learn from Prince Albert's schemes.

The estate workers quickly grew to respect their employer, and, years after his death, one former labourer recalled the Prince's 'kindness of heart and his invariable good humour'.

"If your work pleased him, he said so, and if it did not please him, he said so, but always with the same kind smile, [and he was] always ready to own if he had made a mistake."[24]

In the course of the construction, a fire broke out on the estate, damaging several cottages and huts and threatening the castle itself. Prince Albert joined the workmen in dousing the flames and, later, he and the Queen paid for the damage out of their private funds.

Queen Victoria laid the foundation stone of the new Balmoral on September 1853 – an occasion which was marked by prayer from Mr Anderson, the minister at Crathie Kirk, followed by great festivities – and three years later the fairy-tale castle was complete.

The Queen adored her 'dear paradise in the highlands' where she adopted an exaggerated 'Scottish-ness', covering the floors and walls with tartan and insisting that her sons dressed in kilts during their stay. Balls were no longer the stately affairs of the English aristocracy but rather traditional country dances where the Queen and her children would happily swirl around the room with the ghillies and labourers, far more freely than would have been possible in London. Every Sunday afternoon, the Queen and Prince Albert walked arm-in-arm through the countryside, while their children ran about them, chatting happily to the local people as they passed.

These beautiful settings were not merely a façade of happy domesticity. Within them, Alice grew up in a close-knit family, spending far more time with her parents than was typical for royal children, and learning from their example of concern for their tenants and the local poor. Every morning when the Queen was in residence, a group of five women arrived at Balmoral to have their baskets filled with bread, meats and other foods from the royal kitchens, so that within one week thirty-five families had been fed. The sick, too benefited from their royal neighbours. The Queen had employed a nurse for her staff but, more often than not, she was sent to anyone in the region, requiring attention.

Alice learned, too, the importance of being accessible to the people as she often accompanied her mother to visit the widowed or bereaved. Many times, on hearing sad news of one family or another, the Queen personally intervened: a widow had a leaking roof, and the Queen arranged for it to be re-thatched; an elderly couple had been evicted by their landlord, and, seeing them standing helplessly at the side of the road, the Queen provided them with a new cottage; a mother had lost a son, and Alice went with the Queen to offer what comfort she could. On one afternoon alone, Alice, Vicky and the Queen's friend and lady-of-the-bedchamber, Jane Churchill, went for a walk and, according to the Queen:

"…stopped at the shop and made some purchases for poor people and others;…walked up the hill to [the home of Mrs Farquhason and she walked around with us to some of the cottages…Before we went into any, we met an old woman who…was very poor and eighty-six years old…I gave her a warm petticoat…I went into a small cabin of old Kitty Kear's…she sat down and spun; I gave her also a warm petticoat…We went into three other cottages and…to see old Mrs Grant…to whom I gave a dress and handkerchief."[25]

Much as Alice enjoyed these encounters with 'ordinary' people, she took even greater pleasure in the family events celebrated within her own home. Christmas at Windsor was particularly magical, thanks largely to the influence of Prince Albert who introduced many German traditions to Britain, including decorating the tree, which was suspended from the ceiling and decked with coloured candles and artificial snow. Gifts were laid out on separate tables for the household and members of the family, and, following the religious service, a large and often noisy family dinner was held.

On birthdays and anniversaries, the children entertained the guests with masques or tableaux, which they prepared and performed with gusto. On one occasion, according to the visiting Baroness Bunsen, they produced a representation of the Four Seasons:

> "...First appeared Princess Alice as the Spring, scattering flowers, and reciting verses, which were taken from Thomson's Seasons; she moved gracefully and spoke in a distinct and pleasing manner with excellent modulation, and a tone of voice sweet and penetrating like that of the Queen."[26]

On another occasion, the subject was Little Red Riding Hood where, again, Alice was called upon to recite verses from memory.

It was common practice for members of the Royal Family not only to receive but also to give gifts on their birthdays. When the family was staying at Balmoral on the Queen's birthday, May 24th, a carriage packed with presents was sent around the local villages, and every woman within a five mile radius was given a new dress, a pound of tea and two pounds of sugar.

The children's birthdays were also celebrated with parties and dances, and were such happy occasions that Alice's governess Miss Hildyard commented that:

> "The whole family indeed appear to advantage on birthdays...no tradesman or country squire can keep one with such hearty affection and enjoyment."[27]

As at Christmas, tables were set out filled with gifts from the household and members of the extended family, the most interesting, perhaps, being a pet lamb, which Alice received on her fifth birthday, to the consternation of Lady Lyttelton:

"One present I think we all wish to live farther off: a live lamb, all over pink ribbons and bells. He is already the greatest pet, as one may suppose. Princess Alice's pet lamb is the cause of many tears. He will not take to his mistress but runs away lustily, and will soon butt at her, though she is most coaxy, and said to him in her sweetest tones, after kissing his nose often: 'Milly, dear Milly! Do you like me?'"[28]

An even greater surprise awaited her the following year when, just six months before his death from scarlet fever, the composer, Johann Strauss I, composed the 'Alice Polka' in her honour. The merry dance was performed for the first time at Buckingham Palace five days later.

Animals were an integral part of Alice's childhood. All the Queen's homes were filled with beloved pets who were as much a part of the family as the royal children. Hardly a portrait was painted without one dog or another being depicted in an affectionate pose; and Queen Victoria, a staunch opponent of vivisection, not only donated large sums to animal charities but was also the first royal patron of the R.S.P.C.A. Even on the day of her coronation, the Queen had returned home to bathe her King Charles spaniel, Dash; and when Prince Albert arrived in England, he was accompanied by his faithful black greyhound, Eos, whose death caused him immense grief and whose bronze statue still stands at Osborne. Prince Albert also had a fondness of birds and insisted that none of the nests in the gardens were ever disturbed. The children were encouraged to care for any wounded creatures that they came across, and an injured sparrow was a particular favourite. Prince Albert was also keen to prosper the farm at Windsor Castle, where various rare breeds of cattle and sheep were housed. Beyond the palaces, the children were taken to the Zoological Gardens in Regents Park, where Alice was especially delighted an Indian tigress. Years later, Alice would foster in her own children the same love of and concern for the welfare of animals.

From the Scottish Highlands to the heart of London; from the Isle of Wight to the towers of Windsor, Alice's childhood was filled with such varied and happy experiences that, years later, she was able to write to her mother with absolute sincerity:

> "What a joyous childhood we had and how greatly it was enhanced by dear, sweet Papa and by all your kindness to us."[29]

Chapter 3 –
A Vain Little Thing

Alice had not remained the baby of the family for long. When she was sixteen months old, a younger brother, Alfred (Affie), was born, to be followed almost two years later by a second sister, Helena (Lenchen). Over the next decade a further four siblings – Arthur, Louise, Leopold and Beatrice – completed the family.

The shift from being the youngest, and the natural process of finding her place in the domestic hierarchy bridled a little of her early self-confidence but did not dampen her enjoyment of receiving praise and attention.

'A vain little thing', according to her mother, she was at times over-excitable, and, even from an early age, shocked the Queen by her lack of inhibition. When she was only five-years-old, Lady Lyttelton recorded:

> "Just had to interrupt an incipient coquettish flirtation begun by Princess Alice with Mons. Nestor while he dressed her hair!"[30]

Although she could be as boisterous as her brothers in their games, Alice also enjoyed the more feminine arts of dressing up in fashionable clothes and fine jewels. As early as her fifth birthday, Lady Lyttelton observed her 'tripping about, blushing and smiling at all her honours,' proudly displaying her new lace dress and a new set of pearls; she treasured the gifts of jewellery that she received from her parents on her birthdays; and, to the frustration of her governess, she was delighted when her lessons were interrupted by a visit from the dressmaker.

For the first few years of her life, Alice's education was solely under the charge of Lady Lyttelton in the nursery, but soon she was attending lessons with Vicky, and, while could not compete with her elder sister's aptitude for learning, she 'read well', had a ready grasp of languages, and displayed gymnastic, artistic and musical talents – she soon became a particularly competent pianist, who would later accompany the composer, Brahms, and who delighted in listening to performances by Agnes Zimmermann and other acclaimed pianists of the day. Under the supervision of Lady Lyttelton, the unpunctual Mme Rollande was selected to teach French; the frail Mlle Grüner taught German; a dancing master, Joseph Lowe, trained Alice and her sisters in the necessary accomplishments of the ballroom, and also instructed them in callisthenics – the most up-to-date form of exercise for girls in that era. Virtually every other subject was consigned to the care of the much-loved Miss Hildyard, a parson's daughter, whom the children affectionately named Tilla.

Lessons began between eight and eight-thirty in the morning and continued until six in the evening, broken throughout the day by frequent physical and outdoor activities – and, as Lady Lyttelton complained, by the arrival of couturiers, painters or visiting theatre troupes and the necessary rehearsals for the family tableaux. Frequently, the Queen or Prince Albert sat in on a lesson to monitor the children's progress, and in the event that one of their tutors was absent, the Queen was happy to take over the class herself. Extra-curricular activities were a vital aspect of the children's education. Alongside visits to the Botanical and Zoological Gardens, Miss Hildyard occasionally took her charges to lectures from well-known scientists and academics.

Apart from dancing, there were several necessary accomplishments required of a princess, the most important of which was the ability to converse with people of many different backgrounds. Placing chairs in a circle, Alice and her sisters practised moving around the room, addressing imaginary ambassadors, princes or politicians with appropriate questions and comments to initiate a conversation.

Within the sheltered world of the palaces and mixing with few other children, Alice became particularly close to her elder siblings. Vicky, with whom she shared a room, became her role model and confidante, and though Alice was somewhat overshadowed by her elder and more precocious sister, there was never, according to their friend, Louise of Prussia, "...the least semblance of a disagreement...[Alice's] individuality was less decided and prominent than that of her sister and she had a special charm of childhood grace."[31]

Nor was Alice afraid to correct her sister, when she felt that she was in the wrong. Vicky, who was as prone to bursting into tears as Alice was, was sobbing one evening after being reprimanded, and Miss Hildyard overheard Alice sighing,

"Oh Vicky! How can you be so naughty?"

In spite of her somewhat self-righteous indignation, Alice was equally capable of misbehaving. One afternoon, she and Vicky noticed a maid black-leading the fire grate and, under the pretext of learning how it was done, asked her to give them the polish. Rather than applying it to the grate, they seized the poor girl and rubbed it all over her face until she fled from the room and, by chance, ran straight into Prince Albert. That evening, members of the household caught sight of the Queen leading her two eldest daughters by the hand to the servants' quarters to apologise to the unfortunate maid where they were told to apologise to the unfortunate girl before using their pocket money to buy her an entirely new set of clothes – including a hat, gloves and shawl – to compensate for the dress they had stained.

More often than not, though, it was Bertie, rather than Vicky, who was Alice's 'partner in crime'. Together they sneaked off to the Swiss Cottage to smoke cigarettes – a habit which the Queen detested, and one which resulted in a severe reprimand when it was discovered by

Miss Hildyard – and, on the frequent occasions when Bertie was banished to his room, 'Alee', as he called her, crept up to whisper to him and to pass biscuits beneath the door. Bertie returned the favour when it was Alice's turn to be reprimanded, and throughout their lives they would champion each other's cause when either one of them was out of favour with their mother.

> "She is like Bertie in many ways," the Queen commented – and a comparison to Bertie was never a compliment! – "but has a sweet temper and is industrious and conquers all her difficulties."[32]

So devoted was Alice to Bertie that she kept a lock of his hair in a locket around her neck and, whenever he was absent, she missed him so much that she cried herself to sleep.

It was soon clear, however, that if Vicky had inherited her father's brilliant brain, Alice had inherited his heart. Her kindness and awareness of the needs of others was frequently commented upon by members of the suite for whom she bought presents with her saved pocket money and the earnings from the sale of her fruit and flowers.

> "At Christmastime," recalled a German member of the household, "she was most anxious to give pleasure to everybody, and bought presents for each with her own pocket money. She once gave me a little pin cushion, and on another occasion a basket, and wrote on a little card with a coloured border (always in German for me), 'For dear Frida from Alice', and brought it to me on Christmas Eve. I felt that she thought how much I must have missed my home that day."[33]

Once when Bertie made a rather cutting comment about one of his mother's very tall dressers, Alice responded within earshot,

51

"It is very nice to be tall. Papa would like us all to be tall."

Her concern for others went beyond the confines of the palaces. She was genuinely interested in the lives of the tenants at Osborne and Balmoral whose homes she often visited; and on at least one occasion she left the family pew during a church service to sit with the lowlier members of the congregation[34].

Her sensitivity and empathy was not without disadvantages, since, combined with her passionate nature, it frequently sank into sentimentality and tears. She sobbed when her parents departed for a tour; and could hardly bear to be parted with Lady Lyttelton, when she resigned as Superintendent of the Nursery, causing both the Queen and Prince Albert to speak of her as, "Poor, dear little Alice."

The melancholy which often accompanies hypersensitivity, was, though, but one aspect of a personality that was more commonly dominated by cheerfulness and an exquisite sense of humour. Prince Albert called Alice 'an extremely good and cheerful child', and, according to Louise of Prussia, she was:

"...charming, merry and amiable...[Her] cheerful disposition and her great power of observation showed themselves very early in the pleasantest manner, and she had a remarkable gift for making herself attractive to others."[35]

Lord Greville, too, described seven-year-old Alice as 'a singularly attractive child' and he added:

"I doubt whether any childhood or youth was ever more joyous and bright, or ever gave a livelier promise of that which was afterwards so amply fulfilled."[36]

Nonetheless, like her father, Alice was prone to moods of sadness, springing from her profundity and the desire to delve beyond the superficial. One moment she might delight in pretty dresses and jewellery, but the next she was bewildered by the most profound questions of the meaning and purpose of suffering and life itself. Music and art moved her immensely, and in her lifelong quest for the aesthetic, she closely resembled Prince Albert, who also combined the practicalities of duty with a deep-rooted soul-searching and sense of the Infinite.

Unsurprisingly, Alice adored her father as the one person who truly understood her, and his example became the yardstick by which she would measure her progress for the rest of her life.

> "It makes me feel myself so small, so imperfect when I think that I am his child and so unworthy of being it."[37]

The hours she spent in his company became her happiest memories, and she would look back on them always with a deep sense of gratitude and nostalgia. Unfortunately, as the Prince's responsibilities increased, he had less and less time to spend with his family but his absences merely strengthened Alice's admiration, particularly when she saw the fruits of his labours, the greatest of which began when she was seven years old.

During his tours of numerous factories and farms, it had occurred to Prince Albert that the many technological advances of the Industrial and Agricultural Revolutions could not only increase production and make life easier for workers but also contribute to international peace by bringing people together to share their ideas for the benefit of humanity. The Prince had observed, too, that much of the ugliness of the overcrowded cities could be ameliorated by combining art and science to create havens of industrial activity in aesthetically pleasing settings. By 1850, he had formed an idea of presenting a 'Great Exhibition' of the most innovative and beautiful designs, comprising contributions from people of different nations.

The amount of planning and preparation required for such a venture was immense but, while Prince Albert, with Queen Victoria's unreserved support, threw himself wholeheartedly into forming a Royal Commission to oversee the project, there were many who did not share his enthusiasm and were quick to pour scorn on his plans. Xenophobes claimed that it was madness to encourage foreigners to travel to Britain since they would undoubtedly cause chaos and spread revolutionary ideas.

"The strangers...are certain to commence a thorough revolution here," Prince Albert wrote in disgust, "to murder Victoria and myself and to proclaim the Red Republic in England...For all this I am to be responsible, and against all this I am to make efficient provision."[38]

Undeterred, he pressed on, organising a competition to invite designs for a building to house the exhibition. After sifting through various suggestions, the Royal Commission awarded the contract to the architect and landscape gardener, Joseph Paxton.

Paxton, who had designed the pioneering conservatories at Chatsworth House in Derbyshire, had put forward a proposal for an enormous glass construction – the Crystal Palace. While Prince Albert enthused, many scientists and Members of Parliament sneered that such a building would be far too flimsy to withstand storms or wind, and contemptuously added that, since there would be very little interest in the exhibition anyway, the entire plan was doomed to be an expensive failure.

Prince Albert remained optimistic but as the day of the opening approached, he met with further disappointment. One by one, the European monarchs and princes declined an invitation on the grounds that security in Britain was too lax and the country was haven for exiled anarchists. Even the heir to the throne of Prussia, who had found refuge in Britain during the uprisings of 1848[c], sent a cautious reply and only after a rather terse response from Prince Albert did he agree to attend. His decision would have far-reaching consequences for Alice and her sister, Vicky[d].

The Great Exhibition was officially opened by Queen Victoria on 1st May 1851 and, to the delight of the Royal Family and the humiliation of the critics, it proved an instant success. The foreigners converging on the city were, according to Lord Macaulay, all 'respectable and decent people'; and Alice witnessed crowds of visitors wandering in awe through the nineteen acres of the impressive glass palace, enjoying the beauty of the building with its pink crystal fountain and indoor trees. A hundred thousand displays were on view, from plush French tapestries to Stevenson's hydraulic press, and from the renowned Kohinoor Diamond to a bed with a timer to eject its sleeping occupant.

> "I made my way into the building," wrote Macaulay, "a most gorgeous sight; vast; graceful; beyond the dreams of Arabian romances. I cannot think that the Caesars ever exhibited a more splendid spectacle."[39]

Queen Victoria was even more overwhelmed and gushed to Uncle Leopold that it was:

> "...the greatest day in our history...the most beautiful, imposing and touching spectacle ever seen, and the triumph of my beloved Albert. Truly it was astonishing, a fairy scene. Many cried, all felt touched and impressed with devotional feelings. It was the happiest, proudest day in my life and I can think of nothing else. Albert's dearest name is immortalised with this great

[c] See Chapter 4
[d] See Chapter 5

conception, his own and my own dear country showed she was worthy of it. The triumph is immense..."[40]

Alice, too, stood in awe of her father's ability to bring his magical dream to fruition in the face of so much mockery and opposition. Undoubtedly, she was still more impressed when the Prince, realising that the £2-3 price of admission was preventing many working people from attending, arranged for alternative tickets to be made available for only a shilling. From then on, the numbers of visitors rose to an average of almost fifty thousand per day and, within a very short time, the exhibition had paid for itself and presented a glorious image of Britain to the world. Such a moment of triumph was surely in Alice's mind when, fourteen years later, she wrote to her mother:

"The longer I live, the more I see of the world, the deeper my tender admiration grows for such a father...You can understand with what pride and love I talk of him...Dear beloved Papa, he never half knew how much, even when a foolish child, I loved an adored him."[41]

In the midst of the triumph, as Alice stood with her family on a plinth in the Crystal Palace, it must have seemed to observers – and to Alice herself – that her privileged upbringing in a loving and healthy environment where her talents were nurtured, had created an idyllic childhood, but, while Alice would always look back nostalgically to those happy days, she was learning, too, the responsibilities and very real dangers of being born into a 19th century royal family.

Chapter 4 – Our Little Riots

One bright afternoon in May 1849, six-year-old Alice was returning along Constitution Hill from her mother's birthday celebrations when suddenly, from the middle of the cheering crowds, an unemployed Irishman, William Hamilton, stepped forwards and fired a pistol point-blank at the Queen. Fortunately, the gun had not been properly loaded and failed to fire but for Alice it was a rude awakening as to the perils faced by royalty.

A year later, an even more frightening incident occurred while Alice and her brothers, Bertie and Affie, were returning with the Queen from a visit to her uncle, the Duke of Cambridge. As the carriage moved through a crowded thoroughfare, a man named Robert Pate stepped forwards and violently struck the Queen with the brass end of his cane. Instantly, the angry crowds seized the attacker but it was several seconds before the Queen regained sufficient consciousness to stand up and announce to the horrified onlookers that she was not seriously hurt. Nonetheless, the episode was shocking for her children and, indeed, for the Queen herself, who observed that it was brutal for a man to strike a defenceless woman, and an assault with a stick was far more cowardly than if he had attempted to shoot her! Some days later, still suffering the after-effects of the attack, she wrote to King Leopold:

> "I have not suffered except from my head, which is still very tender, the blow having been extremely violent, and the brass end of the stick fell on my head to make a considerable noise. I own it makes me nervous out driving, and I start at any person coming near the carriage, which I am afraid is natural."[42]

To protect herself from further blows to the head, the Queen often carried a green silk parasol that was lined with chain-mail, but such a precaution did not remove the constant danger to which she and her family were exposed.[e] Frequently throughout Alice's childhood disconcerting letters arrived at the palace, threatening to kidnap or murder the royal children, and, while it was assumed that the majority of these were written by 'mad men', Prince Albert took them very seriously.

> "The last thing we did before bedtime," wrote Lady Lyttelton, "was to visit the access to the children's apartments to satisfy ourselves that all was safe. And the intricate turns and locks and guard rooms, and the various intense precautions, suggesting the most hideous dangers, which I fear are not altogether imaginary, made one shudder! The most important key is never out of Prince Albert's own keeping, and the very thought must be enough to cloud his fair brow with anxiety."[43]

As if threats from madmen and would-be assassins were not distressing enough, Alice and her family were also aware of the perennial possibility of revolution.

Throughout the early months of 1848, unrest was sweeping through Europe and parts of South America. Rapid industrialisation, inadequate housing, unjust working conditions and overcrowding had led to discontent which turned the cities into the ideal recruiting ground for socialists and communists in their search for supporters. This was the year in which Karl Marx and Friedrich Engels produced their *Communist Manifesto,* urging the 'workers of the world' to unite against the bourgeoisie and ruling classes. Although the pamphlet

---

[e] There were in fact no less than seven attempts on Queen Victoria's life throughout her sixty-three year reign. The Prince of Wales was shot at in Belgium; and Prince Alfred was shot in the back on a tour of Australia.

was not directly responsible for the events which overtook Europe that year, it was symbolic of the emergence of a new group of social revolutionaries who viewed the monarchy and all it stood for as an enemy of the people.

In a turbulent political climate, when the upper classes were held responsible for the poverty of the masses, any indiscretion or crime on their part could produce a spark to ignite the flame of revolution. Such was the case in France in 1848.

The previous summer, a sordid tale of murder and adultery across the Channel reached the ears of Queen Victoria. Shortly before dawn on Monday 18th August 1847, blood-curdling screams shattered the silence of the Hôtel Sébastiani, the Parisian residence of the Duc and Duchesse de Praslin. Startled into action, servants scrambled along the corridors to the rooms of the thirty-year-old Duchesse, only to find the doors bolted. As they struggled to force the locks, the screams gradually faded until the door opened from the inside and the Duc appeared in the entrance. Behind him, amid overturned furniture covered in blood, the Duchesse – her throat half-cut, her hands slashed and her head bludgeoned by a candlestick – lay gasping her last.

The Duc, feigning shock, was quick to state that this was the work of an intruder but, within minutes of the arrival of the Sûreté Nationale, it was established he was the culprit. Not only were his blood-stained clothes and hunting knife found in his adjoining room but the whole of Paris knew he had a definite motive for murder.

Behind of their façade of domestic harmony, the Duc and Duchesse de Praslin had, for more than five years, endured a strained co-existence. Amid rumours of child abuse, the Duc had forbidden his volatile wife from playing any part in their children's upbringing, handing over all authority for their welfare and education to their English-trained governess, Henriette Deluzy, who was rumoured to be his lover. While the hysterical Duchesse ranted and raved, French newspapers gloated in reporting details of the alleged affair until, at last, under pressure from his father-in-law, the Duc was compelled to send the unfortunate Henriette on her way. Far from easing the situation, her departure served only to increase the tension in the household, culminating in the frenzied attack on the 18th August.

"What a mess!" sighed King Louis Philippe as the Duc de Praslin, still protesting his innocence, was brought before a Court of Peers and found guilty of murder. To appease the public's demand for justice, he was condemned to death but before the sentence could be carried out he poisoned himself with arsenic and died in agony six days later.

There, the domestic tragedy might have ended, but these were unsettling times and a scandal involving a well-known aristocrat was enough to shake public confidence in an already teetering monarchy.

"This horrid Praslin tragedy is a subject one cannot get out of one's head," Queen Victoria recorded. "The Government can in no way be accused of these murders, but there is no doubt that the standard of morality is very low indeed in France, and that the higher classes are extremely unprincipled. This must shake the security and prosperity of a nation."[44]

Her anxiety was justified. Within six months, the security of the nation would be shaken to the core.

In February 1848, the Queen received the alarming news that King Louis Philippe, father-in-law to her Uncle Leopold, had been compelled to abdicate and was fleeing the country disguised as a common citizen. Within days, a bedraggled band of royal refugees reached England, where Queen Victoria provided them with a home at Clairmont in Surrey. Far from being grateful for such hospitality, the discontented guests lodged numerous complaints while, to Prince Albert's annoyance, making little effort to use the time of their exile to good effect.

Meanwhile, the unrest across the Channel, spread into the orderly nurseries of Buckingham Palace and Windsor Castle as the children of the Queen's French cousins irked the staff by their disruptive behaviour, and unsettled the royal children with stories of their perilous escape from the revolution.

Even without these first-hand accounts, Alice would surely have realised that these were dangerous times. Revolution spread from France to Italy, Denmark and Germany, while civil war erupted in Switzerland. The Austrian Emperor was compelled to abdicate in favour of his eighteen-year-old nephew, Franz Josef; and the heir to the Prussian throne fled to England, disguised as a merchant. The danger of similar scenes being enacted in Britain moved ever closer as riots broke out in various cities and a feeling of unease swept the country.

"Our little riots are a mere nothing and the feeling here is very good," Queen Victoria reassured Uncle Leopold, but a month later she was far less convinced as she wrote of the 'awful sad and heart-breaking times…and the future is very dark.'

Prince Albert was so alarmed at the prospect of imminent revolution that he began boarding up the windows of Buckingham Palace and preparing escape routes for his family. Although he attempted to shield his wife and children from his fears, the atmosphere was so tense that so sensitive a child as Alice could not have failed to pick up on it.

Towards the end of March, anxieties increased when it was announced that the Chartists[f] were preparing a mass demonstration in London on 10th April. Although

[f] The Chartists, adherents of 'The People's Charter' of 1838, were a group of working men demanding political reform.

the Chartists themselves were not perceived as a threat, it was feared that a gathering of such magnitude could easily turn hostile and lead to further riots or even revolution. Prince Albert was in a quandary: to leave the city now would be tantamount to fleeing, whereas staying could leave the Queen and his children exposed to violence. After much reflection and a good deal of persuasion from ministers, he finally decided that the wisest course was to evacuate his family to the safety of Isle of Wight. Typically, however, he was equally concerned with remedying the cause of the dissatisfaction and, once settled at Osborne, he wrote earnestly to the Prime Minister, Lord Russell, that:

> "I have enquired a good deal into the state of employment about London, and I find, to my regret, that the number of workmen of all trades out of employment is <u>very</u> large, and that it has been increased by the reduction of all the works under Government owing to the clamour for economy in the House of Commons…Surely this is not the moment for the tax payers to economise upon the working classes…I think the Government is bound to do what it can to help the working classes over the present moment of distress."[45]

In the event, the precautions proved unnecessary. Far fewer people than expected attended the Chartists' meeting, which passed off peacefully without disturbance. Within a few weeks, the Royal Family returned to London and, as the year progressed, the European revolutions petered out and calm was restored.

Nonetheless, at only five-years-old, Alice had learned that royalties lived a perilous existence; and, having had her first glimpse of revolution, she was about to experience her first taste of the horrors of war.

By the mid-19th century, the crumbling Ottoman (Turkish) Empire was proving too great a temptation for European predators, who were intent on gaining greater control in the region, under the guise of protecting persecuted Christians. The new French President, Louis Napoleon, was among the first to stake a claim by promising assistance to the Catholic Church in Palestine in the hope that in return he would gain support for declaring himself Emperor Napoleon III.

Seeing the success of the French operation, Tsar Nicholas I of Russia initiated a campaign to regain Orthodox rights in the Ottoman lands and, when the Turks raised no objections, he went further and attempted to take control of the Dardanelles. Despite opposition from Britain, France and Austria, who encouraged the Turks to reject the Russian demands, the Tsar's armies, ostensibly under Ottoman supervision, occupied the Principalities of Moldavia and Wallachia on the banks of the Danube with the intention of pressing his case more forcefully.

Concerned that the Russian presence might have an adverse effect on British trade with the Turks and the trade routes to India, ministers in London watched these manoeuvres with alarm, and, by June 1853, 'the Eastern question' was building up to a crisis. Queen Victoria confided to her uncle in Belgium that she was confident that war could be avoided but, four months later, the Turks suddenly turned on the Russian invaders. Within weeks, the Russians retaliated by destroying the Turkish squadron at Sinope, provoking an outcry among the British public who demanded a firm response from the government. Still, the Queen hoped that the situation could be resolved through negotiation and continued to exchange letters with the Tsar, who less than a decade earlier had been such a welcome guest at Windsor.

Despite an ultimatum and the outbreak of war with the Turks, over a year passed before the Russians agreed to evacuate the Danubian Principalities but, by this time, the joint forces of Britain, France and Sardinia were determined to put an end to the Tsar's intervention in the region once and for all. In September 1854, an allied expeditionary force landed in the Crimea and besieged Sebastopol, where the Russian Black Sea fleet was stationed. Britain and her allies were at war.

From the safety of their nursery, the royal children listened with fascination to stories of heroism, which inspired songs and poems such as Tennyson's epic *The Charge of the Light Brigade*:

> *Half a league, half a league,*
> *Half a leage onward,*
> *All in the valley of Death*
> *Rode the six hundred.*
> *'Forward, the Light Brigade!*
> *'Charge for the guns!' he said:*
> *Into the valley of Death*
> *Rode the six hundred...*
>
> *...When can their glory fade?*
> *O the wild charge they made!*
> *All the world wondered.*
> *Honour the charge they made,*
> *Honour the Light Brigade,*
> *Noble six hundred."*

Inspired by such tales, Alice and her siblings eagerly joined the war effort, accompanying their mother to visit the casualties who had been brought back to London, and selling their own paintings to raise funds for wounded soldiers and the families of the dead.

The newspapers, however, told a story very different from that described by the poets. For the first time in history on-the-spot journalists and photographers sent graphic reports of the sufferings of the British troops, which contrasted sharply with the imagery of heroic battles. Lice-ridden and covered in vermin, injured men lay on filthy, rat-infested floors as there were far too few beds to accommodate the number of casualties. Infection spread rapidly; gangrene was rife; and it was soon apparent that far more British soldiers were being killed by typhus and cholera than by injuries received in battle.

'The sick appear to be tended by the sick, and the dying by the dying,' a witness observed; while one of the doctors complained that,

> "...The wretched beggar, who wanders about the streets of London in the rain, leads the life of a prince compared with the British soldiers who are out here fighting for their country."[46]

In response to the public demand for action, the Secretary of the War Office, Sidney Herbert, authorised Florence Nightingale to travel to Scutari with thirty-eight companions to nurse the wounded. 'The Lady with the Lamp' rapidly became the focus of British propaganda as romantic versions of her work appeared in the press:

> "She is a 'ministering angel' without any exaggeration in these hospitals, and, as her slender form glides quietly along each corridor, every poor fellow's face softens with gratitude at the sight of her. When all the medical officers have retired for the night and silence and darkness have settled down upon those miles of prostrate sick, she may be observed alone, with a little lamp in her hand, making her solitary rounds."[47]

In actuality, the death rates increased with the arrival of Florence Nightingale, who came into frequent conflict with more experienced nurses who had been working in the squalid conditions since the beginning of the war. Nonetheless, although her contribution to the immediate welfare of her patients was negligible, her

65

administrative abilities and relentless letter-writing highlighted the plight of the ordinary soldiers, and her harrying of the Government led to improvements in nutrition, sanitation and supplies for the troops.

Florence Nightingale was the heroine of the hour and, as exaggerated stories of her care for the sick and wounded proliferated, Queen Victoria asked to meet her at the home of her doctor, James Clark, where, Prince Albert recorded in his diary,

> "She put before us all the defects of our present military hospital system, and the reforms which are needed. We are much pleased with her; she is very modest."[48]

Shortly afterwards the Queen invited her to Balmoral before writing to her, enclosing a brooch, 'the form and emblems of which commemorate your great and blessed work, and which, I hope, you will wear as a mark of the high approbation of your Sovereign!'[49]

Florence Nightingale's work captured the public imagination, and numerous fund-raising events were staged in her honour. Within a few years, the donations reached £45,000, which was used to establish the Nightingale Fund for training nurses at St. Thomas' Hospital in London.

Eleven-year-old Alice followed the nurse's adventures with such fascination that she and Vicky decided to run away to Scutari to assist her. Of course, their plans did not materialise but the example of the 'lady of the lamp' inspired in Alice an interest in nursing which would continue to the end of her life.

For now, though, she had a more immediate experience of illness when, in the summer of 1855, her younger sister, Louise, contracted scarlet fever. Although outbreaks were common particularly among children, it is possible that Louise caught the illness from one of the wounded soldiers since the measles-like infection was known to spread rapidly through military bases.

As soon as the fever was diagnosed, Prince Albert insisted that the usual precautions were taken – Louise was isolated and confined to bed while the visiting King of Portugal was lodged on a yacht to avoid contamination. Nonetheless, within a short time Louise's brothers, Leopold and Arthur, contracted the illness and eventually Alice, too, fell victim to the disease.

It has often been suggested that Alice's constitution was permanently weakened by the illness, resulting in many of the physical problems she suffered in later life. This, though, is unlikely since the strain was not particularly virulent, and, despite the former belief that scarlet fever is responsible for all kinds of latent maladies which might manifest later in life (most notably photosensitivity), modern medical science finds no evidence to support this claim. Princess Helena (Lenchen), later recalled that Alice 'recovered quickly but for some time afterward a certain delicacy was observable'[50], but that is no reason to suggest that the weakness or delicacy persisted beyond a normal period of recuperation; and it must be remembered that, at the time, Alice was on the verge of puberty, when many young girls acquire 'a certain delicacy'.

The year of Alice's illness did, however, mark a turning-point in her life which might well account for the slowness of her recovery. Although she was, as yet, unaware of it, the idyll of her childhood was rapidly spiralling towards its conclusion, and, within a short time, she would face the trauma of separation from two of her most beloved siblings.

Chapter 5 –
The Real Separation from Childhood

When so many royalties had declined an invitation to the Great Exhibition, Queen Victoria and Prince Albert were relieved that Prince Wilhelm of Prussia eventually decided to attend. His presence not only signified respect for the remarkable achievement but also, unbeknown to Alice, provided Prince Albert with an opportunity to further a long-held dream.

At the time, Germany did not yet exist as a unified nation but comprised a collection of independent kingdoms and grand duchies of which Prussia was rapidly becoming most dominant. Prince Albert cherished the dream that one day the various states would unite under a liberal Prussian leadership so that Germany could become a powerful force for peace and culture throughout the continent. He had studied the subject in detail and had written a now lost treatise on the subject, 'entitled "The German Question Explained" in which he propounded a scheme for a federated German Empire with an Emperor at the head.'[51]

Throughout Prince Wilhelm's sojourn in England during the revolutions of 1848, Prince Albert had found him to be a congenial and intelligent man with whom it was possible to discuss his hopes for the future. For his part, the Prince was grateful for the Royal Family's friendship and declared that, 'In no other State or country could I have passed so well the period of distress and anxiety through which I have gone.'[52]

This friendship between the princes boded well for a future alliance between their two countries and, what was more, made Prince Albert aware of an opening through which his own liberal ideals might one day take root in Germany.

Three years later, when Prince Wilhelm returned to England for the Great Exhibition, he brought with him his children: twelve-year-old Louise, who began a lifelong friendship with Alice, and nineteen-year-old Frederick Wilhelm (Fritz), who stood in awe of the spontaneity of the British Royal Family, which differed quite starkly from the stiffness of his native court. Although nine years her senior, he was particularly mesmerised by the intelligence and precocity of ten-year-old Vicky who, unlike the majority of Prussian princesses, was clearly well-educated, widely-read and capable of conversing on all manner of subjects in fluent German or English.

Prince Albert was similarly impressed by the young prince in whom he recognised many of the qualities which he valued most highly. Fritz was intelligent and serious-minded, with liberal opinions, an eagerness to learn and a willingness to listen to advice. It was obvious to Prince Albert that there could be no better way of securing a peaceful future for a united Germany than to cultivate high ideals in this future King and ensure that he found a like-minded helpmate who would support him in bringing to fruition the dream of a pacific and prosperous nation. Who better to play that role, thought Prince Albert, than his own eldest daughter, Vicky?

As Vicky was still a child at the time of the Great Exhibition, and Prince Albert had no intention of forcing her into marriage against her will, he did not mention the subject to her, but continued to maintain correspondence with Fritz and, with the support of Queen Victoria, nurtured a plan to bring the young people together. As the months passed, Fritz developed a filial affection for Prince Albert and became increasingly appreciative of the way in which the Government and Crown operated in Britain, viewing it as an ideal to which Germany could aspire. Moreover, as he came to know the family better, he could not fail to be impressed by the obvious devotion of Vicky's parents, when his own parents' marriage was anything but an example of domestic harmony.

Meanwhile in Berlin, Fritz's parents had also recognised the benefits of such a match and, despite initial opposition from Prince Wilhelm's brother, the King of Prussia, they were equally eager to bring the young people together. All were agreed, however, that no pressure should be placed on Vicky and Fritz; instead they should be given opportunities to meet in the hope that their blossoming friendship might develop into mutual love. It did not take long for those hopes to be realised.

In the early autumn of 1855, Fritz visited Balmoral where, after almost a week in the remote romantic setting, he summoned the courage to approach the Queen and Prince Albert, requesting their permission to propose to their eldest daughter. Though the Queen's delight was tempered by consternation about fourteen-year-old Vicky's immaturity and a desire that 'all the simple unconstraint of girlhood' should continue for as long as possible, both she and Prince Albert gave their consent on condition that Fritz did not tell Vicky of his intentions until after her confirmation the following spring.

Fritz readily agreed but, in spite of his best efforts to keep the secret, his parents were eagerly awaiting news of the outcome and it was almost inevitable that the story should leak out. As congratulatory messages began to arrive from Prussia, Queen Victoria, fearing that Vicky might discover what had been agreed and think that her future had been decided without her knowledge, decided to rescind her stipulation and invited Fritz to propose directly.

On the afternoon of 20th September 1855, Fritz accompanied Vicky and her parents on a ride up the craggy Highland paths to Craig-na-ban where, as Queen Victoria recorded in her diary:

"...he picked a piece of white heather (the emblem of good luck), which he gave to her; and this enabled him to make an allusion to his hopes and wishes as they rode down Glen Girnock..."[53]

Vicky coyly accepted his proposal and so began what was to become one of the greatest royal love-matches in history. The ever-romantic Queen Victoria was delighted; and, although it perfectly suited Prince Albert's hopes of securing a liberal influence in Prussia, he assured his mentor, Stockmar, that it was not politics which had persuaded him to encourage Fritz's suit, but rather 'it was my heart.'

The following day, Prince Albert was suddenly afflicted with severe rheumatism, which spread so painfully from his left shoulder to his back and right arm that he could not even hold a pen, and was left, in his own words, 'a cripple'. Considering his highly sensitive nature and the strength of his affection for Vicky, it is not too far-fetched to suggest that this sudden attack sprang from his reluctance to accept that her childhood was nearing its conclusion and his happy family unit was soon to be divided.

If Prince Albert was so affected by the prospect of parting with his daughter, the discovery of what had taken place left Alice utterly devastated. Deeply hurt that she had not been warned of the plans, the thought of parting with her closest sister and confidante caused her to break down in tears. It is highly likely that she, whose sensitive nature so resembled that of her father, had an equally strong physical reaction to the news, which accounts for the 'certain delicacy' that followed her recent bout of scarlet fever.

Although, due to Queen Victoria's stipulation that the wedding could not take place until after Vicky's seventeenth birthday, Alice had two years left in which to enjoy her sister's company, it was already obvious that their world was changing rapidly and the security of childhood was drawing to a close. Vicky was no longer simply a confidante and playmate, but rather the fiancée of a foreign prince who would one day inherit a throne. Her evenings were no longer spent with Alice, but rather with her father, who was busily preparing her for life as a future Queen.

Unlike many royalties of the day, Prince Albert did not view his daughters merely as vehicles through which dynasties might be continued. He recognised the importance of their intellectual and political opinions and the benefits they could bring to the countries they served. Such responsibility required intensive training and so, from the moment that Vicky's engagement was officially announced, he spent one hour each day introducing her to political and historical ideas.

> "She comes to me every evening between six and seven, when I put her through a kind of general catechizing," he wrote to Fritz. "In order to make her ideas clear, I let her work out subjects for herself, which she then brings to me for correction. She is at present writing a short compendium of Roman history."[54]

Alice, who adored her father, would have loved such attention, but Vicky's studies served only to emphasise her imminent departure; and, to matters worse, two of her brothers were also on the point of leaving home.

In 1856, at his own request, twelve-year-old Affie began preparing for a career at sea and was allocated his own residence at Royal Lodge, under the supervision of a Royal Navy commander. For Bertie, Affie's departure came as a double blow: now he was not only deprived of his closest companion but he also suffered the humiliation of seeing his younger brother being granted a modicum of independence while he remained at home, straining under the instruction of his overbearing tutor, Frederick Gibbs.

Realising Bertie's frustration and aware of his attraction towards a military life, Prince Albert sought to ease his situation by promising that, if he would apply himself more seriously to his studies and undertake a series of university courses, he could then begin training with the Grenadier Guards. Bertie agreed and soon he, too, was allocated his own residence, White Lodge in Richmond Park, as plans were made for a series of educational tours, which would take him across the Continent and as far afield as the United States of America.

This gradual but definite disintegration of her close-knit family was incredibly painful for Alice, who clung desperately to the security of her childhood, and who found any separation from her siblings or parents deeply distressing. When Vicky and Bertie accompanied their parents on a formal visit to France, Alice was too overcome to greet them on their return to Osborne. While her brothers waited on the beach to greet the travellers, and her sisters came out of the house to welcome them home, 'poor, dear Alice,' remained indoors and, as the Queen recorded, 'was quite upset at seeing us.'[55]

Now, though, with Vicky's wedding approaching, Alice had to face up to the inevitability of change. Realising that she had no alternative, she worked to overcome her emotions and to suppress the passionate nature. The effort required was enormous for a child who would burst into tears at the slightest provocation, and, though the Queen admired her determination to overcome her natural impulses, in later years her stoicism was occasionally mistaken for coldness. Perhaps so sensitive a soul could only deal with painful emotions by suppressing her feelings and distracting herself from them by acquiring ever-increasing commitments and duties; and in this, as in so many aspects of her character, she grew daily more like the father whom she adored.

The New Year, 1858, began with a flurry of activity as the final preparations were underway for Vicky's wedding. On 15th January, as guests began to arrive from all over Europe, the Royal Family left Windsor for Buckingham Palace.

> "We took a short walk with Vicky, who was dreadfully upset at this real break in her life; the real separation from childhood!" the Queen wrote that evening in her diary. "She slept for the last time in the same room as Alice..."[56]

Fortunately for Alice, the next nine days were filled with festivities and the comings and goings of so many guests that there was little time for self-pity; and as the morning of the 25th January dawned to the sound of bells ringing out across the city, she was ready to play the role of bridesmaid with finesse and grace. Wreathed in flowers and dressed in pink satin decorated in Newport lace, she entered the Chapel Royal in St. James' Palace, hand-in-hand with her younger sisters, Louise and Lenchen, to witness Vicky serenely pronouncing her vows and preparing to begin a new life in a foreign country.

Days of celebrations followed, postponing the inevitable departure for just over a week but the delays could not continue forever, and on a dull February morning the time came for Alice and siblings to say their goodbyes. After spending a few brief moments with the Queen, Vicky and Fritz walked into the Audience Chamber where a broken-hearted Alice was waiting with the rest of the family. Everyone, including the newly-weds, wept, and Queen Victoria was so overcome by grief that she could not even bear to accompany the couple to the ship which would take them to Germany. Prince

Albert and Bertie travelled with them to Trinity Pier and, within an hour, both Alice and Queen Victoria sat down to write to Vicky:

> "..it is cruel, very cruel – very trying for parents to give up their beloved children and see them go away from the happy peaceful home – where you used to be all around us!...You, though always our own dear child and always able to be at home in your parents' house, are no longer one of the many, merry children who used to gather so fondly around us...Poor, dear Alice, whose sobs must have gone to your heart – is sitting near me, writing to you."[57]

When Alice eventually dried her tears, she would realise that in losing a sister her own position had significantly altered. Now, as the eldest daughter at home, she would gain new privileges and be expected to play a more prominent role in the public duties of the Royal Family. Vicky's departure had certainly been traumatic, but it had also paved the way for Alice to step out of her shadow, to mature in her own way and to demonstrate her own innate talents more fully than ever before.

Chapter 6 –
A Very dear Companion

Queen Victoria had no intention of allowing any detail of Vicky's new life to escape her notice. Her daily letters to Berlin were filled with questions to which she expected prompt replies. If the responses did not come immediately or were insufficiently thorough, Vicky could be sure to receive a reprimand, demanding a fuller account of her everyday life, right down to descriptions of the clothes she was wearing and the furniture in her rooms. So excessive were the Queen's expectations that eventually Prince Albert had to intervene, explaining that the poor girl could not possibly settle in her new homeland while her mother continued to require so much of her attention.

By now, though, with Vicky far away in Prussia, the Queen was able to focus more clearly on her second daughter, and she was happily surprised to discover how quickly and easily Alice filled the void left by her elder sister.

"She is a very dear companion," she wrote fondly to Vicky. "She is really very good, so amiable, so gentle, so obliging and so humble."[58]

It was typical of Queen Victoria that as her admiration increased, so too did her perception of Alice's physical appearance. Now, the child, who had once been nicknamed Fatima, was 'graceful' and 'quite grown up; very pretty and with perfect manners in society, quite ladylike at cercléing.' Most impressive of all, though, in the Queen's opinion, was the beneficial influence which Alice had over her elder brother.

Suffocating in the seclusion of White Lodge, the Prince of Wales continued to distress his parents by his failure to live up to their expectations – or, more especially, his inability to resemble his father. Repeatedly, throughout Bertie's childhood and youth, Prince Albert was held up as the paradigm to which he should aspire but, at the same time, he was kept keenly aware that he could never hope to attain such a standard of perfection.

Confused and disheartened, Bertie made little effort to accommodate his parents' wishes, and despite his eagerness to pass the necessary military examinations to join the Guards Regiment, by the age of seventeen, he had no more aptitude for study than he had had when he was a small child. Rather than appreciating his natural talents for geniality and diplomacy or his flair for style and individuality, his parents simply could not understand why he had not inherited Prince Albert's diligence. There were times when the despairing Queen blamed herself and her Hanoverian ancestry for his failings, once remarking that he was her caricature, but this only added to her exasperation that he would not, or could not, adapt to her and Albert's attempts to mould him into an ideal prince.

> "Oh! Bertie, alas! That is too sad a subject to enter on," she complained to Vicky. "...He vexes us much. There is not a particle of reflection or even attention to anything but dress! Not the slightest desire to learn..."[59]

Fortunately, Bertie had a reliable supporter in Alice, who not only defended him and praised his qualities but was also the one person in the family to whom he would listen. According to the Queen, she had 'much influence with him', and it was becoming increasingly apparent that this influence was beneficial to Bertie himself, and helped to smooth the relationship between him and his parents.

Clearly, in Vicky's absence, Alice's unique gifts had begun to shine, and, just as she had earned her mother's admiration, it would not be long before she was making an equally favourable impression on the public.

One Monday evening in early September 1858, the royal train, en route from Osborne to Balmoral, stopped in Leeds where the Queen had been invited to open the new Town Hall. The occasion was particularly memorable for Alice, since this was her first official engagement; and it was equally memorable for the people of Leeds, since it was the first time that a reigning monarch had officially visited the town[g].

The train drew into the station at six-fifteen and, as Alice stepped onto the platform, she and her younger sister, Lenchen, were presented with bouquets by the Lord Mayor's daughters before participating in a procession through the crowded streets. The Loiners[h] had turned out in force to present a rapturous welcome and no expense had been spared in the preparations for the visit. The thoroughfares were festooned with greenery, wrought into wreaths spelling out the names of Alice and her siblings, and even palm trees had been brought in to mark the occasion.

> "Nowhere have I seen the children's names so often inscribed," the Queen observed. "On one large arch were even 'Beatrice and Leopold,' which gave me much pleasure."[60]

It was, however, the warmth of the crowds which made the occasion so unforgettable. As Alice left the station in the royal carriage, she was overwhelmed by the numbers of people who had gathered from all over the county and beyond.

> "There arose such a cheer, as has seldom been heard before," wrote a reporter from *The Times*. "It was a cheer, not only of the thousands to whom [the Queen] was visible, but the cheers of all along the line of route; it was caught up and passed from

---

[g] Queen Victoria had previously visited Leeds – which did not become a city until 1893 – in 1835, two years prior to her accession.
[h] Loiners = people of Leeds

street to street, and into places far removed from where the Queen would pass – one long sustained outburst of loyal enthusiasm."

That evening, the Royal Family stayed at Woodley House, the home of the Lord Mayor, whose striking appearance made a great impression on the Queen, and an even greater impression on Alice's governess:

"Such a picturesque Mayor," Queen Victoria wrote to Vicky that evening. "He looked like a Doge painted by Titian. Miss Hildyard is in ecstasies about him."[61]

The following morning, the enthusiastic applause resumed when Alice accompanied her parents to Woodhouse Moor, where thousands of Sunday School children had assembled to sing a selection of hymns. From there, the royal party progressed to the Mayor's woollen mill – a visit of specific interest to Prince Albert, who had seen the machinery used in the mill at the Great Exhibition – before arriving at the Town Hall for the official opening. That evening, after knighting the Lord Mayor, the Queen and her family left the town and continued their journey to Balmoral.

At fifteen-years-old, Alice's grace and composure had won the affection of the crowds, and in the months that followed she would continue to rise in her mother's estimation. Now, she was considered sufficiently mature to join her parents for dinner once or twice a week; and just as Prince Albert had tutored Vicky prior to her marriage, he now focussed more intently on Alice's education. Each evening she was invited to spend an hour alone with him to discuss history, politics and literature to enable her to form opinions, which would, it was hoped, serve her well in her future role – whatever and wherever that might be.

For Alice these evenings were sheer delight so it was hardly surprising that Prince Albert should remark that she was always 'most attentive'. Unfortunately, however, due to his many responsibilities, he was often late for her lesson and sometimes failed to arrive at all. While Alice accepted the situation with good grace, her disappointment in his absence was a mild foreshadowing of the events which would soon unfold to take him from her forever.

For now, though, unaware of the impending tragedy, Alice was relishing the swansong of her childhood. These were the halcyon days, which she would look back on for the rest of her life – a time when she was able to form her own ideas, develop her personality and blossom into maturity, while still unburdened by the responsibilities of adulthood.

In the spring of 1859 as she approached her sixteenth birthday, plans were underway for Alice's confirmation in the Church of England. Apart from its religious significance, the sacrament was a major stepping-stone in the life of a princess, marking the transition from childhood to early adulthood. Once a young lady had been confirmed she was considered old enough to attend balls and, quite often, preparations began for marriage.

Though acutely aware of the sacrament's practical aspects, the Queen and Prince Albert were more concerned with its spiritual importance. Prayer and faith were central to their household – on being informed that her uncle had died and she was now Queen, the eighteen-year-old Victoria's immediate response had been, 'I ask your prayers on my behalf,'; and later she commented, 'It is hard that I cannot always hear my children say their prayers'. No matter where the family was staying, Sunday services were meticulously observed, and it had been perfectly natural for Prince Albert to mark the opening of Osborne House with a hymn and a prayer. A clergyman from the Isle of Wight recalled an occasion when he was visiting an invalid and noticed a woman sitting by the sickbed reading quietly from the Bible. Only when the woman rose to leave, did he recognise Queen Victoria.

Neither the Queen nor the Prince had, however, any interest in the mere show of religion. Concerned more with the spirit than the letter of the law, Queen Victoria had little time for black-clad bishops and was most put out by the long, dreary sermon muttered inaudibly by the Archbishop at Vicky's confirmation. She was equally dismissive of excessive piety and would tell her children and grandchildren that it made little difference whether they said their prayers kneeling down or lying in bed.

"I am quite clear," she had written of Vicky, "that she should be taught to have great reverence for God and for religion, but that she should have the feeling of devotion and love which our Heavenly Father encourages His earthly children to have for Him, and not one of fear and trembling. ; and that thoughts of death and afterlife should not be represented in an alarming or forbidding view...and not think that she can only pray on her knees, or that those who do not kneel are less fervent and devout in their prayers."[62]

Unimpressed by sham-holiness or the trappings of religion, she was distressed to realise that her presence at Whippingham Church on the Isle of Wight was distracting the congregation from the service, and consequently arranged for a private Prayer Room to be set up in Osborne House, furnished with an unostentatious pulpit and altar.

This devotion to Christianity did not, however, provoke bigotry or self-righteousness, and both the Queen and Prince Consort were anxious to promote the rights of people of different denominations and faiths. During their stays at Balmoral, they were happy to attend Presbyterian services; during a visit to Ireland they were conducted around the schools by the Roman Catholic Archbishop of Dublin; and, in later life, Queen Victoria would acknowledge the festivals of her Indian servants, and write frequently to her generals and ambassadors, reminding them to respect the customs and rites of native peoples across the Empire.

'One must be tolerant,' she wrote, and, true to her word, would raise no objections when three of her granddaughters chose to convert to Orthodoxy.

Prince Albert was equally broad-minded in respect of other denominations. In spite of his personal distaste for 'Popish' ceremonies, he and the Queen were horrified when, in 1850, the Pope's re-establishment of a Roman Catholic hierarchy in England led to an upsurge of anti-Catholic feeling.

"Sincerely Protestant as I am," the Queen wrote to her aunt, "...and indignant as I am at those who call themselves Protestants, while they in fact are quite the contrary, I much regret the unchristian and intolerant spirit exhibited by many people at public meetings. I cannot bear to hear the violent abuse of the Catholic religion, which is so painful and cruel towards many good and innocent Roman Catholics."[63]

When the government attempted to pass the Ecclesiastical Titles Bill, prohibiting the re-establishment of Catholic dioceses, Prince Albert went out of his way to calm the situation and succeeded in having the Act postponed. When it did come into force the following year, it was never implemented, thanks largely to the Prince's influence.

Within the Church of England, too, the Queen and Prince Albert encouraged tolerance, rejecting the paternalistic approach of some Evangelicals who wished to impose puritanical laws such as the prohibition of gambling and the sale of alcohol. While supporting what they saw as Christian reforms such as the abolition of slavery and the reduction of working hours for children, they refused to countenance any measures which would impinge on individual freedom of choice.

The Queen was, nonetheless, firmly committed to a simple faith and pressed her children to accept God's will with absolute trust. In the era of Darwin's *Origin of the Species,* when science appeared to be contradicting fundamental beliefs, she believed it was better not to baffle the mind with too many questions and she would later urge one of Alice's daughters not to delve too deeply into questions which might undermine her faith.

In this, Prince Albert differed from the Queen, for, notwithstanding his poetic temperament, he was also a rationalist whose scientific studies reinforced his spiritual beliefs. He encouraged his sons and daughters to consider opposing arguments in order to reach their own conclusions; and he saw the hand of God at work in each new technological advance or scientific discovery. On a practical level, he recognised, too, the importance of putting his faith into action, as his numerous philanthropic schemes and his determination to use his gifts for the good of others were inspired primarily by his religious beliefs.

It was of the utmost importance to the Queen and the Prince Consort to ensure that their children were well prepared for confirmation – the sacrament in which they would commit themselves to the faith in which they had been baptised. In the weeks leading up to the ceremony, high-ranking clerics tutored and tested them to ascertain that they fully understood the importance of the rite; and they were expected to spend the eve of the service in quiet contemplation. The night before Bertie was confirmed, for example, his brother, Affie, was kept away from him so that 'so that the right atmosphere shall not be disturbed.'

Considering the extent of her later spiritual seeking, Alice undoubtedly approached her confirmation with great seriousness. Like her father, she was both profoundly contemplative, constantly seeking answers to spiritual questions, and, at the same time, committed to correcting her perceived faults and living her faith through service to others.[i] Her diligence in preparing for the sacrament earned her father's respect and her mother's admiration, as, while the Queen sighed wistfully that it was a pity that the ceremony could not be carried out in Germany where it was performed with greater reverence, she noted with satisfaction that, following Alice's examination, both Prince Albert and the Dean of Westminster, Richard Chenevix Trench, were 'much pleased and satisfied with her.' The Archbishop of Canterbury, too, observed Alice's sincerity, noting that she was 'too intrinsically religious by nature to ever be affected by the mere outward form of worship'.

Alice was not so pious, though, as to be immune to the lure of beautiful jewellery and dresses. To mark the occasion, she purchased for herself a diamond necklace and earrings, for which the Queen and Prince Albert made a contribution of £1,000, and she was delighted at being presented with the Royal Family Order and a cameo of her parents surrounded by diamonds.

The ceremony took place on 21st April 1859, after which the Queen reported to Vicky that her sister showed such a deep feeling and was 'altogether so dear, and good, and charming'.

Now she had officially made the transition from childhood to adulthood, and, though she and her mother

---

[i] It is hardly surprising that, several decades later, following Alice's example, one of her daughters, Grand Duchess Elizabeth of Russia, would found an Orthodox order intended to combine the attributes of the Biblical sisters, Martha and Mary, by practical service and meditative contemplation. See *Most Beautiful Princess* by Christina Croft

were reluctant to accept it, the time had come to consider her future and the possibility of marriage.

Chapter 7 –
Her Future is Still Undecided

Three days after her confirmation, Alice celebrated her sixteenth birthday – an occasion which the Queen marked with a sigh of relief that there were as yet no plans for an imminent betrothal. The pain that the Queen had felt at Vicky's departure and the problems Vicky faced on her arrival in Berlin prompted her to the decision that her younger daughters would not be allowed to marry until they were at least eighteen years old. This suited Alice perfectly. By now she had adjusted to Vicky's absence and, thoroughly enjoying the benefits of her status as the eldest child at home, she was in no hurry to find a husband, particularly when news from Berlin created an alarming image of marriage.

In spite of her love for Fritz and his unerring devotion, life in Prussia had not turned out to be quite as idyllic as Vicky had dreamed. By the time of her wedding, Fritz's father, Prince Wilhelm, was acting as regent for his elder brother, who had suffered a stroke and was no longer deemed capable of ruling. Surrounded by ministers and courtiers who viewed the English princess with suspicion, Prince Wilhelm made it clear that his daughter-in-law's sole purpose was to provide a son to continue the Hohenzollern dynasty. Although he treated Vicky with courtesy and kindness, far from appreciating her brilliant intellect or welcoming her political opinions, he was convinced that women had no place in politics, and should confine themselves to pleasing their husbands and producing children.

For Vicky, who had been so carefully groomed to play an important role in the country's future, such attitudes were both baffling and frustrating. While she tried to accommodate the mores of the Prussian court, she could not deny her intelligence or upbringing and found it stifling to remain silent about matters that were close to her – and her father's – heart. To compound her frustration, Fritz, who shared her liberal views, was repeatedly prevented from participating in affairs of state, and, when Vicky pressed him to stand up to the government ministers, she was accused of attempting to dominate him to mould him to her English ways. In truth, there were times when her tactless comparisons of England and Prussia aroused a good deal of antipathy, and the situation was exacerbated by her regular correspondence with her mother, who frequently reminded her that she was first and foremost an English princess.

If the political scene was frustrating, the tension within the royal household was positively excruciating for Vicky. The rancour between Fritz's parents presented a stark contrast to her experience of her own parents' happy marriage, and she found their frequent rows and public disagreements both shocking and painfully embarrassing. Like Vicky, Fritz' mother, Princess Augusta, held strong liberal views and a desire to influence politics, but her attempts to intervene in the government of the country served only to arouse her husband's anger and increase their mutual animosity.

> "...Her life here is as disagreeable as it can be, and it does not improve her health," Vicky told her mother. "If only there are no more scenes; it is so painful to witness..."[64]

The Princess' health issues were more psychological than physical, as her moods swung from one extreme to another in a manic-depressive manner. Initially, Vicky both pitied and admired her, and in return the Princess Augusta confided in her and treated her with such kindness that Vicky happily referred to her as a 'second mother'. Within a short time, however, her endless demands and erratic behaviour became virtually unbearable.

> "...You do not know how difficult it is to be her friend," Vicky confided in Queen Victoria, "for she is always her own enemy!...I must acknowledge that I make many sacrifices for I am always at her beck and call all day long – whenever she wants me, whether it be morning or evening, I go but I look forward with dread to some future day when, as last year, being really faint and sick and unwell, I could not be there at all hours and as [she] is rather tyrannical, she did not like that..."[65]

Though Vicky was reluctant to admit it, it soon seemed clear that the Princess, who had initially been in favour of the marriage, now resented her daughter-in-law's influence over Fritz. Whether the young couple's mutual devotion was a constant reminder of her own dysfunctional marriage, or she simply saw Vicky as a scapegoat to bear her own unhappiness, Princess Augusta began to undermine her at every opportunity, even to the extent of attempting to alienate her from her own children.

Whether or not Alice was aware of these domestic tensions, reports of Vicky's first experience of childbirth did not escape her horrified notice. Despite Queen Victoria's insistence on the administration of chloroform, the labour was so tortuous and protracted that for a while it was feared that neither mother nor child would survive. Disagreements between the attending English and German doctors aggravated the difficulties, and when at last, with the help of forceps, the baby was born in the breech position he appeared not to be breathing. In a desperate effort to revive him, the doctors shook him so frantically that the nerves in his neck were damaged and, as a consequence, his arm failed to develop properly, leaving the future Kaiser Wilhelm II with a humiliating handicap for the rest of his life.

> "The detail which the courier brought us yesterday," Prince Albert wrote to Baron Stockmar, "gave us our first information of the severe suffering which poor Vicky had undergone, and of the great danger in which the child's life hovered for a time."[66]

Queen Victoria's half-sister, Feodore, was even more horrified:

> "Oh! My dear Victoria," she wrote, "I feel all the anxiety and pain you have suffered. It is so dreadful to know what a young creature has had to go through – one's own child, whom we have protected from every ill, guarded against every evil; now we see them in danger and tortured by pain."[67]

While the Queen attempted to shield her younger children from the details of Vicky's ordeal, Alice understood that her sister's sufferings had been extreme, and consequently she was left with such a terror of having children that she announced she would 'rather have none'.

> "Our dear Alice," the Queen told Vicky, "has seen and heard more (of course not what no one can ever know before they marry and before they have had children) than you did, from your marriage – and quite enough to give her a horror rather of marrying."[68]

Nonetheless, neither Alice nor her parents could conceive any other future for a princess than that of a wife and mother, and, in an age where there were so many unhappy royal marriages, the Queen felt it was a 'sad necessity' to find a husband who would at least ensure her daughter's happiness.

It is a testament to the love that the Queen and Prince Albert bore their children that, unlike many royal parents, neither could countenance the idea of forcing any of them into a loveless marriage, no matter how beneficial such a dynastic arrangement might be. On the contrary, a great deal of time was spent studying the characters and backgrounds of similarly-aged royalties and arranging meetings in the hope that mutual attraction might form and develop into love. So it was that, even before Alice's sixteenth birthday, the Queen had enlisted Vicky's help in scouring the courts of Europe for available princes who might one day prove worthy contenders for Alice's hand.

Vicky began the search 'close to home' and within a short time she had furnished the Queen with a collection of photographs of suitable German princes. The Queen viewed them all with a discerning eye and decided:

"Beauty I don't want though I should be glad of it when it's there; but nice manly, sensible, healthy, gentlemanlike appearance is essential."[69]

The first to arouse a passing interest was Fritz's cousin, Prince Albrecht (Abbat) of Prussia. Six years older than Alice, he had once been considered as a possible partner for Queen Victoria's cousin, Princess Mary of Cambridge, of whom the Queen was beginning to despair. As she neared her thirtieth birthday, Mary's forwardness and impropriety convinced her family that it was 'time to get her married' but, though various princes had been suggested, her obesity, ungainly manner and lack of attention to her appearance seemed to be deterring potential suitors. Abbat was added to her list of possibilities but Queen Victoria, whom he had greatly impressed while visiting Osborne, dismissed the idea. Abbat was too young for Mary, she said, and wondered whether he might be more suited to Alice.

No sooner had the thought crossed the Queen's mind than she recalled the scandal surrounding his parents, whose marriage had ended in divorce some months after his mother had left her unfaithful husband to take up residence with a former coachman. Initially, on account of the family's disgrace, the Queen dismissed Abbat from her list, but later, realising that his background was not so different from that of Prince Albert, she was prepared to reconsider and told Vicky not to discard him completely. In the event, nothing came of the idea. Abbat remained single until the age of thirty-six when he married the nineteen-year-old Princess Marie of Saxe-Altenburg.

Meanwhile, Queen Victoria continued to study the photographs and read Vicky's descriptions of the princes with whom she came into contact. Although not particularly clever, Prince William of Baden was 'an excellent person'; Prince Leopold of Hohenzollern-Sigmaringen was especially appealing but unfortunately happened to be a Roman Catholic; and, as the search extended beyond Germany, religion again prevented the Queen from pursuing a possible match with the recently widowed Catholic King Pedro of Portugal.

In the autumn of 1859, Queen Victoria cast her eyes towards the Netherlands where the heir apparent, William, Prince of Orange, was just three years older than Alice. Vicky diligently began to ask questions of those who knew him, and quickly discovered that he had recently been staying in Baden where his dissolute behaviour had earned him a very bad reputation. While the Queen hoped that the stories of his gambling and drinking had been exaggerated, she continued to make further enquiries, all of which sadly confirmed that 'the Orange boy' was not at all suitable for her daughter. Though disappointed, she was not entirely surprised, since his father, who lived apart from his wife, had, she claimed, set him a very bad example. Even when her own Lady of the Bedchamber, Jane Ely, spoke highly of him, and Vicky somewhat priggishly attempted to defend his behaviour by blaming his 'bad, loose habits' on 'bad company and never having associated with people of his own rank', the Queen was not convinced. Lady Ely, she said, was swayed by her friendship with William's mother, and, in response to Vicky's descriptions of the eighteen-year-old prince's 'nice blue eyes, white teeth, and good hair', she retorted:

> "...he is 20 and not 18 – and the 'white teeth' I fear cannot be his own, as he had bad ones when we saw him three years ago. Poor boy, great allowances must of course be made for him."[70]

These allowances did not, of course, extend to considering him as a future son-in-law and the Queen was relieved that she had not told Alice of her investigations, which might have resulted in dashed hopes or disappointment.

No sooner had the Prince of Orange been discounted, however, than suddenly, at the end of December 1859, he announced his intention of visiting Windsor the following month. Queen Victoria was horrified. The arrival of a foreign prince in a household where there lived a princess of marriageable age, would inevitably lead to speculation about the purpose of his visit. Stories linking his name with Alice's would circulate so quickly that it would be virtually impossible to keep the rumours from Alice herself, and, what was worse, they might deter more appropriate suitors from paying her any attention.

Under the circumstances, the Queen and Prince Albert felt it was necessary to warn Alice of the negative reports they had heard about William to prevent her from developing any romantic notions. Alice, who had never met the prince, responded impassively, grateful, perhaps, for her parents' honesty and relieved that she was not being pressurised into falling in love with a stranger. Still, the Queen was disconcerted by the thought that the visit could give rise to stories of an imminent engagement and was greatly relieved when Prince William announced publicly that he considered himself too young to marry, thereby quashing any speculation.

The visit, though uneventful, altered the Queen's perception of the young man. Comparing him favourably with her eldest son, she was impressed by his impeccable behaviour and intelligent conversations with Prince Albert. William, however, was far more attentive to the younger children – two-year-old Beatrice and her brothers – than he was to Alice, and he went on his way, leaving Alice to continue her carefree existence, unburdened by the prospect of an imminent departure to a foreign court.

By now, though, Alice was far too astute to be unaware of her mother's quest. Prince Albert's warning about the Prince of Orange was evidence enough that her parents were busily studying the backgrounds of possible suitors, and, as she neared her seventeenth birthday, she could not forget that, at that age, her elder sister was married. Still, she hoped to cling to the vestiges of childhood and postpone the separation from her family for as long as possible.

"...Only the day before yesterday," Queen Victoria wrote to Vicky, "she said she could not dream or think of going away from us – or from here!"[71]

Her reluctance to leave was understandable. Now, according to her mother, she was physically fitter and stronger than she had ever been; she relished her father's attention, was on excellent terms with her mother, and the intimacy she enjoyed with them both was more rewarding than at any other time in her life.

"Alice has become a handsome young woman of graceful form and graceful presence," Prince Albert wrote to Baron Stockmar in January 1860, "and is a help and stay to us all in the house."[72]

A few days later after this letter was written, Alice accompanied her parents to the State Opening of Parliament for the first time – yet another stepping-stone along the path of royal duties and an acknowledgement of her maturity. By the beginning of 1860, changes were clearly afoot, and a whole new way of life was appearing on the horizon.

"My dearest Uncle," Queen Victoria wrote to the King of the Belgians on 25th April 1860, "I write to you on this paper today, as it is our good Alice's birthday – her seventeenth! She is a good, dear, amiable child, and in very good looks just now. Her future is still undecided, she is quite free, and *all* we wish is a good, kind husband – *no* brilliant position (which there is not to be got), but a quiet, comfortable position."[73]

Alice's future might have been undecided but by now the Queen had narrowed down the list of potential husbands to three: Abbat and two young princes who indeed seemed to offer a 'quiet comfortable position' and at whom she might well have been hinting in her letter.

For some time, the Queen had been making discreet inquiries about the family of Prince Charles, brother and heir of the Grand Duke of Hesse-and-by-Rhine. Her initial interest centred around Prince Charles' only daughter, Anna, whom she briefly considered as a bride for Bertie, but by autumn 1859 she had switched her attention to Anna's brothers, Louis and Henry – in particular, the elder of the two – as serious contenders for Alice's hand.

The princes had first impressed the Queen fifteen years earlier in Coburg, and even then, although they were still children, she had considered them as future prospects for her daughters. Now she needed a more recent appraisal and, as usual, Vicky was enlisted to supply her with photographs, which proved sufficiently impressive to merit further investigation. Conveniently, their mother, Princess Elizabeth, was a first cousin of Vicky's father-in-law, so, with Fritz's help, it did not take long to obtain the most up-to-date information, including the unfortunate rumour that Louis had already formed an attachment to 'Maroussy', a daughter of the Duke of Leuchtenberg.

Pressed by the Queen to discover more, Fritz approached one of his uncles and casually asked if the rumour were true. On receiving the reply that that there was no possibility of Louis marrying the girl since the Leuchtenbergs were deemed to be of an inferior rank, Fritz mentioned 'in passing' that none of his four English sisters-in-law was married and they would certainly be worth Louis' consideration. In response, his uncle remarked that Louis' mother would be delighted if her son should marry one of Queen Victoria's daughters, since that was exactly what she had been hoping would happen.

Though mildly relieved by this news, Queen Victoria, with her typical dislike of snobbery, commented that it was ridiculous to view the Leuchtenbergs as inferior; and, what was more, whether or not Louis were permitted to marry, if he had already given his heart to Maroussy he couldn't possibly be considered as a suitor for Alice.

Meanwhile, however, Prince Albert had broached the subject of the Hessian princes with his mentor, Stockmar, whose son provided further photographs and the assurance that the young men were of excellent character. Although not entirely convinced, the Queen became more optimistic and decided that a meeting was in order but several anxious months were to pass before she could contrive to bring the young people together.

In the meantime, stories of Louis's feelings for Maroussy resurfaced and no sooner had Fritz warned the Queen about the rumours than Louis and Henry announced their intention of visiting England for the Ascot races. Once again, as with the arrival of the Prince of Orange, Queen Victoria was thrown into a panic. If the rumours about Maroussy were true, there could be no possibility of Louis marrying Alice but the visit might well attract speculation which would deter other suitors.

The brothers' arrival at Buckingham Palace on 1st June 1860 did little to dispel Queen Victoria's anxieties. While she found them 'gentleman-like, natural and pleasing', she was desperate to uncover the truth about Louis and Maroussy, without revealing her hopes for a match with Alice. In the days that followed, her admiration for the Hessians increased to the point where she described them as 'the nicest young men I have seen for very long', but so too did her anxiety as she observed that Louis and Alice were thoroughly enjoying one another's company, and feared that this might lead to disappointment.

"You will imagine my agitation not to do too much and yet not to neglect anything,"[74] she wrote to Vicky; and, a couple of days later, her agitation became more intense when her Aunt Augusta, Duchess of Cambridge, broached the subject of Maroussy directly.

While driving back from the races, the Duchess asked Louis whether the Leuchtenberg princess was truly as beautiful as she had been led to believe.

"Yes," he replied, leaving the fretful Queen with no alternative but to heed Prince Albert's advice to simply sit back and wait to see how events would unfold.

> "...but I own with the best intentions," she told Vicky, "it is impossible for me to help thinking of it constantly, first thing of a morning and the last at night....I put my trust in Providence to order all for the best but the uncertainty is trying."[75]

Alice, meanwhile, oblivious of her mother's distress, was quietly enchanted by the 'manly' prince who was paying her a good deal of attention. While she couldn't fail to realise that any visiting prince might be viewed as a potential husband, her parents had told her nothing of their inquiries and had spoken of him only in general terms to avoid placing her under pressure. Moreover, since his visit coincided with that of the King of the Belgians and several other royalties who had come to attend the races, Louis could be seen as just another guest rather than someone with whom she was expected to fall in love. In such a relaxed atmosphere, Alice and Louis were perfectly comfortable in each other's company, and, though onlookers were keenly observing them for any sign of a blossoming romance, unruffled Alice's composure and grace not only impressed her mother, but also won Louis' heart.

Interestingly, Leeds, the town in which Alice had made her first official public appearance, would play a part in another major event in her life. Her first evening with Louis was spent at a concert performed in Buckingham Palace by the recently-formed Yorkshire Choral Union, conducted by its founder, Robert Senior Burton, organist at Leeds Parish Church[j].

Throughout the week that followed, as the Hessians dined at the palace and accompanied the Royal Family to the races, the incessant rain dampened everyone else's enjoyment of Ascot but it made little difference to Alice and Louis, whose mutual attraction was becoming strikingly obvious. Unsurprisingly, after so short a time, no specific plans came of their meeting but Louis gave Alice his photograph and asked for one of her in return – a sure sign of his deepening affection.

"There is no doubt that…Louis and Alice have formed a mutual liking," Prince Albert wrote to Stockmar, "and although the visit fortunately has

---

[j] At Prince Albert's invitation, The Yorkshire Choral Union would go on to perform at the Crystal Palace the following year.

passed over without any declaration, I have no doubt that it will lead to further advances from the young gentleman's family. We should not be averse to such an alliance as the family is good and estimable, and the young man is unexceptional in morals, manly, and in both body and mind distinguished by a youthful vigour...The Queen and I look on as passive observers, which is undoubtedly our best course as matters stand."[76]

Prince Albert might have been content to remain a passive observer but the Queen was far less patient when it came to her daughter's future. While acknowledging the wisdom of Albert's attitude and agreeing that it would be unseemly for Alice to appear desperate for Louis to propose, she was exasperated by Louis' inaction and, on hearing that Prince Albert had not pressed him to speak of his intentions but had casually invited him to return in the autumn, she petulantly accused him of 'not caring what happens to our children.'[77]

To add to her troubles, no sooner had Louis departed than Prince William of Baden arrived in England, hurling her into her habitual agitation at the thought that *he* might propose to Alice while the situation with Louis remained unresolved.

If Prince Albert remained unperturbed and refused to intervene, the Queen would not allow Vicky to rest until the situation was resolved. Having urged her to discover exactly what Louis thought of his recent holiday, the Queen was gratified to hear that he had thoroughly enjoyed the visit, and, what was more, Vicky had made contact with his mother, Princess Elizabeth, who was still eagerly hoping for a match. By the middle of July, Princess Elizabeth was able to inform Vicky that her son was filled with admiration for Alice and trusted that his suit would not be 'met with indifference'. The same day, Louis himself wrote directly to Prince Albert, requesting permission to approach Alice directly when he returned to England in the autumn. Deeply impressed by his courteous behaviour, the Queen and Prince Albert rejoiced at this development and now needed only to ensure that this was precisely what Alice wanted.

By happy chance, Louis' letter coincided with a telegram from Prussia, announcing that Vicky had given birth to a little girl. In celebration of the event, Alice and her sisters prepared a meal for their parents in the Swiss Cottage, after which Prince Albert took Alice aside to tell her that Louis intended to propose.

"To dear Alice," wrote the Queen, "it was a very eventful day, as Papa told her all, and…you will hear how joyfully these news were received by the dear child."[78]

Suddenly Alice's reluctance to leave home and her fears about marriage and childbirth were forgotten. Although their meeting had been brief, Louis had captured her heart, and, on that summer's day, amid the salty sea air and the scent of magnolia, the future seemed even more thrilling than the past. Now she could look forward to Louis' return and eagerly anticipate life as a married woman.

Even the Queen, reluctant as she was to part with another daughter, could barely contain her excitement as she wrote to the King of the Belgians:

"…I venture now to confide a secret to you – the details of which you shall hear verbally from us when we have the happiness of seeing you in October. It is that our surmises respecting Louis of Hesse have turned out to be true, and that we have reason to hope that this affair will be in due time realised. The feelings are very reciprocal on both sides, though nothing definitive will be settled till the young people meet again, probably later this Autumn (but not in Germany). Please do not say anything about it to anyone. Your very great kindness and affection for our children has induced me to mention this to <u>you</u>, who moreover saw the first dawning of these prospects."[79]

Chapter 8 –
A Very Dear Good Fellow

The cold, wet summer of 1860 flew by through the annual migration from the Isle of Wight to Scotland, where the Royal Family paused en route to Balmoral to review a magnificent display of over twenty thousand Scottish Volunteers at Holyrood House in Edinburgh. On a rare sunny day in the middle of such a dull year, Alice, seated in a carriage with her mother and grandmother, drove past crowds of over two hundred thousand people, not one of them yet aware of the reason for the radiance of her smile.

Alice's cheerfulness lightened the dismal days at Balmoral where, as Prince Albert complained, there was such an 'utter absence of any summer' that it was necessary to have fires lit in the house 'and if you go out you get frightfully wet'. Her joy helped to ease, too, her grandmother's distress over the news of the recent death of her elder sister, 'Great Aunt Julia'.

Returning to the Isle of Wight in September, the Royal Family spent only three days at Osborne before travelling to Gravesend to embark on a long-awaited trip to Prince Albert's native Coburg. The prospect of the holiday was filled with excitement – not only would Alice have the pleasure of seeing her father's relations in his childhood home, but there would also be a happy reunion with Vicky and the opportunity to meet her new baby daughter, Charlotte. To add to the cheeriness of the occasion, the people of Gravesend had gone to great lengths to give the royal party and wonderful send-off. Every street from the railway station to the pier was festooned with flowers, bunting and banners, and every window was crowded with smiling faces, cheering loudly as the carriage passed by. A decorative arch, emblazoned with the Royal Crest, had been constructed at the entrance the pier, along which over a thousand guests sat at either side of a red carpet.

As the Queen boarded the *Victoria & Albert*, the royal standard was raised and a flotilla of brightly-decorated boats escorted the yacht from the harbour. Following a serene sea-crossing, the royal party made its way through Belgium in an atmosphere of joyous anticipation when suddenly a message was brought to the train which would change the mood dramatically: Prince Albert's stepmother was gravely ill and it would therefore be advisable to postpone the visit for at least a few days. 'We hoped that this was merely a temporary alarm,' wrote the Queen, and, since the train was already en route to Coburg, postponement was impossible.

At Verviers, a second telegram arrived announcing that the Dowager Duchess had died at five o'clock that morning. Prince Albert was devastated. Only a few days earlier, he had received a letter from his stepmother, describing her excitement at the prospect of seeing him again, but now, as bright summer clothes gave way to the black crepe of mourning, her death cast a shadow over what was to be his final visit to Coburg.

The gloom was lightened a little by the arrival of Vicky and her children, but observant Alice couldn't fail to notice that Prince Albert's melancholy deepened as he revisited the scenes of his childhood. Several times, he seemed to be on the point of tears as though a premonition were telling him that this was the last time he would ever see his home.

On the afternoon of October 1st, a further ominous event occurred. While Prince Albert was attending to family business, Alice had spent the day with Vicky and their mother, sketching the beautiful scenery in the golden light of early autumn, before strolling back towards the road where they expected to be overtaken by the Prince Consort's carriage. Instead, they were met by Prince

Albert's equerry, Colonel Ponsonby, who informed them that the Prince's carriage had been involved in an accident. There was no cause for alarm, Ponsonby said, as the Prince had escaped unharmed but, as he recounted the details of what had happened, the extent of the danger became frighteningly apparent. While approaching a level-crossing, the sound of a train had startled the horses and caused them to bolt, leaving Prince Albert no option but to leap from the fast-moving carriage.

At once, the Queen and her daughters hurried to the scene only to be warned to avert their eyes to avoid the dreadful sight of the overturned carriage, a seriously injured coachman, and the remains of one of the horses which had run directly into the path of the train.

Hearing that Prince Albert had been taken to the home of Baron Stockmar, the Queen and Princesses hurried to see him and were greatly relieved to hear him making light of his injuries.

"He was quite cheerful and talking," the Queen recorded, "and giving an account of this fearful accident, and, as it proved merciful and Providential escape."[80]

The doctor assured the family that the Prince's wounds were not serious and would leave no lasting scar, but, though no one, least of all the Queen, was prepared to believe it, Prince Albert was already sinking into a decline which would have far more devastating consequences than anyone could have realised. At the time, though, Queen Victoria was so grateful for his 'providential escape' that she founded a charity to assist young men and women in apprenticeships and to enable them to set up their own businesses.

After the shock of the accident and her father's obvious sorrow at leaving Coburg, the long homeward journey was brightened for Alice by further news from Louis. In cold, rainy weather, the royal party broke the journey in Mayence, where they spent the night in a dull hotel on the edge of a railway line. At eleven o'clock the following morning, Louis parents arrived, having made the long trip specifically to speak with Alice's parents.

> "[His mother] was most friendly and kind;" wrote the Queen. "[His father] very civil and amiable but painfully shy."[81]

Arrangements were made for Louis forthcoming visit to England, and Prince Albert agreed to approach the Prussian Prince Regent to obtain permission for him to be granted a leave of absence from his military duties for the duration of his stay.

This brief meeting proved to be the only highlight in an otherwise difficult journey, for, no sooner had Prince Albert recovered from his accident, than the Queen fell ill with a sore throat and fever, which was undoubtedly a delayed reaction to the shock of the Prince Consort's accident, and which left her confined to bed for several days, leading to a brief postponement of the last stage of the journey home.

Eventually, the family reached England and, as October faded and November dawned, the difficulties of the holiday gave way to excitement at the prospect of Louis' return. While Alice could think only of his forthcoming proposal, the Queen fluctuated through her usual gamut of emotions: first eager expectancy and the hope he would 'brush up his English' before the visit, then alarm and anxiety as she recalled her sorrow at Vicky's engagement, and agitation at the thought of having to 'take a stranger into the family.'

Vicky was equally pessimistic, describing the two years of her own engagement as a most awkward and trying time.

> "By showing one loves one's 'future' with all one's heart and longs (as one must do if one loves him) that the day of the wedding were nearer, one

is afraid of showing ingratitude to one's parents and one's home, and one feels so shy and wretched and always between two fires."[82]

She could only take comfort from the thought that, since Alice was older than she had been at the time of her engagement, and their parents had been through the situation before, everything would be far less stressful for Alice than it had been for her.

Louis, accompanied by his brother, Henry, arrived at Windsor in time for luncheon on 24th November. At once the Queen observed that he was far more nervous than he had been during his previous visit, and despite his best efforts to speak English, his mastery of the language had not greatly improved. More disconcertingly for Queen Victoria, days passed and, though Alice was bright and happy in his company, he had not yet summoned the courage to propose. At length, with mounting impatience, the Queen urged Prince Albert to broach the subject with Louis, who responded with such nervous agitation that Prince Albert offered to arrange a time when the young couple could speak privately together. Louis gratefully accepted the offer but, in the end, it turned out to be unnecessary when, a day earlier than expected, he finally spurred himself into action.

During the course of dinner on the evening of 30th November, Louis, even more nervous than usual, was clearly steeling himself to act. As the company left the table, he spotted Alice standing alone by a chimney piece and took his chance to speak with her. The ever-vigilant Queen had not failed to notice their whispered conversation but, with uncharacteristic tact, she passed by and spent the evening dispelling her tension by crocheting until at last:

"...Alice came to our room, much agitated and we told Papa. We then sent for dear Louis to Papa's room, where we went in with Alice and here the confirmation of what had occurred took place, and which was very moving as poor Louis was so completely overcome with his feelings as to be unable to say a word; he seemed quite overpowered. Dear Alice was a good deal upset too – but very quiet and sensible and reasonable."[83]

From that moment, the Queen received Louis into the family with great affection and, typically, her appreciation of his appearance increased in proportion to her appreciation of his qualities. The previous year she had described him as 'not handsome' but now, as she repeatedly wrote of his good looks, she could hardly find sufficient adjectives to praise him. 'Dear Louis', she said, was 'quick', 'intelligent', 'unaffected', 'natural' and 'taking an interest in everything'; and he and Alice were 'not at all sentimental but like two happy children – adoring one another and all full of fun and play.'

This childlike quality also appealed to Prince Albert, who delightedly wrote to Vicky of the 'great Alician event' and informed Stockmar that:

"We like [Louis] better every day, because of his unaffectedly genial and cordial temper, his great modesty, and a very childlike nature, united with strict morality and a genuine goodness and dignity."[84]

Sadly, Louis' childlike innocence, which was at the time so endearing, would later become a source of great irritation to Alice and cause a good deal of friction in their marriage.

For now, though, life was filled with wonder and excitement as she and Louis were, in her father's words, 'as happy as mortals can be.' The wedding was planned for 9th June the following year, and congratulatory telegrams and letters poured in from around the world – the only sour note coming from Vicky's mother-in-law, whose own dissatisfaction led her to resent happiness in others. Callously remarking that she disliked both Louis and his mother, she claimed that she could not understand what all the excitement was about. It would not be the last time that the Prussian Crown Princess would find reason to snipe at Alice, but her words were of little consequence at a time when she and Louis were absorbed in the first thrilling flush of love.

In the midst of their joy, however, Prince Albert was once again afflicted by illness. In an almost identical replay of the symptoms he had suffered following Vicky's engagement, within a couple of days of Alice and Louis' betrothal he was suddenly too weak to even hold a pen. As before, though, his symptoms gradually subsided, leaving Alice free to delight in Louis' company.

Throughout the darkening days of November and December, they travelled everywhere together, attending functions, taking tea with the visiting French Empress, and spending their evenings contentedly in the company Alice's parents as Prince Albert attempted to instil in Louis some of his own ideas about German politics. The rain, which had blighted much of the year, continued into the winter but, as the Queen wrote to her uncle, 'perpetual sunshine' emanated from the young lovers, who were '*so* happy, so devoted to each other, that it does one good to see it'.

Christmas that year was especially delightful for Alice. From Windsor, the Lord-in-Waiting, Viscount Torrington, reported to *The Times* that:

> "Even as in a public bazaar, where people jostle one another, so lords, grooms, Queen and princes laughed and talked, forgot to bow, and freely turned their backs on one another...I never saw more real happiness than the scene of the mother and all her children: the Prince Consort lost all his stiffness. Altogether a jolly Christmas."

Louis, who was not 'in the least in the way', contributed to the joy of the festivities and was, as Prince Albert told Vicky, '...an accession. He is a very dear good fellow who pleases us better and better daily.'[85]

As 1860 drew to a close the new year was filled with the promise of a wonderful future for Alice. Tragically, it was a promise that would never be fulfilled. Already dark clouds were gathering and events were about to unfold which would permanently alter Alice's life, her outlook and her temperament, and turn her almost overnight from a carefree young girl into a serious-minded and responsible woman.

Chapter 9 –
Everything Has Changed

Throughout Alice's life, 'Grandmama' – the Duchess of Kent – had been an almost constant presence and a source of much affection for the royal children. The once fraught relationship between the Queen and the Duchess, which had marred the early years of Victoria's reign, had been replaced by mutual affection and the restoration of a bond which had been so severely tested in the days of 'the Kensington System'. Following the departure of Lehzen and the removal of John Conroy from the Duchess of Kent's household, Prince Albert had done much to bring the Queen and the Duchess together, and from the moment that Alice was born, her fond grandmother was a significant member of the family who showered her grandchildren with love.

> "For the past two years," Prince Albert wrote in 1861, "[Queen Victoria's] constant care and occupation have been to keep watch over her mother's comfort, and the influence of this upon her own character has been most salutary."[86]

The Duchess frequently accompanied the Royal Family on their annual migrations and had her own suites of rooms in their palaces, but the Queen had also given her the picturesque Frogmore House on the Windsor estate as a permanent home. Alice frequently visited her there and enjoyed many happy hours, playing the walnut piano in the lilac-coloured sitting room while her grandmother listened with delight. Revelling in the antics of her grandchildren, the Duchess was present at every birthday party, joined in the celebrations for Alice's engagement, and was as much a part of Alice's life as her parents and siblings were. Being in good health, she participated, too, in many formal events, becoming a popular figure with the public and greatly loved by her ladies-in-waiting and other members of her household.

By 1861, however, the Duchess had suffered a series of bereavements which gradually undermined her constitution. In 1856, Prince Karl of Leiningen, her son by her first marriage, suffered an aneurysm and died at the early age of fifty-two.

> "Poor Mama is chiefly to be commiserated, who thus sees her only son quit the world before herself," Prince Albert wrote to his stepmother. "She is much bowed down but composed and touching in her sorrow."[87]

Four years later, the death of her last-surviving sister, Julia, affected her deeply and, in the early months of 1861, her health began to decline. In February, feverishness and a painful swelling in her arm prevented her from accompanying the Royal Family to Osborne; and, in early March, her doctors performed surgery to drain a deep-rooted abscess. The operation had little impact on the inflammation and soon other sores and swellings appeared, convincing her doctor, James Clark, that she was suffering from cancer. Clark, unwilling to cause distress, kept this diagnosis to himself but, while Queen Victoria repeatedly assured herself that, apart from the sores, her mother was in good health, she was already aware that something was seriously amiss. Several times she urgently pleaded with Vicky to bring her children to visit her grandmother before it was too late:

> "Don't delay your visit, don't delay bringing both children – God knows when you could again show them to your beloved grandmother...it is a duty which you owe her, your only grandmother, who has ever been so kind to you."[88]

For Vicky, however, abandoning everything to return at once to England was simply impossible. Only two months earlier the King of Prussia had died and, as

Fritz' father succeeded him, Vicky was elevated to the position of Crown Princess. In the midst of adapting to the responsibilities of her new role, and unaware of the seriousness of the Duchess' condition, she promised to visit in the summer.

On 12th March, Alice and her parents visited the Duchess at Frogmore and, while the Queen was distressed by the appearance of yet another sore, she confidently wrote to Vicky that there was no immediate cause for alarm. Alice, who was now spending her evenings reading to, or playing the piano for her grandmother, visited again on the 14th and there appeared to be no deterioration. Reassured by the doctors that her mother's life was not in danger, the Queen continued her duties, including, on 15th March, inspecting the new gardens of the Royal Horticultural Society in South Kensington. Following a tour of the gardens, the Queen returned to Buckingham Palace, leaving Prince Albert to his discussions with members of the society. He was still in Kensington when an urgent message from the Duchess' doctor arrived, urging him to return home as quickly as possible. The doctor was waiting for him at the palace and informed him that his mother-in-law's health had suddenly deteriorated and her condition was now so critical that it would be advisable for the family to go at once to Frogmore. All plans were immediately cancelled and, at seven o'clock in the evening, Alice and her parents anxiously boarded a specially commissioned train to Windsor.

At Frogmore, they found the Duchess in a great deal of pain. Throughout the long night, the Queen frequently returned to her bedside as she drifted in and out of consciousness until she was no longer able to even recognise her own daughter. By dawn it was clear that she was fading rapidly, and, at ten o'clock in the morning, with Alice and Prince Albert by her side, she died peacefully, holding the Queen's hand.

This was Alice's first direct experience of death but, in the wake of her mother's all-consuming grief, she had little time to express her own shock and desolation.

> "Oh! the sickness of heart, the agony," the Queen wailed, "the thought of the daily, hourly blank was and is unbearable."[89]

Guilt for their years of estrangement overwhelmed her, and the thought of how close they had been in recent times left her so bereft and bewildered that she could barely function. Putting her own feelings aside, Alice dutifully did all she could to comfort her mother, and, her efforts did not go unnoticed:

> "Dear good Alice," wrote the Queen, "was full of intense feeling, tenderness and distress for me, and she...loved 'Grandmama' so dearly."[90]

So great was their sorrow that neither the Queen nor her daughters attended the funeral, fearing it would all be 'too much', but when a red-eyed Prince Albert returned and assured them that it had all been carried out perfectly, Queen Victoria's grief only intensified.

For days and weeks and months, her mourning continued unabated.

> "She is greatly upset and feels her childhood rush back upon her memory with vivid force," wrote Prince Albert, "Her grief is extreme...In body she is well, though terribly nervous...she remains almost entirely alone."[91]

Frequently bursting into tears, she neglected her duties and suffered such a complete breakdown that Prince Albert was compelled to assume all her responsibilities while trying to ease her pain and organise the Duchess' estate. Often the stress proved too much for him and he urged Alice to 'go and comfort your mother.'

In an effort to raise her spirits, Alice accompanied her for a drive in a rubber-wheeled carriage, as the noise of metallic wheels grated on the Queen's nerves; and each evening she sat with her, quietly trying to support her as she wallowed in her memories and repeatedly relived the Duchess' final hours.

The preparations for Alice's wedding, which had once been so joyful, now became a trial for the Queen, who dreaded meeting anyone outside her immediate family and would have preferred to retire from public life altogether. 'Everything has changed since that fearful blow,' she told Vicky; and, for Alice, 'everything' included any possibility of enjoying the prospect of her forthcoming marriage.

With great reluctance, the Queen attended a meeting of the Privy Council on 1st May to formally announce Alice's engagement and arrange an official request for her dowry. Two days later, when the request was conveyed to the House of Commons, Disraeli responded in a typically sycophantic manner:

> "The interest which this House takes in the domestic happiness of Her Majesty must be increased when we remember that it relates to the accomplished Princess whose good fortune it will be in another land to represent in a manner gratifying to all Englishmen the character of her country. That lady, as is well known to public opinion and by her private conduct to many – to the country generally, and to this House – has already shown a disposition so eminent for its good qualities, and an intelligence so bright and winning, that I am sure it will not be a mere formal ceremony on the part of the House of Commons when they express in the most cordial and unanimous manner the satisfaction they feel, and their readiness to consider in a manner

becoming the occasion the recommendation brought to our notice in the Message from the Crown."[92]

With the support of the Prime Minister, Palmerston, Parliament agreed to a £30,000 dowry and an annuity of £6,000. Although this was considered a very generous settlement, it was clear that Alice's financial situation in Hesse would never compare with the fortune which Vicky would one day inherit.

"She will not be able to do great things with it,"[93] Prince Albert remarked.

Alice, though, was happy with her lot, and looked forward to a forthcoming visit from her fiancé to alleviate the gloom which now pervaded the royal household. Her mother did not share her excitement. Prior to the Duchess' death, she had been happy about the prospect of seeing Louis again but now she 'dreaded' his coming since, as she told Vicky, she was, 'quite unfit and unable to be cheerful.'

Louis' arrival on May 18th did little to lift the gloom. Hardly had he settled into Osborne House than he contracted measles and had to retire to his room for several days. Alice endured this 'trial with her usual sweet temper and patience' but, within a short time, her eight-year-old brother, Leopold, was also confined to bed with a far more serious illness.

Leopold's health had long been a cause of concern. At the age of two, he had fallen on his face and bled so profusely that he was forced to remain in bed for a fortnight. Since then, all the typical bumps and bruises of childhood that normally pass unnoticed, had resulted in profuse bleeding and swellings in his joints, which at times left him crippled with pain. Often he was too ill to accompany the rest of the family on their travels and it was obvious to his parents that something was seriously amiss. It was not until 1860, when Leopold was seven-years-old, that James Clark finally diagnosed the inherited condition: haemophilia.

Lacking the protein, Factor VIII, the blood of a haemophiliac fails to clot, so even a minor cut could prove fatal and the slightest knock could lead to agonising bleeding into the joints. A few weeks before Louis' visit, Leopold had suffered from haematuria, and now he experienced a series of nosebleeds and became, in the words of his sister, Lenchen, 'very seriously ill'.

For Alice, Louis' visit was marred not only by anxiety about the invalids, but also by the atypically tense relations between her parents. Having previously witnessed only their mutual devotion and her mother's readiness to yield to Prince Albert in everything, she was distressed to observe a sudden distance and irritability between them. Moreover, it was painful to realise that, as her mother's mental state became increasing fragile, so too did her father's health – and this, without a doubt, was at the heart of the tension in their relationship.

The Queen's typical response to any upsetting situation or emotional trauma was to weep copiously and complain of the stress to her 'nerves'. This was not simply a histrionic display to gain attention, but a virtually uncontrollable psychological reaction. At such times, she could not bear loud noises or excitement, and felt so helpless that her only recourse was to withdraw from company to bemoan her fate and lament the human condition. So it was that, around the time of Vicky's wedding, she wrote page upon page of her sorrow; and so it was that, after the death of the Duchess of Kent, she could not be consoled or cajoled into finding relief. Her relief *was* her suffering. The more tears she shed, the more, she believed, she demonstrated the extent of her love, and thereby assuaged the guilt she felt for any past disagreements or resentment.

For years, Prince Albert had supported the Queen through her bouts of nerves and her periods of violent emotion but now even he could no longer endure her excessive and seemingly self-indulgent grief. Exhausted by his own physical ailments and stressed by the burden of so many responsibilities, he told her it was time to put an end to her mourning as there were duties requiring her attention. More poignantly, in the light of subsequent events, he questioned how she would cope if something even worse were to befall her – a tragedy which, it seems, he already suspected was about to happen.

In response, Queen Victoria bombarded Vicky with a stream of letters, complaining not only of her overwhelming grief but also of the fact that men were incapable of understanding such powerful emotion.

Prince Albert had a quite different reaction to emotional trauma, and one which the Queen found equally difficult to comprehend. No matter what was happening in his personal life, his overriding sense of duty would not permit him to relinquish his responsibilities. On the contrary, the greater his stress, the harder he worked, as though by taking control of external affairs he might somehow ease his inner turmoil and distract himself from his thoughts. As a child, he had thrown himself into his studies to combat the confusion he felt at being abandoned by his mother; and, in the early years of his marriage, he devoted himself to reorganising the palaces to relieve the frustration of having his talents stifled. Sooner or later, however, his suppressed emotion inevitably exploded in a variety of physical symptoms, most of which left his doctors baffled as to their cause. Thus, after both Vicky's and Alice's engagements, as the Queen vociferously bewailed the loss of her daughters, Prince Albert remained stoically silent, only to suffer such intense rheumatic pains that he could not even raise his arm.

The Queen's melodramatic sobbing and constant reliving of sad events have often been viewed as so self-indulgent that even Prince Albert lost patience with her unrestrained grief. At the same time, though, through her eyes, many of the Prince's physical ailments were simply the result of hypochondria and a lack of 'pluck'. Throughout all the years she had known him, he had been suffering from one kind of malady or another. On one of his earliest visits to England, he had, while recovering from sea-sickness, fainted during a dance. In the first few months of their marriage, he had difficulty adjusting to the late hours and late breakfasts, which he found difficult to digest (as indeed at the time he found the Queen's imperious behaviour difficult to swallow) and which left him with a feeling of exhaustion for the rest of the day. Stomach-cramps and digestive disorders regularly plagued him; and, when he contracted an otherwise minor infection, his symptoms were usually far worse and lasted far longer than would normally be expected. Queen Victoria, who was proud of her strong constitution, had as much difficulty understanding his illnesses as he did understanding her 'nerves'.

In former years each accepted the other's physical or psychological responses to events, and their differences created a balance: Prince Albert supported the Queen through her mood swings and mental anguish, and in return she sympathised with his physical ailments. By the spring of 1861, however, as the Queen was overwrought by the death of her mother, and Albert's physical symptoms had intensified, neither was capable of sustaining the other. It therefore fell to Alice to offer emotional support to both of her parents, and the effort involved impinged upon her own happiness.

While trying in vain to comfort her mother, she was also aware that her father's health was failing. Now he had toothache with no apparent cause, followed by

117

abscesses on his gums, weight loss, hair loss, swollen ankles, muscle and joint pain, extreme cold, exhaustion, and the familiar digestive disorders. He was also uncharacteristically cantankerous, looked older than his forty-one years; and, ever since his visit to Coburg the previous summer, he was frequently depressed and convinced that he was dying. He had been particularly attracted to a William Branks' book *Heaven our Home,* and, after reading from it, told the Queen:

"We don't know in what state we shall meet again, but we shall recognise each other and be together in eternity. I am certain of that."

Rather than retiring to regain his strength, Prince Albert worked even more frenetically, as though he wished to achieve all he could in the little time he believed he had left. In the middle of May he visited Bertie at Cambridge, and suddenly, at the end of the month, announced that the family must return to London from Osborne in order to be present for the opening of the Royal Horticultural Gardens on 5th June.

The Queen, relishing the seclusion of the Isle of Wight, was horrified:

"Papa insists on our going to Town for no earthly reason but that tiresome horticultural garden – which I curse for more reasons than one – and have to leave poor little, sick Leopold behind here in his bed which makes me sadly anxious and adds to my low spirits!"[94]

To appease Prince Albert, she reluctantly returned to Buckingham Palace but she could not bring herself to appear in public for the official opening of the gardens and opted instead for a private viewing earlier in the day. Later that afternoon, Alice and her siblings accompanied their father to the opening where onlookers were shocked at how tired and ill he looked. None of them was as yet aware that this would be his final public engagement in their city.

"Am ill, feverish with pains in my limbs and feel very miserable," he wrote in his diary in the middle of June but still he continued his engagements, entertaining numerous visiting royalties including Louis' mother. He worried about Leopold; followed the disconcerting events in Italy, Austria and the United States; and held countless meetings with ministers to advise them on domestic and foreign affairs. The weather might have been warmer and drier than the previous year but neither heat nor sunshine brought him much joy as his letters made frequent references to how ill and exhausted he felt.

In an otherwise fraught and challenging summer, the only highlight for the Royal Family was a visit from Vicky and her family from the end of June until August. Unfortunately, even this cheery reunion served as a reminder to the Queen of her 'great loss'.

> "This happy family meeting with our children and grandchildren, while our dear Alice's bridegroom is still here, makes me long and pine for *her*, who would have been so happy and so proud."[95]

For Alice, seeing her sister again was sheer delight. Not only was Vicky able to help comfort their parents but also this was the first time that the sisters had met since Alice's engagement had been officially announced. Now, as a soon-to-be-married woman, Alice could confide in Vicky just as she had done when they were children, and the Queen had no doubt that their conversation would turn to the intimate details of married life. Shortly before the visit, she wrote anxiously to Berlin:

> "Let me caution you, dear child, again, to say as little as you can on these subjects before Alice (who has already heard much more than you ever did)…I am very anxious that she should know as

little about the inevitable miseries as possible, so don't forget, dear."[96]

Whether or not the warning was heeded, the sisters enjoyed their time together. Vicky revelled in being once more at Osborne with all its memories of her happy childhood; and for Alice, the visitors' presence helped to ease the pain of Louis' departure for Germany in early July. The only discordant note came from a telegram from Baden-Baden, summoning Fritz home immediately as his father had been the victim of an assassination attempt. A student had fired a pistol point blank and had come so close to killing the King that the bullets actually passed through his collar. Fortunately, apart from a relatively minor wound to his neck, he was unharmed and recovered so quickly that Fritz was soon able to resume the holiday.

When the time came for the Prussians to leave, the Queen and Prince Albert bade them farewell 'with heavy hearts.' The following day, to commemorate the Duchess of Kent's birthday, Alice and her parents visited the mausoleum at Frogmore which, the Queen told her uncle, was:

> "...so airy, so grand and so simple that, affecting as it was, there was no anguish or bitterness of grief, but a feeling of repose." [97]

Prince Albert was equally satisfied by the solemnity and serenity of the place, telling Vicky that it was very beautiful and 'just what it should be'. Within a short time, he, too, would be laid to rest at Frogmore.

Chapter 10 –
A Strange Sort of Presentiment

On 21st August 1861, Queen Victoria and Prince Albert boarded the *Victoria and Albert*[k] at Holyhead en route to Ireland. Travelling with them were Alice, Lenchen and Affie, who had returned only three days earlier from a naval posting aboard the veteran of Trafalgar, *HMS Euryalus,* which had taken him as far afield as South Africa and the West Indies. On a calm sea, there was great excitement aboard the royal yacht as Affie described his adventures, and all three siblings eagerly looked forward to seeing their elder brother again.

As Prince Albert had promised, Bertie was spending the summer stationed with the Grenadier Guards in the Curragh Camp in County Kildare. The posting was basically a reward for his good behaviour, for, despite his inaptitude for learning, he had done his best to apply himself to his studies at Oxford University and had made an excellent impression on his hosts during a recent tour of Canada and the United States. Now, he was reading Constitutional Law at Cambridge, and Prince Albert felt it was only fair to grant him his dearest wish for a military attachment during the summer vacation. Disregarding the misgivings of some of his tutors, who feared his fellow-officers might have a detrimental influence on the young prince's morals, Prince Albert designed a programme by which his son would have the opportunity to master the skills of a military command and, through his own efforts, earn regular promotions. During the visit to Ireland, Prince Albert would have an opportunity to discover how well his programme was working.

The royal yacht docked at eleven-thirty in the evening and, following a comfortable night at the Vice-

[k] The royal yacht *Victoria & Albert* was launched on Alice's birthday – 25th April 1843

Regal Lodge, Prince Albert set out to visit the camp. To his delight he found that Bertie had adapted extremely well to army discipline and, although his progress was slower than he had predicted, he was proving to be a proficient officer. Onlookers observed the joy and pride in Prince Albert's eyes as the Prince of Wales competently demonstrated his new skills with professionalism and dignity. It was a rare occasion when Bertie so impressed his father but, in that proud moment, Prince Albert was unaware that alongside his enjoyment of military life, Bertie was also relishing the favours of an actress named Nellie Clifton, whom his fellow officers had smuggled into his room to initiate him into the pleasures of the flesh. The consequences of what seemed to Bertie and his companions nothing more than a light-hearted liaison would prove to be far more devastating than he could ever have imagined.

On the 26th August, the Prince of Wales joined the rest of the family to celebrate his father's forty-second birthday at Killarney House, the home of the Earl of Kenmere. By now the friction between the Queen and Prince Albert had eased and 'the dearest of days' was made all the happier since it was the first time in several years that both Affie and Bertie had been present for the occasion. Although Prince Albert missed Vicky and his younger children, who had remained in England, they had sent lovely gifts, which he received with delight, alongside a drawing from Alice which pleased him immensely. That afternoon, the family travelled to Killarney where they were greeted by a crowd of over ten thousand people and an impressive firework display. The next day, as they were taken out on the lake in a boat rowed by eight oarsmen, they were struck by the sheer beauty of the place which had, Queen Victoria remarked, exceeded her highest expectations.

That night, they stayed at Muckross Abbey, home of the Lord Lieutenant of Kerry, who had gone to great lengths to ensure that his guests would have a comfortable and quiet stay, in rooms overlooking the lake. Alongside imported Persian carpets and Parisian curtains, he had specifically order a piano from London for Alice to play. She was so delighted with its tone that she requested the name of the maker and, on discovering it was manufactured by Messrs Allison and Sons of Wardour Street at a cost of only thirty-two guineas, she promised to be a client of the company in the future.

The restorative scenery and the genuine warmth of the crowds, made the visit to Ireland so memorable that the Queen requested ivy and ferns to be sent to Osborne as souvenirs; and, by the time the Royal Family departed for Balmoral on 29th August, all were agreed that the trip had been most beneficial to Prince Albert's health and to Queen Victoria's nerves.

After the turmoil of the past few months, the late summer days drifted into an atmosphere of serene contentment. The weather was particularly clement that year and, when Louis arrived at Balmoral in far better health than he had been at Osborne, he and Alice were able to spend much of the time outdoors. Throughout his six-week stay, they walked and rode in the glens, visited the tenants and endeared themselves to the local people. Only one problem clouded their vision of the wonderful future they would share: the question of where they would live once they were married.

Plans were underway for a new palace to be constructed for them in Darmstadt but it would take two years to complete, and, in the meantime, the Queen felt it was only right that her daughter should be provided with a home befitting her station. She approached Louis' uncle, the Grand Duke of Hesse, with a formal request that the young couple be allowed to live in the existing palace in

Darmstadt until their new home was ready but the eccentric Grand Duke refused outright and suggested instead that they should settle with Louis' parents.

"The rudeness and stupidity of this is too great!" huffed the Queen, who instantly decided that the only solution was for Alice and Louis to spend a good deal of time in England until the new palace was completed. Louis had no objections to the plan, which suited Queen Victoria perfectly, for it would save her a good deal of the trauma she had felt at Vicky's departure.

Meanwhile, as Alice and Louis enjoyed the autumnal days, the Queen was again preoccupied with finding a suitable bride for the Prince of Wales. Although she had been impressed by his bearing and behaviour in Ireland, she was under no illusions that Bertie had suddenly been transformed into her ideal of a prince. Both she and Prince Albert concurred that he would easily yield to temptations of the flesh, and so, to prevent him from 'falling', he needed a beautiful wife as soon as possible. Louis' sister remained a possibility, as did Princess Elizabeth of Wied, whom the Queen favoured despite Vicky and Stockmar's rather 'disappointing' accounts of her appearance and manner. To his mother's chagrin, however, when Bertie was shown her photograph, he professed no interest whatsoever in her.

A far more suitable prospect was sixteen-year-old Alexandra of Denmark, who was, in Vicky's opinion:

> "...the sweetest girl who ever lived, and full of life and spirits...She has always been strong and healthy as possible and has never ailed anything in her life except having the measles...I own Princess A. of Holstein is the only one of these princesses for whom I feel portée – it would be dreadful if this pearl went to the horrid Russians."[98]

Negotiations with Alexandra's parents were soon underway and, though the Queen feared that Bertie was unworthy of such a 'pearl', she was eager to find a way to bring them together.

The perfect opportunity arose in late September when the Prussian Army was carrying out a series of manoeuvres in the Rhineland at the same time as Alexandra and her family were holidaying in the region. With Vicky's help, arrangements were made for Bertie to observe the manoeuvres, ostensibly to further his military education but in reality to enable him to meet the Danish princess. Vicky, of course, was on hand to furnish her mother with details of what took place during the meetings, and on 26th September she reported that, although Bertie was a little disappointed that Alexandra was not quite as beautiful as he had been led to believe, he was 'pleased' with her and she had made an impression on him 'though in his own funny, undemonstrative way.'

When Bertie returned to Balmoral a few days later, the impatient Queen was frustrated by his lack of passion. 'I don't think he is…capable of enthusiasm about anything in the world,' she complained to Vicky but, relenting a little, conceded that, while he was unlikely to open his heart to his mother, he was sure to do so to Alice, who remained his closest confidante.

Unsurprisingly after so brief an encounter, Bertie was not ready to make a commitment and, though the Queen bemoaned his lack of fervour, Prince Albert sensibly concluded that it was impossible to compel anyone to fall in love. His solution was simple: Alexandra and her parents should be invited to Windsor. If Bertie then decided that he wished to marry her, he must propose at once; if not, he must tell her so, since any other course of action would be ungentlemanly. Of course, it was vital to discover Alexandra's opinion, and so, once again, Vicky was enlisted to contact her mother, Princess Louise, to find out what kind of impression Bertie had made on the young princess. When the Royal Family returned to Windsor at the end of October, Princess Louise replied that her daughter had been greatly impressed by the Prince of Wales and was eager to meet him again. Prince Albert forwarded the letter to Bertie at Cambridge, and he and the Queen were optimistic that it would lead to a happy conclusion.

For Prince Albert, the return to Windsor marked a return to his onerous commitments and, though he arrived home in good spirits, several international crises as well as his continuing involvement in the country's domestic affairs quickly began to exhaust him. Throughout the autumn and early winter, he was preoccupied, too, by family matters which not only required a great deal of his time but were also emotionally draining.

Alongside making arrangements for Alice's wedding and her future life in Hesse, he began preparations for the establishment of a separate household at Marlborough House for the Prince of Wales. His greatest concern, however, was for his youngest son, Leopold, whose health continued to cause immense anxiety. After contracting measles during the summer, Leopold had suffered from a series of nosebleeds and had been confined to bed for over a month. With winter rapidly approaching, Prince Albert feared that the cold and damp might exacerbate his condition and eventually decided that the warmer climes of the south of France would be more conducive to his recovery. Under the care of his doctor, Theodore Gunther, and a Groom-in-Waiting, Sir Edward Bowater, Leopold left Windsor on November 2nd, but before he and the party had reached their destination in Cannes, Sir Edward fell ill and was unable to travel for several days. By the time that Leopold and his attendants reached Avignon, it was clear that Sir Edward's condition was serious, leaving Prince Albert in the difficult position of having to make precautionary arrangements for Leopold's care in the event that his 'minder' should die. [1]

Meanwhile, news had reached Windsor that Vicky had caught a chill at her father-in-law's coronation and, despite several days' bed-rest, her recovery was so slow that she was regularly being bled. The Queen and Prince Albert were so alarmed at the number of leeches being used that they even considered sending their own doctor, William Jenner, to Prussia in the hope that he might prescribe a more beneficial treatment.

Stressed and exhausted by so many concerns and commitments, Prince Albert's health rapidly declined. The incessant rain of November exacerbated his rheumatism; his teeth ached; digestive disorders prevented him from eating; and in the gloom of the season his familiar melancholy returned. The Queen, feeling equally low-spirited, was so worried that she urged him to relinquish some of his duties but he simply *could not* stop working. Perhaps it was his only means of distracting himself from a sense of foreboding and the awareness that he had little time left to accomplish all he hoped to achieve.

Prince Albert was not alone in his sense of foreboding. The Queen was also tormented by two portentous conversations she had had with the ghillie, John Brown, before leaving Scotland. Brown had described how he had lost three brothers and a sister within six weeks – all victims of typhus fever; and, as the royal party was leaving Balmoral, he said that he looked forward to seeing the Queen again soon and added ominously that he hoped that, in the meantime, there would be no deaths in her family.

These conversations gained a new significance in early November when news arrived from Lisbon that

---

[1] Sir Edward Bowater did not recover from his illness. He continued on to Cannes, where he died on 14th December 1861.

Prince Albert's cousin and friend, Prince Ferdinand of Portugal, had died of typhoid, and his brother, King Pedro, was suffering from the same illness. The King's death a short time later plunged both the Queen and Prince Albert into a deep depression as they contemplated the briefness of life and the ease with which families can be torn apart.

"It shows how uncertain life is!" the Queen sighed to Vicky, before going on to describe the conversations with Brown:

"But here are 2 deaths already. These 2 coincidences struck me so much...that they keep returning to my mind like as if they had been a sort of strange presentiment."[99]

Within a month the Queen would realise quite how tragically accurate her premonition had been.

Chapter 11 –
Mute Distracted Despair

In mid-November 1861, a disturbing rumour came to Prince Albert's attention: Bertie's behaviour in Ireland the previous summer was, it was said, the talk of all the gentlemen's clubs in London. It did not take long for the omniscient Stockmar to confirm the story, and, as the details of the liaison with the actress emerged, Prince Albert was shaken to the core. All his efforts to protect Bertie's innocence had been in vain; the anticipated engagement to Alexandra could be jeopardised; and, if the press should hear of the escapade, the reputation of the monarchy, which he had safeguarded so diligently for the past twenty years, would be tarnished in an instant. Then, there was the possibility that the actress could be pregnant, or could resort to blackmail; but most wounding of all for Prince Albert was the betrayal of his trust. Against the advice of Bertie's tutors, he had trusted his son to behave impeccably in Ireland but now it seemed that his faith had been misplaced and Bertie might well have embarked on a course which would lead him into debauchery.

Queen Victoria, though deeply shocked by the news, was more concerned about its effect on Prince Albert. 'I never saw him so low,' she told Vicky, explaining that his lack of sleep was caused by, 'a great sorrow which upset us both greatly – but him especially and it broke him right down.'

Worried, worn out, wracked with neuralgia and unable to eat or sleep, Prince Albert took up his pen and, 'with a heavy heart', wrote to his eldest son. Though deeply disappointed, he assured Bertie that he only wished to help him but, in return, Bertie must explain every detail of what had taken place, if not to his father, then to his 'Governor', General Bruce.

A few days later, on 22nd November, despite his pain and exhaustion, Prince Albert travelled to Cambridge to speak to Bertie in person. In the pouring rain, father and son walked through the Madingley countryside where Prince Albert warned of the dangers of such folly, and a duly repentant Bertie admitted that he had 'yielded to temptation' but would be far more circumspect in future. So engrossed were they in their conversation that they soon found themselves completely lost and by the time they eventually found their way back to civilisation, the drenched and shivering Prince Consort was utterly exhausted to the point of near collapse.

Still shivering and aching, he returned to Windsor that evening, and over the next few days, he dragged himself through his engagements in an effort to conceal quite how ill he felt. If the Queen was reluctant to accept the seriousness of his condition, perceptive Alice was all too aware of his rapid decline and, in an effort to raise his spirits, barely left his side.

"Good Alice is a very great comfort," the Queen wrote. "She is so devoted to dear Papa and reads to him and does everything she can to help and cheer me!"[100]

By the end of the month, an international crisis added to Prince Albert's woes. For some time he had been anxiously watching the conflict in America, afraid that Britain could be dragged into the war. Towards the end of November his fears came close to being realised. A few weeks earlier, a captain of the Northern States' navy forcibly boarded and searched a British mail ship, the *Trent,* and arrested two Confederate (Southern States) agents. When the *Trent* returned to England at the end of the month, news of what had happened led to an outcry in Parliament and outrage among the British public. The

Foreign Minister, John Russell, immediately drew up a letter to be sent to Washington belligerently protesting at this breach of international law and violation of British neutrality. When Prince Albert was presented with a draft of the letter he was horrified, convinced that if it were delivered, war would be inevitably. At once, he set to work redrafting the letter in far more conciliatory terms, which eventually settled the matter without conflict.

By now, though, it was clear that Prince Albert was dangerously ill. Restless and irritable, he wandered from room to room, trying to find some relief from his insomnia, lumbago and neuralgia. He joined Alice and her mother for meals but was unable to eat anything, and, by December 2nd he was too weak to dress, and was reduced to lying on a sofa. Dr Jenner observed that he had developed 'a low fever' but Dr Clark – the same doctor who had misdiagnosed the infant Vicky, and had been involved in the Flora Hastings affair – disagreed, insisting that there was no cause for alarm as he was sure that the illness would pass after a few days' rest. The Queen, seeing only what she wanted to see, gratefully accepted Clark's prognosis and wrote several times to Vicky, telling her not to worry because, although her father's progress might be slow and tedious, he would eventually recover.

Being constantly in his presence, Alice could see what the Queen refused to accept: her beloved father's illness was far graver than his doctors dared to admit. His weakness and pallor were astounding for a man of his age. His mouth was dry, his skin, clammy and ashen, and at times he could barely breathe.

"While Alice was reading the *Talisman* in the bedroom, where he was lying on the bed," the Queen wrote on 4th December, "he seemed in a very uncomfortable, panting state, which frightened us. We sent for Doctor Jenner, who gave him something, and then Mr Brown (of Windsor) came up and was most kind and reassuring and not alarmed. But Doctor Jenner said the Prince *must* eat and that he was going to tell him so – the illness was going to be tedious and that starving himself, as he had done, would not do."[101]

That evening, while the Queen was out of the room, he asked Alice to write to Vicky, telling her that he would never recover.

Over the next ten days, Alice barely left his side as doctors came and went, each offering the assurance that his life was not in danger until, at last, Jenner told the Queen that the Prince was suffering from typhoid. Knowing of Albert's fear of 'the fever', particularly since the recent death of his Portuguese cousins, the Queen insisted that the diagnosis be kept from him, and at the same time reassured herself that the illness need not be fatal – after all she herself had survived a worse case of typhoid in Ramsgate many years earlier.

In fact, with hindsight, Jenner's diagnosis is highly questionable. Having devoted a good deal of his professional life to studying the disease and having written several papers on the subject, it is possible that he simply noted a few similar to symptoms to those which were at the forefront of his mind. Since typhoid is usually transmitted through contaminated water, the drains at Windsor have been blamed as the most likely source of the infection but there is no record of anyone else in the household contracting the disease, which usually spreads in epidemics. Moreover, while Prince Albert had a high temperature and fever, there was no evidence of the purplish rash or delirium which usually accompanies typhoid. Considering the symptoms which had plagued him for several years prior to 1861, it is far more likely that he was suffering from some form of chronic malabsorption syndrome which, exacerbated by exhaustion and stress, eventually led to renal failure and a complete breakdown of his metabolism.

Throughout the dark days of December, the Queen continued to search for any sign of improvement. If Prince Albert smiled, sat up, or took so much as a little broth, it was evidence of his imminent recovery – for, indeed, in her view, he *would* recover, as the alternative was too horrific to contemplate. Nonetheless, the stress of watching over him while carrying out her constitutional duties was exhausting.

"The trial in every way is so very trying," she wrote, "for I have lost my guide, my support, my all, <u>for a time</u> – as we can't ask or tell him anything."[102]

Alice continued to do all she could to entertain her father. She read aloud from the works of Sir Walter Scott, which he greatly enjoyed, and, when he asked to listen to quiet music, a piano was brought to an adjoining room so that she could play for him. One hymn in particular appealed to him *A Strong Tower is our God,* and as Alice played, his eyes often filled with tears. Other times, he joined his hands as though in prayer and on one occasion, Alice thinking him to be asleep, whispered:

"Were you asleep, dear Papa?"

To which he replied with a smile, "Oh no, only I have such sweet thoughts."

Undoubtedly, during those dark days, Alice listened, too, to his instructions in the event of his death. Prince Albert knew that he had not long to live and often he specifically asked for Alice to come to him. Her quiet serenity soothed him and, aware of how the Queen would react to his passing, he surely commended her to Alice's care. After all, it was Alice who had helped him to support the Queen after the death of the Duchess of Kent; and, of all his children, he knew that she was the one who had the capacity to bring comfort to the sick and bereaved, and the strength of mind to take control in a crisis.

It required incredible strength of will for Alice to spend day after day at his bedside without breaking down in tears. Her father was her idol as well as her 'soul-mate' – the only person in the world who completely understood and empathised with her sensitivity and the depths of her thoughts.

"The Princess Alice's fortitude has amazed us all," wrote a member of the household. "She saw from the first that her father's and her mother's firmness depended on her firmness, and she set herself to that duty. He loved to speak openly of his condition and had many wishes to express. He loved to hear hymns and prayers. He could not speak to the Queen of himself, for she could not bear to listen and shut her eyes to the danger. His daughter saw that she must act differently, and she never let her voice falter or shed a tear in his presence. She sat by him, listened to all he said, repeated hymns, and then when she could bear it no longer, would walk calmly to the door, and rush away into her room, returning with the same calm and pale face, without any appearance of the agitation she had gone through. Of the devotion and strength of mind shown by Princess Alice all through these trying scenes, it is impossible to speak too highly."[103]

On 8th December, the Court Circular announced that the Prince Consort had been suffering from a 'feverish cold' for the past week, but 'there are no unfavourable symptoms'. Three days later an equally positive bulletin was published, but on 12th December, there was marked deterioration in his condition. His breathing was laboured and, although he was able to converse logically, his irritation with himself and his state of health increased. Realising that the situation seemed hopeless, Alice suggested that Bertie should be summoned from Cambridge but the Queen, still clinging to the hope of his recovery and convinced that Bertie's misdemeanour was responsible for the illness, refused. The following day, when there was still no improvement, Alice took matters into her own hands and secretly dispatched a telegram telling her brother to come at once.

By the time that Bertie arrived at Windsor in the early hours of the 14th December, his father seemed a little calmer, leading one of his doctors to declare that he had passed through the worst of the crisis and was now on the road to recovery.

"There is a slight change for the better in the Prince this morning," read the daily bulletin, but whether this pronouncement sprang from ignorance or optimism, the apparent improvement was merely the rallying which often precedes death. By noon it was clear that the Prince Consort was dying, and at four-thirty a further bulletin was issued:

"His Royal Highness the Prince Consort is in a most critical state." Alice remained at his bedside until the early afternoon when she accompanied her mother onto the terrace for 'a breath of air'. There, admitting the truth at last, the Queen broke down in tears; and Alice, her own heart breaking, had to put her feelings aside to comfort her mother.

Throughout the evening, as other members of the family gathered around the bed, Alice maintained her vigil, escaping sporadically to give vent to her grief and to strengthen herself for the inevitable outcome. Her mother, likewise, removed herself occasionally to an adjoining room where she was sitting when, shortly after ten o'clock, Alice entered to tell her that the end was near. By the time that Queen Victoria reached for Albert's hand, it was already cold. At ten forty-five he drew three final breaths and was gone.

"I stood up, kissing his heavenly forehead," the Queen recalled, "and called out in a bitter agonising cry, 'Oh, my dear darling!' and then dropped on my knees in mute distracted despair, unable to utter a single word or shed a tear."

In a state of collapse, she was led to a sofa where she sat, pleading with her children and members of her household not to desert her. In the midst of her mother's despair, her sisters' sobs and her elder brother's silent disbelief, Alice remained calm, gazing for a while at her late father before turning to offer assistance to the Queen. With the help of other members of the extended family, she took her mother to the adjoining room and asked the doctors to provide her with an opiate. Once this had been administered, she gave instructions for her own bed to be placed beside the Queen's, and helped the maids to undress her.

Queen Victoria could not sleep. Under the influence of the opiate, she ran along the corridor to the nursery and, taking her sleeping child, four-year-old Beatrice, from her cot, wrapped her in Prince Albert's nightshirt and carried her back to her own bed, where she lay in a daze, trying to comprehend the enormity of what had happened. For Alice, watching beside her, the sight of her mother in such a state was surely an ominous reminder of the fragility of her nerves and the care she would need in the coming months to cope with so great a loss.

In those hours following the death of the father she had loved so deeply, Alice had little time to express her own sorrow, and while she was occupied comforting her mother, there was no one on hand to comfort her. In that moment the world as Alice had known it, came to an end.

In one sorrowful evening the carefree days of childhood had reached their tragic finale.

Chapter 12 –
Strength of Mind & Self-Sacrifice

Paralysed by shock and bewilderment, Queen Victoria withdrew from the world, refusing to see anyone but Alice and the Duchess of Kent's former lady-in-waiting, Lady Augusta Bruce. Numb with grief, she was unable to weep, but then, when her tears burst forth, members of the household claimed they heard her desperate wailing echoing along the corridors of Windsor Castle. Alternatively deifying Prince Albert and lamenting the 'lack of pluck' which led to his demise, she insisted that his shaving water should be changed each morning, and his nightshirt laid out for him each night – it was a practice which would continue for the next forty years.

Black crepe draped every corridor and every item of furniture at Windsor; preparations for Christmas were abandoned, and the Queen discarded the bright colours of the past to don the widow's weeds that she would wear to the end of her life. In the country at large there was a sense of shock and sorrow, too, as people mourned not so much for the death of a foreign prince but for the sorrow of his forty-two-year-old widow and her fatherless children.

It has often been implied that during the early days of her bereavement the Queen was on the verge of insanity. From a modern viewpoint her excessive grief might suggest that that was indeed the case but a glance at the evidence shows that this was far from the truth. In the 19th century, death was treated very differently from how it is dealt with today. Black plumed horses bearing coffins draped in black palls were a common sight, and outlandish statues and headstones cluttered the churchyards. Victorian literature was filled with dramatic death scenes, which the people of the time relished but which now appear overly sentimental – one need only think of the public outpouring of grief at the death of Little Nell in the serialisation of Dickens' *The Old Curiosity Shop,* or the death of Beth in Louisa May Alcott's *Little Women.* In the average middle-class home, gloomy paintings and embroidered inscriptions about the briefness of life hung on the walls; and even the most popular songs of the time wallowed in mawkish morbidity: *'Father's a Drunkard and Mother is Dead',* and *'The Vacant Chair'* to name but two. Rather than being viewed as macabre, dramatic demonstrations of grief were seen as signs of respect for the departed and as evidence of the depths of love they had inspired in the bereaved.

In all aspects of life, Queen Victoria was a passionate woman, and one, incidentally, who was very fond of popular novels, so it is unsurprising that her reaction to the death of Prince Albert appears melodramatic. There is also the possibility that the witnesses who wrote of her 'wailing' at Windsor, were simply following the tradition of writers of the day to demonstrate the extent of her grief. The fact that she snatched the sleeping Beatrice from her cot is often cited as an example of her mental instability but, in that moment, she was under the influence of an opiate, and, in the days that followed, she was sufficiently sane to write coherently to her uncle in Belgium, to think about her children's future, to choose the site of Albert's mausoleum, and to attend his funeral in a dignified manner.

As early as 24th December, the Queen wrote to King Leopold:

> "I am also anxious to repeat one thing, and that one is my firm resolve, my irrevocable decision, viz. that his wishes – his plans – about everything, his views about everything are to be my law! And no human power will make me swerve from what

he decided and wished...I apply this particularly as regards our children – Bertie etc. – for whose future he had traced everything so carefully. I am also determined that no one person, may he be ever so good, ever so devoted among my servants – is to lead or guide or dictate to me. I know how he would disapprove it. And I live on with him, for him; in fact I am only outwardly separated from him, and only for a time."[104]

Clearly, only ten days after Prince Albert's death she had the wherewithal to prepare for a life without him.

It might well be the case, too, that, because she withdrew from public gaze for so long, imaginations, fired by the popular Gothic novels of the era, formed an image of the 'Widow of Windsor' as a demented creature, shrieking in her ancient tower, like Charlotte Bronte's Bertha Mason, Wilkie Collins' 'Woman in White' or even Dickens' Miss Havisham.

The extent of her influence and the length of her reign have often created the impression that Queen Victoria was a formidable woman with boundless self-confidence, but, in reality, she was desperately shy and acutely aware of the distinction between the role she played as sovereign and who she was as a person. As a Queen, she expected her orders to be obeyed and was capable of commanding respect and awe, but behind the role she saw herself as a helpless woman, who needed the support of a strong man. Throughout her married life, Prince Albert had given her the self-assurance necessary to carry out her public duties but, suddenly deprived of his presence, her nerves overcame her as much as did her grief. She spoke frequently of her inability to appear in public 'alone', and even the thought of meeting with ministers filled her with dread.

With the death of Prince Albert, it was obvious that there would be no Christmas celebrations at Windsor that year, and it occurred to King Leopold of the Belgians that it would be most beneficial for the Queen to leave at once for Osborne. Perhaps he believed that typhus might still be prevalent in Windsor Castle, or that distance from the death scene might ease the pain of parting. Either way, the Queen could not bear to abandon Prince Albert's body; and Alice, unwilling to create further upheaval, was equally reluctant to leave. Nonetheless, when she realised that her mother's health depended upon it, she finally persuaded the Queen that it was a necessary move, not least for the sake of the younger children, who might also contract typhoid if they were to remain in the castle. Although Alice would later regret the decision to leave, the Queen yielded, and as the household at Windsor was rapidly sent away, the staff at Osborne hurriedly prepared to receive the royal party just six days after Albert's death.

On the morning before their departure, the Queen, leaning on Alice's arm, walked around the grounds of Frogmore in search of a suitable spot for the Prince's mausoleum. Bertie and Louis, who had travelled to England as soon as he heard what had happened, were waiting for them there and, no sooner was the site chosen, than plans began on a design for his final resting place, where the Queen repeatedly expressed the hope that she would soon join him.

On 19th December a sombre group of black-clad travellers reached Osborne. The sea air might have been conducive to health, and the seclusion might have provided the privacy that the Queen craved, but, if it was hoped that the distance from Windsor would alleviate the pain of her loss, nowhere could have been less effective than the house which Prince Albert had designed. For Alice, the entire estate echoed with poignant memories of her father – from the nursery and Swiss Cottage where he had watched her play, to the private suite where his belongings lay as he had left them, and, on the Queen's instructions, would remain for the rest of her life.

Even in the seclusion of Osborne, it was impossible to ignore the necessity of making arrangements for the funeral. Prince Albert had specifically requested a simple service with no memorials but, despite her insistence on adhering to his plans in every other realm of life, the Queen was not prepared to let her 'angel' be forgotten. In no time at all, his portrait hung over every bed she would ever sleep in; statues of him appeared all over the country; George Gilbert Scott was invited to design the impressive Albert Memorial; and eventually the Royal Albert Hall would ensure his name would live on through future generations.

By the standard of royal funerals, however, the service on 28th December *was* relatively simple. There was no lying in state or torchlight procession as had become customary, and very few foreign royalties attended. Nonetheless, the grenadiers provided a full Guard of Honour and the short procession from Windsor Castle to St. George's Chapel was carried out with all the ceremony of a royal occasion. Wreaths of green moss and violets, which Alice and the Queen had made, were placed on the coffin.

"It was a profoundly mourning and impressive sight," wrote the future Dean of Westminster, Arthur Stanley. "Indeed, considering the magnitude of the event, and the persons present all agitated by the same emotion, I do not think I have ever seen or shall ever see anything so affecting."[105]

Queen Victoria, who had returned to Windsor with her family, survived the service, but, unable to watch the coffin being carried to the vault where it was to remain until the completion of the mausoleum, she and her daughters returned to Osborne the moment the rite was complete.

For two months, Queen Victoria remained out of sight on the Isle of Wight, declaring that she had lost interest in all earthly affairs, but, though the country and government sympathised with her grief, parliamentary business could not be put on hold indefinitely. For several days, official papers requiring the monarch's signature had piled up, delaying the passing of laws and other important business. Under normal circumstances, it would have been natural for the Queen's heir to undertake her duties during her absence, but, as she sought someone to blame for her loss, her eyes fixed on Bertie. His careless and selfish behaviour had, in her opinion, broken his father's heart and therefore he was ultimately responsible for his death.

"I never can or shall look at him without a shudder," she told Vicky and, though Alice did her utmost to persuade her that Bertie was suffering, too, she could never take him into her confidence, or, indeed, completely forgive him.

Moreover, prior to his father's death, arrangements had been made for Bertie to visit the Holy Land, and, since Queen was determined to abide by all the Prince Consort's plans, within a few weeks of the funeral, the Prince of Wales departed with his suite. With Bertie out of favour, and Vicky out of the country, eighteen-year-old Alice was left to shoulder an exceptionally heavy burden. Not only was she to act as an emotional prop to her mother, but also, she saw no alternative but to take on her duties as sovereign. Within days of her father's death, she was busily reading through the numerous messages from ministers, formulating responses and handing them to her mother to sign. It was she who met with the Prime Minister and politicians, and she who arranged for the Queen to sit in a room adjacent to that in which the Privy Council met so that she could hear their discussions without having to be seen.

"It is impossible to speak too highly of the strength of mind and self-sacrifice shown by Princess Alice during these dreadful days," the *Times* reported. "Her Royal Highness has certainly understood that it was her duty to help and support her mother in her great sorrow, and it was in a great measure due to her that the Queen has been able to bear with such wonderful resignation the irreparable loss that so suddenly and terribly befell her."[106]

Commendable and necessary as Alice's actions were, the extent of her responsibilities also provided an escape from her own inner turmoil. She was ever her father's daughter, and, just as Prince Albert had used work as a distraction from emotional trauma, so, too, did Alice suppress her grief by accumulating more and more duties.

"She also gained at this time," wrote her friend, the Grand Duchess of Baden, "...the desire for constant occupation, which in her public as well as her private life became part of herself."[107]

But for Alice, as for her father, in time her suppressed emotions would take a severe toll on her health and ultimately, perhaps, contribute to her early death. More immediately they turned her from a happy bride-to-be, into a serious young woman who no longer even had time to delight in the prospect of her forthcoming marriage.

"It was but natural," her sister recalled, "that during the first weeks of her great sorrow, and of her many new duties, the thought of her own future should be put into the background."[108]

Louis' presence in those first few months did not provide the support Alice needed, quite simply because she was too busy and too preoccupied to open her heart to him. Seeing how busy she was and the extent to which the

Queen now depended upon her, Louis began to wonder whether the wedding would take place at all. Although marriage would provide Alice with an escape from the gloom and responsibilities of the British court, it would be difficult for her to abandon her mother at such a time.

Moreover, in those dark days, Alice was changing rapidly. She was no longer the child who delighted in impressing the father on whom she depended, but rather a competent and independent woman determined to imitate his example of service and self-sacrifice. Of course, her personality had not changed overnight. She maintained her exquisite sense of humour and her capacity to bring comfort to those in need, but now her gentleness was buttressed by a will of iron, and, just as she unstintingly devoted herself to duty, she expected that those around her would do the same.

> "How I grieve for her!" wrote Lady Knightley, who met her at this time. "Her young life crushed and blighted by a weight of care and responsibility of which few have any idea."[109]

As a young girl on whom few people depended, Alice had been deeply attracted by Louis' child-like nature, but now that she had assumed so many responsibilities, would his carefree attitude still hold such appeal? What was more, she had always adored her father but, since his death, both she and the Queen had transformed him into such a model of strength and virtue that, regardless of her fiancé's qualities or how deeply she loved him, would he would ever be able to live up to her ideal of the perfect husband?

Whether or not such questions occurred to Alice, it was agreed that the wedding would take place in the summer. Prince Albert had wished it, and, despite her reliance on Alice, the Queen would abide by her promise 'that his wishes – his plans – about everything are to be my law!'

In February, the Queen signed an official agreement with the Hessians, confirming the dowry and annuity which Alice would receive, and the guarantee that, should Louis predecease her, she would be cared for and provided with a home by the Grand Duke of Hesse. In the meantime, Alice sought to soothe her grief by creating a series of drawings for Louis, but nothing, not even the prospect of marriage, could erase the memory of Prince Albert – a rather macabre memento of whom she cherished:

> "…We went into Princess Alice's rooms," wrote Lady Knightley, "and she showed me a great treasure, a picture of her beloved father, taken after death, with the beautiful face looking so calm and peaceful. There we lingered on, talking in the twilight; Princess Alice lying on the sofa, while I sat in an arm-chair at her feet, and Princess Helena was on the floor at mine, and Prince Alfred perched on the table. We had quite a roomful at dinner, all talking and laughing together."

In April, on Alice's nineteenth birthday, the Queen presented her with a touching gift that her father had specifically commissioned: a gold bracelet engraved with her image and a ship, indicating her forthcoming departure for Hesse. Inscribed was a message, added by the Queen:

"To dear Alice from your loving parents, Albert and Victoria, who though visibly parted are ever united."

It was the last material gift that Alice would receive from her father, and one which she would treasure for the rest of her life.

Chapter 13
A Love Which Increases Daily

The Dining Room of Osborne House had long been the hub of happy family gatherings. When the Queen was in residence, dinner was served each evening at eight o'clock sharp, and she and Prince Albert sat down to eat surrounded by portraits of themselves and their relations. In the summertime, light streamed through the bay windows, flooding the room and illuminating Franz Xavier Winterhalter's most famous depiction of the Royal Family. Created in 1846, and hung for the Queen's thirtieth birthday, the painting shows Victoria and Albert surrounded by their five eldest children in an exquisite combination of domesticity and regal grandeur.

Three-year-old Alice is holding her baby sister, Lenchen, and gazing towards Vicky, while her father's left hand dangles above her, just out of reach. Sixteen years later, that pose might have taken on a new significance as Alice entered the Dining Room on her wedding day: her father was still beyond her reach, and, though she had supported her family in his absence, her eyes were now turned towards a new life in Germany, where Vicky was soon to become Empress.

With its brightness and happy memories, Osborne might have been the perfect setting for a wedding. On July 1st 1862, as Alice entered the Dining Room on the arm of her uncle, the Duke of Coburg, the furniture had been removed, a makeshift altar erected, and a plethora of summer scents emanated from countless flowers. To Queen Victoria and other witnesses, however, the occasion was 'more like a funeral' than a wedding, for, while Alice and her bridesmaids – her three younger sisters and her future sister-in-law, Anna of Hesse – were dressed in white lace, the rest of the congregation was clothed in black mourning. The Queen, out of sight by a window to the left of the altar, sobbed quietly throughout the service as she gazed at the painting of beloved Albert; and the recently-widowed Archbishop of York, presiding over the ceremony in place of the Archbishop of Canterbury who was too ill to attend, also had tears in his eyes.

Without ostentation, the service lasted for just under an hour, after which the Lord Chamberlain, Viscount Sydney, led the bride and groom to the Horn Room to complete the official register. At two o'clock, the guests gathered in a marquee on the lawn for the wedding breakfast, after which they left the island while the Queen withdrew to her rooms where Alice and Louis joined her for luncheon.

It had been a private ceremony with none of the pomp and rejoicing which normally accompanies royal weddings – in fact, there had been so little publicity that, as the royal train bringing the guests caused diversions at stations en route, many people believed that the delays were due to an accident. Nonetheless, gifts arrived from across the Empire, the most outstanding of which was a priceless gold fan inlaid with rubies and emeralds from the Maharajah Dhuleep Singh. Earlier that morning, Queen Victoria had given Alice a prayer book, while 'the Maidens of England' sent a polyglot Bible, with a matching prayer book from 'the Matrons of England'. The Countess of Fife presented Alice with an exquisite jewel casket; and the Duchess of Athol had commissioned an inscribed paper weight surmounted by a royal stag. There were countless pieces of china and table decorations, all, in the Queen's opinion, 'really beautiful things' but no amount of beautiful gifts could make up for the absence of the bride's father.

At five o'clock that evening, Alice and Louis left Osborne House for a three-day honeymoon a few miles away in Appley near Ryde, where a small suite of rooms had been prepared for them in Castle St. Clare[m], the seaside home of the Conservative Party politician, Colonel Vernon-Harcourt. In spite of the lack of publicity, crowds had gathered to cheer them on their way, and, though the weather was overcast, Alice could at last taste the first real joy she had known in seven weary months.

Following the bride and groom in a separate carriage was the Queen's friend and Lady of the Bedchamber, Jane Churchill; Louis' equerry, Baron Westerweller; and General Seymour, former Groom-in-Waiting to Prince Albert, the three of whom were to make up the suite during their stay at St Clare. All three, however, maintained a discreet distance and, after all the hustle and bustle of recent weeks, Louis and Alice were finally able to be alone.

The rain, which poured throughout the honeymoon, seemed barely to touch Alice and Louis as they basked in each other's company. Their mutual delight was apparent to everyone who saw them, and several observers commented that, after so many exhausting months of service, marriage had brought a healthy glow to Alice's cheeks, since she and Louis were so clearly in love. Even then, though, she could not allow herself to appear too happy in the midst of her mother's grief, and despite the briefness of the honeymoon and the short distance from Appley to Osborne, she still made time to write to the Queen, thanking her for her kindness and assuring her of her unchanging love.

Letters, however, were insufficient for the Queen. On only the second day of the honeymoon, she arrived at St Clare with her sister, Feodore, Bertie, Lenchen, Louise and a posse of attendants in tow. What Louis thought of this invasion by his in-laws remains unrecorded but the Queen observed that although Alice had a cold, she was obviously happy and filled with affection for her husband.

---

[m] The crenelated mansion was destroyed by fire in 1960 and subsequently demolished.

The following evening, the newly-weds returned to Osborne House, where a suite of rooms had been prepared for them. Over the next few days they spent much of their time with the Queen. Alice rode out with her daily in the rain, and she and Louis dined with her each evening after which Alice entertained the family by reading aloud or playing her father's harmonium. Repeatedly the Queen observed how happy and 'nice' she and Louis were together and how well they suited one another. So impressed was she by her new son-in-law's attentiveness and sensitivity that, having already raised him from 'Serene' to 'Royal' Highness, she awarded him the Order of the Garter – the highest British Order of Chivalry.

Eight days after the wedding, the time came to leave for Darmstadt and, despite her love for her husband, the prospect of leaving her family and her childhood home was so heart-rending for Alice that she broke down in tears. Now, it was the Queen's turn to offer comfort. The evening before the departure, she soothingly reminded Alice that they would not be separated for long, as she intended to abide by the plan of ensuring that she and Louis would, initially at least, spend several months each year in England.

The next morning, the Queen took the young couple aside to lecture Louis on the importance of taking care of Alice's health. Her daughter, she observed, looked thin and would need looking after; and, in her typical euphemistic manner, implied that this would be especially important when Alice became pregnant. Already, with Vicky's traumatic experience in mind, she had asked her doctor to supply the newly-weds with a detailed letter describing the symptoms of pregnancy and the best means of ensuring a safe confinement – a matter of great importance in an age when approximately thirty-three women out of a thousand died in childbirth. The advice was more timely than anyone yet realised for, by the end of her honeymoon Alice was already in what the Queen liked to call 'an unfortunate condition'. Louis' sensible responses convinced the Queen that she need not worry, and, reluctant as she was to see Alice go, she was satisfied that he would do everything possible to make her happy.

At half past four in the afternoon of 9th July, amid many tears, Alice hugged her mother goodbye, and, after bidding farewell to her sisters and the household, she and Louis left Osborne for the royal yacht, which would take them to Belgium for the first stage of their journey. The sea was calm and by evening they had reached Brussels where they remained overnight before boarding a train for Hesse via Cologne. Three days after leaving England, they arrived at Bingen on the Hessian border, where an official party was waiting to welcome them. Continuing by train through the wine-growing region of Mayence, they boarded a 'gaily-decked' steamer to cross the Rhine before making the final stretch of the journey by rail.

At each station more officials arrived to greet them and, as they neared their destination, Louis' parents and uncle, Grand Duke Ludwig III, boarded the train to accompany them on their entrance into the town. That evening, Queen Victoria, who had been tracking every stage of their travels, recorded with relief that they had safely reached Darmstadt[110].

Despite the heavy rain, which had continued for most of the journey, Alice's first glimpse of her new home could not have been more promising. Enthusiastic crowds had gathered to catch a glimpse of the returning prince and his bride, and, as they processed through the brightly decorated streets, they were showered with flowers. Bands played, and a mounted escort rode alongside the carriage, while girls in white dresses assembled to be presented to the English princess.

"I am really deeply touched by the kindness and enthusiasm shown by the people, which is said to be quite unusual," Alice wrote to the Queen."[111]

The crowds were equally enamoured of her, as reports proliferated of her cheerful but dignified bearing, her prettiness and the graciousness with which she responded to the welcome.

Eventually, they reached the house of Louis' parents, where the rest of the family had assembled, and Alice could begin to familiarise herself with her new relations.

In spite of his refusal to allow Louis and Alice to reside in his palace, the eccentric Grand Duke Ludwig proved to be very accommodating and eager to make Alice feel at home. Having been recently widowed, the fifty-five-year-old Ludwig III empathised with Queen Victoria and, as Alice told her mother, he took a 'warm interest in all my brothers and sisters."[112] On the first evening, he presented her with a diamond bracelet, which he and his wife had chosen several months earlier, and over the next few weeks he would put himself out to show her around the Grand Duchy[n].

While Louis' parents were equally welcoming, it was obvious to Alice that they did not extend to one another the affection that they showed to her. Louis' father, Prince Charles, was first and foremost a soldier, who had preferred to spend time with his regiment than with his wife, whom he considered dull and unattractive – not least because, in a physical response, perhaps, to his lack of affection, she grew increasingly obese with the passing of years. To Alice, however, Princess Elizabeth showed nothing but kindness, quickly earning her love, respect and admiration.

---

[n] Queen Victoria was so impressed by the Grand Duke's hospitality that in 1865 she awarded him the Order of the Garter. His investiture was carried out in the presence of Alice and her father-in-law.

"I admire her also now that I know and understand her," Alice wrote. "There is so much beneath, so much Gemüth [warm-heartedness], tenderness, and delicacy of feeling."[113]

Alice was already familiar with Louis' siblings, Henry and Anna, the former of whom had accompanied Louis on his visits to England, and the latter of whom had been one of her bridesmaids. Henry closely resembled his father in character and appearance, and the better Alice came to know him, the more she enjoyed his cheerful company.

Anna, too, became a good friend, whose 'gentle humble spirit' Alice admired, despite Vicky's extremely unflattering description:

"I do not think her pretty – she has not a fine figure but a passable one…She has an incipient twitching in her eyes…and her teeth are nearly all spoilt…She will never have anything graceful in her deportment…She has a very deep voice and rather a gruff abrupt way of speaking, frowning when she speaks, partly to conceal her shyness and partly to conceal her eyes which are perpetually twitching while she is talking…Her eyes are small and insignificant and she has not much expression in her face. Whether she is clever or not, I have not the slightest idea…"[114]

Their scholarly youngest brother, sixteen-year-old William, was, according to Alice, a connoisseur of art and an historian with a specific interest in ancient Rome.

One of the most fascinating members of the family was Louis' 'clever and amusing' uncle, Prince Alexander. While serving in the Russian army, Alexander had committed the terrible crime of marrying a commoner, Julia von Haucke, lady-in-waiting to his sister, the Tsarina Marie. Having been dismissed from his regiment, he returned to Hesse where his brother, the Grand Duke, eventually gave Julia the title 'Princess of Battenberg'. The couple and their five children settled at the picturesque Heligenberg Castle in Jugenheim, which, despite Alexander's faux pas, would become a regular holiday destination for the Tsar and his family as well as a delightful resort for Louis and Alice.

While Alice was forming favourable impressions of her in-laws, she was making an equally positive impression on them. Just as the crowd had been touched by her cheerful dignity, Louis' family was gratified by her eagerness to listen and learn all she could about her new homeland. As she finally lay down to sleep on her first night in the Grand Duchy, she could rest assured that she had lived up to her father's expectations and made an excellent beginning to her new life as a future Grand Duchess.

Situated about two hundred miles south-west of Berlin, Hesse-Darmstadt (Hesse-and-by-Rhine) was one of the most charming regions of Central Europe. Originally a part of Thuringia, the area had become an independent landgraviate in the 16th century, and, after joining Napoleon's Confederation of the Rhine in 1808, it was elevated to the status of Grand Duchy. Although neither as wealthy nor as powerful as Vicky's Prussian relations, the ruling family of Hesse had made some very prestigious connections. The 18th century, Frederika Louisa had married the King of Prussia; and two years before Alice was born, Louis' aunt, Marie, had married the future Tsar Alexander II, establishing a Russian connection which would continue through Alice's children.

By the time of Louis and Alice's wedding, Darmstadt – a 'dull town with fine wide streets, and the grass growing in them'[115] – had been the most prominent town in the Grand Duchy for over three hundred years,

154

and it was there, on the site of the former Botanical Gardens, that work, partly funded by Queen Victoria, had already begun on the New Palace. In the meantime, though, Alice had to adapt to a far smaller household than would be expected for a daughter of the British Queen. Allocated a small suite of rooms in Louis' parents' house, she was attended by very few servants, which made entertaining visitors very difficult. Nevertheless, she did what she could to arrange the furniture and pictures according to her own taste, and was happy to report that Louis had gone to the trouble of having the rooms decorated in the 'English style.'

For a while, at least, the thrill of being newly married compensated for the lack of space, for, although she hardly dared to tell her grieving mother how happy she was, Louis could not have pleased her more.

"If I say I love my dear husband, that is scarcely enough –" she wrote. "...it is a love and esteem which increases daily, hourly; which he also shows to me by such consideration, such tender, loving ways....what have I done to deserve that warm, ardent love, which my darling Louis ever shows me?"[116]

Moreover, during her first few weeks in Hesse, there was little time to pay much attention to the restrictions of her accommodation. Her days were busy and well-ordered. Rising at seven-fifteen and taking coffee at eight, she usually went out with Louis in the mornings, returning at ten to attend to her extensive correspondence. In this, she was helped by her father's former librarian, Dr Becker, who had come from England to assist in arranging her affairs and would soon be appointed as her private secretary and treasurer. As a member of the ruling family, Alice was expected to be *au fait* with current events and therefore had the 'great bore' of reading the daily newspapers before 'breakfast' at noon. Throughout the afternoon, she received official visitors until dinner at four o'clock, after which she and Louis were able to spend time alone, reading together and discussing their plans for the future. Often, though, Louis' regimental duties kept him away for long periods of time, leaving Alice waiting impatiently for the sound of his footsteps on the stairs when he returned.

After their initial welcome, most of Louis' family were too absorbed in their own lives and commitments to be regular visitors, but his parents were constant companions and, despite her willingness to adapt, it did not take long for Alice to realise that living under their roof was hardly an ideal start to her marriage. Apart from the limitations of space and the realisation that, when winter came and the gardens were out of use, it would be impossible to receive anyone, she clearly felt that she and Louis needed greater privacy.

In an effort to assure her that soon they would have their own home, Louis took her to Stauffenberg where he had acquired a ruined castle, which he was gradually converting into a country house, but the restoration was slow and laborious and it would be a long time before the place was habitable. The Grand Duke agreed to allow the young couple to take possession of a 'ramshackle old schloss' at Kranichstein, about three miles from Darmstadt, as a summer residence, but the place had not been inhabited for almost a hundred years, and even by 1866 it was still only half-furnished. Louis optimistically suggested that, since the Grand Duke was fond of Alice, he might be willing to change his mind about allowing them to live in his palace in Darmstadt, but Alice was far less hopeful, and, after only three weeks of living with her in-laws, she saw no alternative but to inform the Grand Duke that she and Louis would return to England in the autumn so as not to 'incommode our parents any longer.'[o]

In fact, there was a far more personal motive for wanting to return home. By then, Alice realised that she was pregnant and, recalling Vicky's first traumatic childbirth in Germany, would feel safer and more comfortable under the care of her mother's doctors. Aware that the Hessians could take offence at this precipitous departure, she assured herself that they would understand that it was not due to any 'ill will on our part', and, in the meantime, made every effort to visit many towns and cities of the Grand Duchy, sometimes wandering about incognito to familiarise herself with the Hessian culture.

The efficiency of the German transport system made it possible, too, to travel with ease beyond the borders of Hesse-Darmstadt to visit her relatives and friends. In early August, she and Louis stayed in Coburg as guests of her godfather, 'Uncle Ernest'; and the following month they spent time with her mother and siblings who were holidaying in neighbouring Thuringia.

Since early September, Queen Victoria and her younger children had been staying at Rheinhardtsbrunn Castle, which had immediately become a centre for happy reunions. Bertie arrived shortly after the Queen, followed by her sister, 'Aunt Feo', and her former governess, the aged Lehzen. On the 15th of the month, Vicky and Fritz arrived with their children; and five days later, Louis and Alice reached the neighbouring Schweizerhaus, where they were to stay with the Duke and Duchess of Coburg.

While other members of the party disappeared on expeditions, Alice and Louis spent the greater part of the holiday with the Queen, which provided Alice with an ideal opportunity to tell her mother she was pregnant. The Queen observed that she looked thin and drawn but 'for

---

º Interestingly, as family patterns go, Alice's daughter, Alix, also spent the early weeks of her marriage to Tsar Nicholas II, living with her mother-in-law and found the situation extremely difficult.

that there is a good reason', and noted again how happy she and Louis were together. Dining with the Queen, sketching the scenery, enjoying a donkey ride, and driving out through the early autumnal sunshine, little had changed between Alice and her mother since her wedding. As happened so often, though, sad news and illness cast a cloud over the holiday. First came word of the death of Alice's great-aunt, and a few days later, her youngest brother, Leopold, accidentally stuck a pen into the roof of his mouth, which bled so profusely that it eventually had to be cauterised. Contrary to the often-repeated myth that Queen Victoria virtually neglected Leopold, she frequently visited his room and wrote a daily account of her anxious discussions with the doctors, who remained with him night and day until his recovery.

More cheerfully, before leaving Rheinhardtsbrunn, arrangements were finalised for Alice and Louis' return to England in late autumn. It was agreed that, due to their restricted finances, the Queen would send the *Victoria & Albert* to bring them from Antwerp to Gravesend, and they would stay until after the birth of Alice's baby, allowing Louis plenty of time to fulfil his intention of visiting the northern industrial towns of Leeds and Manchester.

Before leaving for England, Alice and Louis still found the time to travel to Baden, where Alice's friend, Louise of Prussia, was now Grand Duchess, and where they also called to see Aunt Feo's 'small' but 'pretty' home. On returning to Darmstadt, they played host to Alice's brothers, Bertie and Arthur, both of whom made an instantly favourable impression on the Hessians and their Grand Duke.

Separation from her family had hardly been as distressing as Alice had feared. Between visits to neighbouring regions, she had spent only about ten weeks in Hesse, and, as the year drew to its close, she eagerly anticipated the return home for what was prove a very eventful stay. Despite the Hessians' sadness at her departure, it was with a happy heart that Alice set sail in mid-November, her only regret being that her father would not be there to greet her.

> "In talking last night," she wrote to the Queen, "Louis said what I feel so often, that he always felt as if it must come right again, and we should find dear Papa home again."[117]

Resigned, though, to his physical absence, she added piously, "In another *home* we shall."

Shortly before ten o'clock in the morning on the first anniversary of Prince Albert's death – Alice joined her sisters and mother in the room where her father had died. A bust of the Prince Consort had been surrounded by fresh flowers, and, as Queen Victoria knelt by the bed, Dean Stanley read from the Gospel of St John:

> *"Let not your heart be troubled: ye believe in God, believe also in me. In my Father's house are many mansions: if it were not so, I would have told you. I go to prepare a place for you. And if I go and prepare a place for you, I will come again, and receive you unto myself; that where I am, there ye may be also. And whither I go ye know, and the way ye know."*

After several more readings and prayers, Queen Victoria stood up and kissed her daughters before preparing for a more formal service at noon; and in the evening, at the exact hour of the Prince's death, a further sermon was read.

Four days later, at seven o'clock in the morning on 18th December 1862, a year to the day since Alice and Queen Victoria had chosen the site, Prince Albert's remains were taken from the vault in St George's Chapel to the new mausoleum which, although still under construction, was sufficiently complete to merit consecration. The coffin, carried by Louis and three of Alice's brothers, was lowered into a temporary sarcophagus, after which the Queen and Alice arrived for a service, led by Dean Stanley, the Bishop of Oxford and the Dean of Christ Church.

"The whole household was there," wrote Dean Stanley. "The Bishop, the two Deans and two or three Windsor clergy were raised on a platform at the east end, immediately above the sarcophagus. The Queen and the children came in when everyone was assembled. They remained inside while the clergy and choir walked around chanting the psalm. The Bishop then read two or three prayers extremely well, and then were sung two hymns...Then was read the deed of consecration prefaced by the Queen herself...Then she and the family passed out and we returned as we came."[118]

The re-interment was the first of three major events which took place during Alice's stay in England and it was appropriate that so solemn an occasion should occur towards the end of a year which had been characterised chiefly by mourning. There was a strange irony, too, in a rather harrowing accident which Alice experienced on the last day of December when, while travelling from Osborne House to Newport, her carriage struck an obstacle and she was thrown out into the road. Although she was badly shaken, neither she nor the baby was harmed but, after all the upheavals of 1862, the accident seemed an appropriate conclusion to such a tumultuous year. As 1863 dawned, she could shake off the events of the past twelve months and look forward to two far happier experiences: gaining a new sister-in-law and becoming a mother.

To his family's relief, Bertie's escapade with the actress in Ireland had not jeopardised the plans for his marriage to Princess Alexandra of Denmark. After months of planning and negotiation between the Danish and British Royal Families, the wedding took place in St. George's Chapel, Windsor, on 10th March 1863. Alice, who was delighted by her new sister-in-law, had designed the crystal lockets engraved with diamonds and coral, representing the red and white of the Danish flag, and wrought into the initials 'A-E–A' for Albert Edward and Alexandra, which Bertie gave to the bridesmaids.

Twenty-one-year-old Bertie and his eighteen-year-old bride looked so happy together that everyone agreed that they made perfect couple, and, although the Queen found the ceremony tortuous as her thoughts inevitably returned to her own wedding day, it was the first truly joyful family occasion since the death of Prince Albert. Of course, at the Queen's insistence, the image of the late Prince appeared in most of the wedding photographs, as though his spectre were hovering over the proceedings, reminding Bertie of his former errors and his duty to live up to his father's high standards of morality.

Following the ceremony, as Bertie and Alexandra left for a honeymoon at Osborne, Alice, who had modestly concealed her pregnancy beneath a cape throughout the celebrations, returned to Windsor Castle to await the birth of her child. By 3rd April, she was feeling decidedly unwell, thrusting her mother into a constant state of agitation in anticipation of 'the event'. The following day, she was so uncomfortable that the Queen summoned Mrs Lilly, the nurse who had been in attendance when Alice herself was born, who instantly sent for the midwife, Mrs Clark, and Dr Charles Locock – the aging obstetrician who had also attended the Queen's accouchements.

As her fretful mother held her hand, Alice's labour continued throughout the evening and into the night, partially relieved by chloroform, which left her 'half-stupefied', until at quarter-to-five on Easter Sunday morning, a daughter was born.

As the Queen wept with relief, a twenty-one gun salute echoed across Darmstadt, and over the next few days the British newspapers kept the public informed of the progress of the baby and her nineteen-year-old mother. Nonetheless, having suffered almost as much as in the process as if she were going through it herself, Queen Victoria made it very clear to Louis that she hoped it would be a long time before he put her precious daughter through such agony again. In that, as in so many matters concerning Alice, she would be disappointed.

On 27th April, the baby was christened Victoria Alberta in a Lutheran ceremony conducted by the Hessian court chaplain, Prediger Bender. A few days later, Louis and Alice took her to Osborne, where Alice completed her recuperation before spending a couple of days with Bertie and Alexandra at Marlborough House and finally returning to Darmstadt.

Their departure grieved the Queen so deeply that she immediately began making plans for their next visit but now, with a child of her own, Alice realised the importance of spending more time in Hesse. As Louis would one day inherit the Grand Duchy, it was vital that he should devote himself more fully to his civil and military duties and, if Alice were to gain the Hessians' confidence, she must establish her family there.

"Out of the ten months of our married life five have been spent under your roof," she wrote rather sternly to the Queen, "so you can see how ready we are to be with you. Before next year Louis does not think we shall be able to come; at any rate when we can we shall, and I hope I shall be able to see you for a day or two in Germany to divide the time."[119]

For all her resolve, within five months, Alice and Louis were back in Scotland to support the Queen through the ordeal of appearing in public for the unveiling of a statue of Prince Albert in Aberdeen. The event passed without incident but it would not be the only time during her stay in Scotland that Alice would be called upon to support her mother.

One cold, rainy evening as the Queen, Alice and Lenchen were returning through the remote countryside to Balmoral, the carriage in which they were travelling repeatedly veered from the road and it soon became obvious that their driver, Smith, was drunk and incapable of controlling the horses. Eventually, after one severe jolt, Alice commented that the carriage was listing, and moments later it toppled over completely, hurling its occupants to the ground. The Queen had fallen on her face and hands; and Alice and Lenchen's clothes had become tangled in the wreckage. The shock was so great that even the seemingly imperturbable John Brown, who was travelling with them, panicked, believing that everyone had been killed. Alice, calmly took charge of the situation, ripping her dress to free herself, before holding out a lantern so that Brown could release the horses, which were fortunately unharmed. In the middle of nowhere, there was nothing to do but to huddle under blankets in the overturned carriage in the hope that sooner or later someone would come to their aid. To their great relief, within half an hour, an aide, who had feared that something like that might happen, arrived with ponies and the bedraggled party was able to return relatively unscathed to the castle.

Once again, Alice's calmness and ability to take charge in a crisis impressed her mother, but it would not be long before the Queen would come to resent the very characteristics on which she had come to depend. While relying on Alice's advice, she had also grown used to her 'obedient' daughter's malleability, and it would come as a shock to realise that Alice was not quite as docile as she had believed. Within a couple of years, Alice's independent thinking would lead to a severe breakdown in their relationship and turn her, in the Queen's opinion, from a 'dear good' and dutiful daughter into a most 'disagreeable' and 'sharp' companion.

Chapter 14 –
How Wonderfully We Are Made

Prince Albert would have been delighted by his lively and intelligent granddaughter and would have thoroughly approved of the manner in which she was raised. Although by royal standards Alice and Louis were not wealthy, they were keen to ensure that Victoria would receive a broad education, and, despite her numerous duties and causes, Alice spent as much time as possible with the child, whose progress was recorded in regular epistles to the Queen. 'Baby's' first tooth, Baby's first words, Baby's first steps, Baby's first Christmas and Baby's first birthday – all were reported in loving detail.

By the time of that first birthday, Alice was again, to the Queen's dismay, in 'an unfortunate condition', but, after spending three summer months in Britain, she spared her mother's nerves by returning to Hesse for the birth. This time, she was attended by Louis' mother, who was 'kindness itself' and 'so discreet'; and on 1st November 1864, after a labour of only four hours, a second daughter was born. Although the Hessians had been hoping for a future Grand Duke, Alice remarked that her being a girl was but a momentary disappointment as she and Louis thought how pretty two little sisters would look together. The baby, who screamed throughout her christening, was named Elizabeth after Louis' ancestor, St. Elizabeth of Hungary[p], but within the family she would always be known as Ella.

Less than two months later, in late January 1865, Alice and Louis took their little girls to Berlin to visit their Aunt Vicky and Hohenzollern cousins. Victoria's

---

[p] It is remarkable how closely Ella's life came to resemble that of St. Elizabeth of Hungary, who, following the death of her husband, gave away all of her possessions and founded a religious order to care for the poor. Ella was canonised by the Russian Orthodox Church and is recognised as St Elizabeth Feodorovna of Russia. See 'Most Beautiful Princess' by Christina Croft

cradle was brought onto the train, while Ella slept in a baby bath in the middle of the carriage, which, Alice assured her mother, was heated by a stove. If the Queen was disconcerted by the thought of travelling with such young children in mid-winter, she was about to receive a far greater shock concerning her two eldest daughters. Prior to the visit, Vicky, who, contravening the mores of the Prussian court, was breastfeeding her own fourth child, had encouraged Alice to do the same for Ella; and, while the sisters were together they actually nursed each other's babies.

Queen Victoria was so horrified that, in her own words, the hairs on the back of her neck stood on end: such an 'animal' practice was demeaning for any woman, but for a princess it was totally unnecessary and disgusting! No matter how vehemently Vicky protested that it benefited the baby, Queen Victoria could only gasp in horror that her daughters had ignored 'the advice of a mother of nine children' and had turned themselves into cows!

Vicky's behaviour was alarming enough, but that Alice had followed her example was positively appalling for the Queen, who had assumed that Alice shared her disgust at the 'details of the nursery'. In the weeks that followed, she would discover how mistaken she had been.

Since reading the accounts of Florence Nightingale's work in the Crimean War, Alice had been fascinated by nursing; and, after tending her father through his final illness, her natural inclination had been to learn as much as possible about caring for the sick and the nature of disease. As early as 1863, she had made a point of visiting the hospital in Darmstadt with a view to raising public awareness and gaining donations to improve the less-than-ideal conditions. The Queen approved of such philanthropy and concern for the welfare of the people, but, with the birth of her children,

Alice's interest had extended into branches of nursing and medicine which her mother considered inappropriate for a woman, and particularly for a woman of her station.

The Queen was not alone in her views. Only a decade earlier, prior to the establishment of the Nightingale Fund, nursing was viewed as a very unsavoury occupation which attracted only the lowest class of society. Dickens' drunken Mrs Gamp was a typical caricature, portraying the prevalent view of untrained nurses as slovenly and incompetent:

> "She was a fat old woman, this Mrs Gamp, with a husky voice and a moist eye, which she had a remarkable power of turning up, and only showing the white of it...She wore a very rusty black gown, rather the worse for snuff, and a shawl and bonnet to correspond...The face of Mrs Gamp – the nose in particular – was somewhat red and swollen, and it was difficult to enjoy her society without becoming conscious of a smell of spirits. Like most persons who have attained to great eminence in their profession, she took to hers very kindly; insomuch that, setting aside her natural predilections as a woman, she went to a lying-in or a laying-out with equal zest and relish."[120]

Unsurprisingly the Nightingale family had initially opposed Florence's chosen career.

Apart from the insalubrious reputation of nurses, the idea that middle or upper class women should have any knowledge whatsoever of human anatomy was anathema to the ideal of the innocent 'angel in the house' – the naïve little woman who was totally dependent on her father or husband. At the same time as Alice was beginning her studies, Britain's first female doctor, Elizabeth Garrett Anderson, was being refused admission to dissecting theatres and prohibited from practising as an apothecary, despite having obtained all the necessary qualifications. In certain medical quarters it was even claimed that women's brains were too small to house too much knowledge, and excessive learning would lead to infertility and hysteria.

Alice, however, was not to be deterred. In early March 1864, she confessed to the Queen:

"I have read and studied a great deal about the human body; about children – their treatment &c. It interests me immensely. Besides, it is always useful to know such things, so that one is not perfectly ignorant of the reasons why doctors wish one to do certain things, and why not. In any moment of illness, before there is time for a doctor to come, one can be able to help oneself a little. I know you don't like these things...Instead of finding it disgusting, it only fills me with admiration to see how wonderfully we are made."[121]

Such was her fascination that Alice quickly became so uninhibited in her conversation that Queen Victoria worried about allowing her younger daughters to visit Darmstadt for fear of what they might hear!

Unruffled, Alice continued her studies, seeking the advice of several forward-thinking doctors, who agreed that breastfeeding was the best means of building of a strong immune system in the baby to prevent dysentery and other childhood ills. When this argument did not satisfy her mother, Alice reminded her that, while the Queen could afford to employ as many staff as she chose, in her own reduced circumstances, hiring a wet nurse would be nothing but an unnecessary expense, which could so easily be avoided.

Ever her father's daughter, Alice was not content to gain a theoretical knowledge without putting it into practice for the good of the people, and she was particularly keen to see improvements for women in childbirth.

Throughout the late 18th and early 19th centuries, in response to the high infant mortality rates and the number of deaths in childbirth, numerous lying-in hospitals had been established, wherein poor but respectable women were attended by doctors and trained midwives. In fact, the primary purpose of many of these hospitals was not to benefit expectant mothers but to provide an opportunity for doctors to train in obstetrics, and, due to their unhygienic methods, the death rates from puerperal fever rose significantly.

"The extent to which these institutions increase the danger of childbirth is now well known," wrote the eminent epidemiologist and statistician, William Farr, in 1842; and Florence Nightingale was in complete agreement, recommending that better provision should be made for women to have their babies at home. By the 1860s, institutes had been established to provide clean linen and other necessities for those who chose to avoid the hospitals, and, when, in 1864, Alice was invited to become the patroness of one such institute – the Heidenreich Institute for Lying-In Women, to which her mother had already made a financial contribution – she willingly accepted the position.

Typically, patronesses donated money and assisted in administration, but Alice was eager to play a far more proactive role. Either through humility or fear of creating a stir in aristocratic circles, she quietly went incognita to the homes of the poor, where she undertook the most menial tasks to assist the new mothers and their babies. Twice, accompanied by her lady-in-waiting, Christa Schenk, she visited a particular family who lived in one room accessible only by a dark ladder. While the mother, who had recently given birth to a fifth child, lay in bed, Alice assisted her husband in cooking a meal and:

"…arranged the bed a little, took the baby for her, bathed its eyes – for they were so bad, poor little thing! – and did odds and ends for her." [122]

Far from seeing herself as a benevolent philanthropist, Alice recognised the benefits she gained from contact with people outside her own class.

"…If one never sees any poverty, and always lives in that cold circle of Court people, one's good feelings dry up, and I felt the want of going about and doing the little good that is in my power. "[123]

This willingness to see for herself the conditions in which people lived, and to venture into areas which many women of her station considered unseemly, enabled her to become involved in another taboo branch of medicine: the care of the mentally ill.

These were the days when psychiatric illness was seen as something shameful, which had to be hidden away. For fear of offending public sensibilities, the immense 19th century asylums were usually situated in the countryside, out of sight from main thoroughfares and approached by winding avenues, giving rise to the expression 'going round the bend'. Within their walls, all manner of patients were housed, from the dangerously insane to the mildly eccentric, and from troublesome adolescents who refused to conform, to unmarried girls who had become pregnant and were 'put away' to avoid bringing shame on their families. Little distinction was made between people with different mental illnesses, while those with learning difficulties were referred to as 'feeble-minded idiots' or 'imbeciles', and deemed incapable of living in normal society.

Nonetheless, the foundation of asylums – literally refuges – was an attempt to improve life for those who, in past decades, would have found themselves in workhouses, prisons or private madhouses, where conditions were often filthy and barbaric, and where inmates were frequently kept chained in solitary confinement. The new asylums of the 19th century were regularly inspected; the patients were attended by doctors and nurses rather than gaolers; and the buildings were equipped with the most modern facilities, including libraries, bakeries, laundries and farms, where the patients could participate in meaningful and therapeutic labour. Rather than using restraints, many forward-thinking doctors believed in 'moral treatment', which involved providing their patients with a daily routine in order to create a sense of discipline and order to rebalance their minds.

When, in 1866, Alice attended a series of lectures about the need for such an institution in Hesse, she took up the cause with gusto, and, in much the same way as the patronage of Diana, Princess of Wales dispelled many myths about AIDS, Alice's support led to something of a reappraisal of mental illness. No sooner had she adopted the cause, however, than she came into conflict with the clergyman who had delivered the lectures and who was hoping to create a distinctly religious establishment.

Typically, many 19th century philanthropists believed they had a duty to impose their own religious ideas and practices on those whom they sought to help. Many of the model factories of the era were founded by pious people who, while providing excellent conditions and housing for their workers, prohibited gambling and alcohol and insisted on regular church attendance for their tenants. Although their motives were well-meaning, Alice, like her parents, opposed this paternalistic approach which, she believed, impinged on individual freedom of conscience. Moreover, contrary to the prevalent view of the time, she viewed mental illness as a medical rather than a spiritual problem and believed, therefore, that it would be better dealt with by doctors than by clerics.

Despite the disagreements, Alice, with her determination and flair for organisation, formed a committee of like-minded supporters and personally undertook responsibility for raising the necessary resources to build and equip an asylum. Having donated 1000 florins of her own money, her first fund-raising activity – a charity bazaar – was so successful that in just four days she had raised sixteen thousand florins[q], and wrote excitedly to her mother:

> "There have been crowds…something quite unusual for the quiet inhabitants of this place. They have shown so much zeal and devotion that I am quite touched by it, as I am more or less a stranger to them."[124]

Already, through her contact with so many people, Alice was gaining more experience in the care of the sick, and, within three months of the charity bazaar, circumstances would contrive to give her an even greater opportunity to develop her medical expertise in the midst of a bitter civil war.

For over fifty years, since the defeat of Napoleon, the German states had been led by Habsburg Austria. By the mid-19th century, however, a sense of German nationalism had emerged, leading to a call for the unification of the different states to create an entirely independent nation. While most Germans supported this idea, two distinct camps had developed with opposing opinions about how the unification should be organised. The German Federation, including Alice's Hesse-Darmstadt, believed in a 'Greater Germany' – the amalgamation of all German-speaking peoples under Austrian leadership. The Prussians, on the other hand, favoured a 'Lesser Germany', independent of Austria and led by the King of Prussia.

---

[q] Approximately £35,000 in today's money.

Prussia's Iron Chancellor, the Machiavellian Otto von Bismarck, was determined to see his kingdom rise to greater prominence, and had long been seeking an opportunity to provoke a conflict which would lead to the realisation of his plan. The opportunity arose in 1866, following the Prussian seizure of the disputed Danish territories of Schleswig and Holstein, the latter of which was governed by Austria. After several thwarted attempts at negotiation, Austria declared war on Prussia and her ally, Italy; and, by May that year, it was it was clear that other German states would soon be dragged into the conflict.

"The cloud grows blacker every day, and the anxiety we all live in is very great,"[125] Alice wrote to her mother, knowing that a costly war could bankrupt the little Grand Duchy. Moreover, since Hesse would side with Austria, she and Vicky would find themselves on opposing sides, as would Louis and his brother, Henry, who was serving in the Prussian army.

To make matters worse, Alice was now six months pregnant and, when Louis left with his troops, she would be 'quite alone', worrying about his safety and that of her children.

> "What shall I do?" she asked the Queen. "...As long as [Louis] comes home safe again – that is all I shall think of. Please God to spare me that fearful anxiety which weighs on me now already; for he having only a brigade could not keep out of danger, like Fritz [Vicky's husband] in Schleswig."[126]

In Berlin, Vicky, who had recently given birth to a fifth child, was equally anxious to avoid a war, which, she believed, had been deliberately orchestrated by Bismarck.

> "Not a day passes," she had told the Queen, "that the wicked man does not with the greatest ability counteract and thwart what is good, and drive on

towards war, turning and twisting everything to serve his own purpose. As often as we are a little hopeful again and see a means of getting out of the fix, we hear shortly after that the means have been rendered unavailable; the tissue of untruths is such that one gets quite perplexed with only listening to them, but the net is cleverly made, and the King, in spite of all his reluctance, gets more and more entangled in it without perceiving it."[127]

In the midst of the national crisis, Vicky faced a more agonising crisis at home. No sooner had Fritz left at the head of his army than her two-year-old son, Sigismund, whom Alice had nursed in Berlin, contracted meningitis. With his father and all the court doctors away, there was no one on hand to alleviate his suffering, and his death on 18th June plunged Vicky into such despair that she commissioned an effigy of the child to be placed in his cot which, to the consternation of the court, she regularly visited.

"I have to bear this awful trial alone, without my poor Fritz," she wept to her mother. "My little darling graciously lent me for a short time, to be my pride, my joy, my hope, is gone, gone, where my passionate devotion cannot follow, from where my love cannot recall him!...What I suffer none can know, few knew how I loved. It was my own happy secret, the long cry of agony which rises from the inmost depth of my soul, reaches Heaven alone."[128]

Saddened by the news, concerned for her sister and anxious about the impending conflict, Alice prayed for peace but prepared for war by gathering supplies and arranging to have her two little girls sent to the safety of their grandmother's home in England. By the middle of the month, the Prussians had crossed the Hessian border and, ten days later, Louis left for the front on a horse provided by the Queen.

Notwithstanding the imminent birth of her baby, Alice at once set to work, procuring rags for bandages, begging her mother for supplies and assisting in the hospitals in the blistering heat of the summer. Alongside the casualties of the battlefield, war invariably led to epidemics, and Alice, who had already seen the effects of smallpox in Hesse, now found herself face to face with cholera victims. Amid the spread of the disease and the echo of the Prussian guns on the palace walls, she went into labour on July 11th when, to her great relief, Louis suddenly reappeared to be present at the birth of a third daughter. The child was named Irène, after the goddess of peace.

Louis' experiences in battle had filled him with such an abhorrence of bloodshed that he urgently pleaded with his uncle to agree to Prussian terms to end the conflict. The Grand Duke, however, was slow to yield and when, after only three days' leave, Louis returned to his regiment, Alice was more frantic than ever, worrying about Louis' safety and appalled by the desolation at home.

> "From all parts of the country the people beg me to do what I can. The confusion here is awful, the want of money alarming; right and left one must help. As the Prussians pillaged here, I have many people's things hidden in the house. Even whilst in bed I had to see gentlemen in my room, as there were things to be done and asked which had to come straight to me. Then our poor wounded – the wives and mothers begging I should inquire for their husbands and children. It is a state of affairs too dreadful to describe."[129]

Food was in such short supply that even the troops were close to starvation and, for three weeks at the height of the conflict, Louis and his fellow officers ate nothing but brown bread.

Such was the devastation that it was almost a relief when the speed and effectiveness of the Prussian advance brought the conflict to an end sooner than expected. After only seven weeks, the resounding Prussian victory at Könnigrätz paved the way to peace. As negotiations began, Fritz returned home swathed in glory for his leadership and military successes but it did not take long for Bismarck to assume all the honours for the victory.

> "I rejoice as a Prussian at the heroic conduct of our troops but my joy is damped with the fear that they have shed their blood in vain," Vicky wrote to the Queen. "With such a man and such principles at the head of our Government how can I look forward to satisfactory results for Germany, or for us?"[130]

Louis was also acclaimed for his courage and leadership but, while victory brought some compensation for Vicky, defeat only created further anxieties for Alice. In August, her children returned from England and, although cholera was rampant in the region, she spent several days with Louis in his regimental quarters where they waited to hear what reparations the Prussians would demand of the states which had fought against them.

Negotiations continued for several months, eventually culminating in the Treaty of Prague by which Austria was denied any further intervention in German affairs, and Schleswig-Holstein was incorporated into Prussia, as was the Kingdom of Hanover, which had, for so long, been ruled by members of the British royal family. Queen Victoria pleaded with Vicky to intercede on behalf of both the King of Hanover and Alice's Hesse-Darmstadt, but, despite her continued affection for her sister, Vicky's reply was uncharacteristically sharp:

"At this sad time, one must separate one's feelings for one's relations quite from one's judgement of political necessities, or one would be swayed to and fro on all sides...they were told beforehand what they would have to expect...as rivers of blood had flowed and the sword decided this contest, the victor must makes his own terms and they must be hard ones for many...We have made enormous sacrifices and the nation expects them not to be in vain. This is the only answer I can give you at present."[131]

Nonetheless, thanks partly to Alice and Vicky's relationship and the high esteem in which Alice was held by the Prussian King, Hesse-Darmstadt fared better than many of its neighbours in that it was allowed to retain its independence. Even so, the Grand Duke was forced to cede large areas of land and pay three million florins in reparation, as well as twenty-five thousand florins every day for six weeks to maintain the occupying Prussian forces. On a personal level, the Prussian seizure of former Hessian lands deprived Alice of a country home – the former property of the late Langravine Elizabeth of Hesse-Homburg which had been promised to Louis. The house, at the foot of the Taunus Mountains, was offered instead to Vicky but, out of loyalty to Alice, she refused to live in it. On a grander scale, the reparation payments virtually bankrupted the Grand Duchy, as Alice told her mother:

"We are almost ruined and must devote all our energies to the reconstruction of our suffering country."[132]

This time, though, Alice's pleas of poverty fell on deaf ears, as the volatile Queen was becoming indifferent to her financial difficulties; and, while one war was over, a more personal conflict between mother and daughter, was gradually reaching its height.

Chapter 15 –
She Should Accommodate Herself To My Habits

Alice's financial difficulties began long before the Austro-Prussian War. As her father had predicted, the £30,000 dowry and £6,000 annuity did not go far for a woman in her position, particularly for one who supported so many charitable institutions and was in the process of building and furnishing a new home.

As early as 1863, Alice told her mother that she and Louis did not 'go about much' as travelling was so expensive. Two years later, they journeyed to Switzerland as private citizens in order to keep the cost to a minimum; and in 1866, when the Queen suggested that Alice might enjoy a specific holiday destination, Alice responded that it would be impracticable 'on account of money'. Following the stresses of the Austro-Prussian War, Alice's doctor recommended that she should take a quiet rest in the mountains but, once again, she had to reply that the expense was too great at such a time.

Queen Victoria had made a substantial contribution to the building of the New Palace, but even then, it proved so expensive that Louis was obliged to take out a loan from Coutts' bank, using the house as surety.

"We must live so economically," Alice told her mother, "– not going *anywhere,* or seeing many people, so as to be able to spare as much a year as we can. England cost us a great deal, as the visit was short last time. We have sold four carriage horses and only have six to drive with now, two of which the ladies constantly want for theatre visits etc.; so we are rather badly off in some things."

In March 1866, the palace, for which Alice had personally designed the furnishings and décor, and which, in Lady Knightley's opinion looked 'like a bad copy of Buckingham Palace', was finally habitable. Though Alice and Louis were delighted by their new home, the expense of its upkeep and the repayment of loans added to their financial burden. Only two months after they had moved in, the builder informed them that he was on the point of bankruptcy and needed them to settle their bills in full 'to save him from ruin' but, as Alice told her mother, she and Louis could 'scarcely manage it'. The cost of the war compounded the situation as there would now be no possibility of further support from the Grand Duke or the councils, leaving them no alternative but to adapt as best they could.

Having grown up in a house filled with servants, Alice was now faced with finding ways to reduce her staff to the minimum. To avoid the expense of dressmakers, she made her children's clothes; and she and Louis educated their infant daughters to postpone hiring a governess for as long as possible.

> "I manage all the nursery accounts, and everything myself, which gives me plenty to do, as everything increases, and, on account of the house, we must live very economically for these next years."[133]

Unsurprisingly, Alice was grateful when her mother sent money for specific occasions but by the mid-1860s the Queen was growing tired of these declarations of poverty and constant requests for more support. When, for example, in 1867 Alice asked for two pearls a year for each of her daughters, the Queen wrote indignantly to Vicky that pearls were far too expensive and:

> "Alice and Louis get money from me for their birthdays and Xmas to help them in furnishing their house – and always more and more is asked for."[134]

Although the complaint was ostensibly about money, the real reason for the Queen's irritation was far deeper-rooted for by then her opinion of her 'modest and humble' daughter had altered dramatically.

A lack of inhibition and unseemly studies were one thing, but to be openly challenged was intolerable to the Queen; and, while her siblings might quietly disagree with their mother, outspoken Alice could not keep silent in the face of a perceived injustice. Her first major *faux pas* came in the autumn of 1865 when she voiced her suspicions about the marriage of her younger sister, Lenchen.

From the moment Alice left home, 'poor dear Lenchen' had taken over as their mother's prop and support, becoming so indispensable that it seemed she would never be permitted a life of her own. Although lacking Vicky's intellect and Alice's grace, Lenchen had many appealing qualities and by the age of nineteen was earnestly hoping to find a husband. It appeared to Alice that the Queen was intent on thwarting that hope, for, although she was not totally opposed to the idea of Lenchen marrying, she set a condition that was likely to deter potential suitors. Having already 'lost' two daughters to foreign courts, she was unwilling to part with a third and therefore insisted that whoever married Lenchen must be willing to settle in England. As a commoner seemed to be out of the question and few foreign royalties could accept such a demand, Lenchen's prospects appeared very bleak until 1865 when the ever-vigilant Vicky unearthed an impoverished prince who met the necessary criterion.

At the age of thirty-four, Christian of Schleswig-Holstein was still single and looking for a bride, and, since his family had lost their lands in the Schleswig-Holstein Wars, he would be more than happy to accept the Queen's offer of a free home in England. In spite of the fifteen-year age difference, Vicky and Aunt Feo were convinced of Christian's 'excellent qualities', so Lenchen was duly dispatched to Coburg to meet him. Just three months later, in December 1865, they were betrothed.

Shocked by the speed of the arrangement, Alice was aghast. Her sister, she thought, was being forced into a loveless marriage with an older man simply to accommodate her mother's desire to keep her in service forever. Moreover, at first sight, Christian was hardly the most attractive of princes. Even Queen Victoria, who favoured the match, was concerned about his poor teeth, his aged appearance, his persistent cough, his lethargy and his addition to smoking. All in all, to Alice, the idea of his marrying Lenchen was utterly preposterous, and she was not alone in her objections.

Bertie's wife, the Danish Princess of Wales, objected so vehemently to his family's part in the Schleswig-Holstein affair that, with Bertie's support, she declared that she would boycott the wedding. When the press caught a whiff of the disagreement, they invented all kinds of outlandish stories, claiming Christian was a madman and a bigamist with numerous children whom Lenchen intended to adopt.

Whenever the Queen met with opposition, her obstinacy increased. Now, as she rallied to Christian's cause, her wrath fell upon Bertie and Alice, her 'undutiful', 'heartless' and 'disrespectful' children. Alice, she said sweepingly, had 'done herself such harm' and 'become so sharp and bitter, and no one wishes to have her in their house.'[135]

Vicky, caught in the middle of the dispute, attempted to pacify her mother by blaming Alice's outspokenness on an 'irritability of nerves', but the Queen was not convinced by the excuse. Even when Alice eventually spoke to Lenchen and, having ascertained that she was genuinely happy with Christian, persuaded Bertie and Alexandra to attend the wedding, the Queen's opinion of her continued to deteriorate.

Although the Austro-Prussian War prevented Alice from travelling to England for the ceremony, she was happy that her children were able to attend and, on the day itself, sent warmest greetings to her mother, asking for God's blessing on the marriage. This, though, was but a temporary lull and the saga was far from over, for when Alice discovered that Lenchen was to receive an equal annuity to her own – and it was rumoured that the Queen intended to raise Lenchen's to £18,000 – as well as a free home and a £100,000 gift from her mother, she was deeply rankled and complained of the arrangement to her siblings. Her sister, Louise, lost no time in spreading Alice's complaints and when news of what had been said reached the Queen she was so incensed that she made it clear that Alice and her family would not be welcome in England that year.

Matters came to a head in January 1867 when the Queen inadvertently mixed up two letters – one to Alice and one to Vicky – and placed them in the wrong envelopes. The letter intended for Vicky reached Alice, who was shocked to read a long list of grievances about her behaviour. Not wishing to exacerbate the situation, she immediately wrote to Vicky, expressing her remorse and asking her to tell the Queen that she regretted causing such distress.

Embarrassed by her mistake, and placated by the humble response, Queen Victoria instructed Vicky to:

> "Tell dear Alice that now she properly and lovingly owns she is much grieved at what she did and said (I will truly believe out of hastiness and imprudence) that I will forgive and forget and receive her with open arms – and am indeed looking forward to seeing her for, I hope, a good two months in the middle of June with dear Louis and the darling children."[136]

Despite this professed willingness to forgive and forget, the Queen immediately launched into a further tirade: Alice had gossiped too freely; she never wrote lovingly of Lenchen; she had criticised Christian; she was jealous of her sister; she was irritable and sharp; and if she were to come to England, she had better behave well, as her mother's nerves could not stand any more mischief. In conclusion, the mother of nine children decided that the only explanation for Alice's behaviour was her exhaustion from having so many (three, at the time!) 'large' children, one after another.

A couple of weeks later, the Queen was still ruminating over Alice's faults. Until recently she had been happy to follow Alice's advice and had been grateful for her support, even embarking on excursions quite simply because 'Alice advises it'. Now, though, her view of the Hessians' previous visits to England was clouded by her annoyance. Ever since her marriage, she decided, Alice had become so domineering and officious that she had made herself very unpopular with the entire household.

> "When [she] came the last two times she grumbled about everything – and Louis also sometimes – the rooms, the hours, wanting to make me do this and that...If Alice wishes to come she should accommodate herself to my habits."[137]

Therein, though she was unwilling to admit it, lay the real root of the Queen's disgruntlement. The dispute about Lenchen's marriage was but a minor upset compared to Alice's inability to accept her mother's refusal to resume the public role which she had abandoned since the death of the Prince Consort. In this, Alice was doing precisely what her father would have done, and undoubtedly following the instructions he gave her from his deathbed. Knowing how Queen Victoria had reacted to the death of the Duchess of Kent, Prince Albert surely realised how she would respond to his own demise, and it is almost certain that he urged Alice to ensure that her mother would fulfil her obligations as Queen.

In fact, Queen Victoria had not by any means neglected all her duties. She continued to work diligently through official papers and took a keen interest in domestic and foreign affairs. Disraeli, ever her champion, reported that:

"There is not a dispatch received from abroad, or sent from this country abroad, which is not submitted to the Queen...and it may be said that her signature has never been placed to any public document of which she did not know the purpose and of which she did not approve...Cabinet Councils are reported...by Minister to the Sovereign, and they often call from her critical remarks, requiring considerable attention...There is probably no person living who has such complete control over the political condition of England as the Sovereign herself."[138]

It was even recorded in Parliament that:

"It is a circumstance worthy of observation that...during all the years during which necessarily she has lived in comparative retirement, she has omitted no part of that public duty, which concerns her as Sovereign of the country."[139]

Nevertheless, without her husband beside her, she felt totally incapable of appearing in public alone. So reclusive had she become that for five years after Albert's death, she could not even bring herself to appear at the Opening of Parliament, leading the republicans to question whether she served any purpose whatsoever. Even the most loyal monarchists, who had initially sympathised with a grieving widow, were becoming exasperated by her invisibility; and, such was the feeling in the country that a sign had been fixed to the gates of Buckingham Palace:

'These commanding premises to be let or sold, in consequence of the occupant's declining business.'

Obviously, ministers and members of her family were anxious about this potentially damaging state of affairs but few had the courage to tell the Queen directly of their concerns until Alice gently declared that it was time for the mourning to stop.

> "Try and gather in the few bright things you have remaining," she wrote. "You have the privilege...in your exalted position of doing good and living for others...Forgive me, darling Mama, if I speak so openly..."[140]

But the Queen could not forgive such honesty. Feeling angry and misunderstood, she sighed to Vicky:

> "As time has worn on and my life has become alas! a sad reality I have naturally tried to make that sad life as bearable as I can, and I think those who truly love me are anxious that I should be kept as quiet as possible, and able as much as possible to do what I have found to suit and comfort me."[141]

Without mentioning his name, the Queen had inadvertently raised another cause of contention between herself and Alice: the influence of her favourite servant, John Brown. First and foremost among those who 'truly loved' her, was the ubiquitous ghillie who was devotedly ensuring that she was being 'kept as quiet as possible' even to the extent of sometimes preventing her own children from seeing her.

Ironically in the light of later events, it was Alice who first thought of bringing Brown to Osborne. As Prince Albert's ghillie, he had proved himself to be a loyal and trusted servant, and, recalling how much her mother had enjoyed the pony trap rides which he had organised at Balmoral, Alice hoped that his presence would not only be a reminder of happier days but would also help to shake the Queen out of her seclusion.

A couple of years after the Prince Consort's death, Brown arrived at Osborne House and within a short time had persuaded the Queen to take daily rides, during which mistress and servant conversed as freely as equals. Initially, Alice and her siblings were relieved by Brown's ability to distract her from her endless mourning; and the Queen so was delighted to have found such a devoted servant who anticipated all her needs that she quickly promoted him to the permanent position of her 'personal servant for out of doors'.

Had Brown remained out of doors, Queen Victoria's children would have been content, but as her dependence upon him increased, so too did his sense of his own authority. Viewing himself as the Queen's sole protector, he was soon taking charge of the rest of her staff and even issuing orders to her family. If he deemed the Queen too tired to receive visitors, he had no qualms about telling princes and princesses that they could not see her; and, in his rough-spoken manner, would brusquely announce which of them would be permitted to join her for dinner. Frequently, her children were kept waiting while he and the Queen talked freely together on any subject he chose, while they were compelled to confine their conversations to themes which would not upset her. Most troublesome of all, though, to Alice, was the manner in which he cossetted the Queen, pandering to her whims and supporting her refusal to resume her public duties.

With tension mounting in the household, it did not take long for rumours to spread about the nature of the relationship between the Queen and her personal servant. Often they disappeared for hours into the Scottish Highlands, giving rise to stories that Brown was a medium who was helping her to make contact with Albert; or more salaciously that mistress and servant were lovers and had even secretly married. Caricatures of the Queen bathing, while Brown stood in attendance, appeared in popular papers, and just as she had once been labelled 'Mrs Melbourne', now she was mockingly called 'Mrs Brown', but, unabashed the Queen was happy to allow the sale of photographs of herself with her Highland Servant, and no amount of cajoling or criticism could persuade her to discard 'so devoted' and 'so true' a friend.

Amid the tension and gossip and being told what to do, Alice's brothers grew to resent Brown's presence so intensely that Vicky suggested that all the Queen's children should sign a petition asking for him to be removed from the household. Once again, though, it was Alice who bore the brunt of her mother's anger for daring to broach the subject directly.

"She is vain and conceited," the Queen huffed, "and...when she comes here...she is dissatisfied and disagreeable."[142]

Shocked by the change in her once-pliable daughter, Queen Victoria could only dismiss her assertiveness as arrogance brought on by her contact with Louis' Russian relations and the company she was now keeping.

'Alice is very fond of amusing herself and of fine society,' she told Vicky, and it irked her immensely to hear that the King of Prussia thought highly of Alice, since she, 'has already too good an opinion of herself; it spoils her and then she expects it elsewhere which she can't get.'[143]

Repeatedly over the next few years, the Queen returned to the same theme, reiterating her annoyance at Louis and Alice's attempts to press her into resuming her public duties.

"Good Alice & Louis tire me – they are not quiet enough and always are astonished that I cannot do what I used to do,"[144] wrote the forty-nine-year-old Queen, who was already referring to herself as a 'poor old woman'.

Nonetheless, despite their disparate views and the underlying tension between their contrasting characters, the Queen and Alice continued their regular and affectionate correspondence; and with each passing year, Alice stated more emphatically how grateful she was to her parents for the happy childhood, to which she longed more than ever to return. Her independent spirit and outspoken views might have compromised her relationship with her mother, but combined with her soul-searching and inner dissatisfaction, they would place an even greater strain on her relationship with Louis. The joy she had expected to find in marriage and the fulfilment she had hoped to find in Hesse had not materialised, and, as her life became increasingly disappointing to her, she longed more than ever to return to the carefree days of the past.

Chapter 16 –
The Uncertainty of Life

The initial euphoria in the weeks following Alice's wedding soon faded and, as the novelty of becoming a wife and mother wore off, the blissful early years of marriage gave way to disenchantment and the painful awareness that Hesse would never truly be home, and Louis could never provide the fulfilment she craved.

Alice's commitment to philanthropic causes had never prevented her from enjoying beautiful clothes, scintillating conversation and fascinating company. Even as a child, the Queen had called her a 'vain little thing', who delighted in dressing for special occasions, and loved to receive compliments on her pretty appearance. As a young woman that aspect of her character had not changed. It must be remembered that she was particularly close to her brother, Bertie, whose love of the 'high life' was legendary; but, like her father, Alice has often been misrepresented as a rather sombre stereotype of the Victorian philanthropist – serious and humourless – when, in reality, in both cases, nothing could be further from the truth.

In Prussia, Vicky frequently attended balls and receptions where she came into contact with many foreign royalties, and, at the time of her wedding, Alice probably expected that life in Hesse would be the same. It did not take long to realise how mistaken she had been. Far from the grandeur of the Prussian Court, the Grand Ducal family lived frugally, and there was few society functions at which she might shine. Repeatedly, she expressed her surprise that her charities were so well-supported since the people were normally quite unenthusiastic and kept themselves to themselves. Having grown up among so many siblings, it came as a shock, too, in the early years of her marriage to find herself quite alone in her rooms while Louis attended to his regimental and civil duties, leaving her with no close companions for hours or even days at a time. Unsurprisingly, she revelled in any opportunity to meet with interesting people in glamorous settings, and when her mother complained that she was becoming too fond of 'Society', Vicky defended her by explaining that:

"If Alice…is fond of amusement and fine society it is only because there is none in Darmstadt."[145]

This might not have been such a burden had she had the resources to pursue her aesthetic passions, but financial restraints prevented her from visiting places which she longed to see; and, despite her determination to contribute all she could to the welfare of the Grand Duchy, nostalgia prevented her from ever feeling truly at home.

Nonetheless, Alice might still have found fulfilment in Hesse, if Louis had been the compatible companion that she had thought he would be, but, once the first oceanic flourish of romance had waned, she came to the sorry conclusion that they actually had very little in common.

To many Victorian women, Louis would have been the ideal husband – faithful to his wife, whose opinions he valued and whose wishes he tried to accommodate; and loving towards his children, who adored him, and with whom he loved to play. He was still a 'manly' man, as Alice's parents' had first noted – a strong swimmer who once saved a woman from drowning in the sea; and a courageous soldier who earned the respect and loyalty of his regiment. Unfortunately, while Alice recognised that his fidelity was a rare blessing, and his courage in the face of battle was an admirable quality, his devotion was not enough to satisfy her deepest needs. Too contemplative and intelligent to settle into the role of a doting wife who was content to live solely for her

190

husband, she soon felt frustrated by the constraints of marriage and Louis' inability to share her deepest longings, intellectual curiosity and spiritual seeking.

"I certainly do not belong by nature to those women who are above all *wife;*" she told her mother, "but circumstances have forced me to be the mother in the real sense, as in a private family, and I have had to school myself to it, I assure you, for many small self-denials have been necessary."[146]

Unlike Alice, who was constantly proactive, Louis was content to adapt to circumstances and settle for whatever life brought his way. The financial restraints, which so irked her, seemed not to bother him; and, in the early weeks of their marriage, while she was becoming increasingly stifled by their living arrangements, he was quite happy to remain in his parents' house until the New Palace was completed. It was Alice who decided to approach the Grand Duke to tell him of their intention to return to England; and it was she who made virtually all the decisions concerning the furnishing and décor of their new home. While she longed for at least *some* opportunities to appear in society, Louis, she told her mother, was a home-loving man, who was satisfied to spend his time quietly with his family.

"...Our life must be rather dull sometimes for a young man of spirit like him,'[147] she told her mother in 1865, but a few years later, commenting that at home he had only '...me, the governess and children as *Umgang* [company]', she added that this didn't bother him, since he was such a 'home bird'.[148]

More poignantly, though, for Alice, Louis had neither the interest nor the ability to engage in the deep conversations which she found so stimulating. The discussions she had enjoyed with her father had stirred her intellect and fed her desire to delve beneath the superficial into the most profound metaphysical questions about the nature of life, the basis of religion and the meaning or purpose of suffering. Being able to speak of these subjects was not only a pleasure but also a necessity for her, for only through discussing the questions which intrigued and tormented her could she find any real sense of intimacy or connection. Louis, however, for all his willingness to read the books that she recommended, had no natural inclination to probe such complex issues. Nor could he fully empathise with Alice's aesthetic yearnings; while he gladly supported all her endeavours, art was of little consequence to him and he often fell asleep during their musical evenings.

Even when it came to raising their children, their differences gradually began to emerge. Louis could not understand why Alice did not want them constantly in her company, while Alice was so taken aback by the enjoyment he took in joining their games that at times it appeared he was more like a son than a husband. In the midst of wars, duties and financial crises, the childlike quality, which had initially been so endearing, became increasingly exasperating for her as she, exhausted by the responsibilities she had chosen to undertake, longed for a strong supporter, just as her father had been to her mother.

Underlying all the petty disparities, *this* was the major issue which neither Louis nor Alice could resolve or perhaps even fully comprehend. Quite simply, no matter how well-meaning and devoted he might be, and no matter how deeply Alice loved him, Louis could never live up to the venerated image that she had created of her father.

> "The older I grow the more perfect and touching and good, dear Papa's image stands out before me," she told the Queen. "Such an *entire* life for duty, so joyously and unpretendingly borne out, remains for all times something inexpressibly fine and grand! With it, how tender and gay he

192

was!...He *was* and *is* my ideal. I never knew a man fit to place beside him, or so made to be loved and admired."

Although she had adored him since childhood, Alice's idealisation of Prince Albert had intensified since his death. In the months immediately after his passing, she had been so absorbed in caring for her mother, dealing with ministers and preparing for her wedding that there had been little time to come to terms with his loss, but, in subsequent years those suppressed emotions resurfaced and created a *perfect* man with whom no one, not even her husband, could ever compete.

It wounded Alice deeply to realise that even after his death her father continued to be misrepresented or criticised, but when, in 1866, following the success of General Grey's account of the early life of Prince Albert, Queen Victoria commissioned the German scholar, Theodore Martin, to write his biography from the years since his marriage, Alice opposed the idea. Unwilling to have such treasured memories made public, she told the Queen that she doubted the wisdom of such a venture. Queen Victoria, however, had set her mind on correcting the erroneous descriptions of the Prince and ensuring that a more accurate image of him would be preserved for posterity. When the book was eventually published, Alice changed her mind and, recognising its value, wrote effusively to the Queen that:

> "People can only be better for reading about dear Papa...To me the volume is inexpressively precious...as a record of life spent in the highest aims, with the noblest conception of duty as a leading star."

As she became more dissatisfied with her marriage, Alice's longing to return to her homeland and the happy world of her romanticised childhood, became ever more pronounced.

"I ever look back to my childhood and girlhood as the happiest time of my life," she wrote in 1869. "The responsibilities, and often the want of many a thing, in married life can never give unalloyed happiness."[149]

With each year her nostalgia increased and her letters became more expressive of her yearning to return to the past. While visiting Scotland in 1876, she wrote of the relief of being back amid familiar scenery where she felt her father's presence so strongly, for, '...no home in the world can become quite what the home of one's parents and childhood was."[150]

Although Louis could do nothing to alleviate Alice's inner turmoil, he clearly understood what lay at the root of her discontentment. It is unlikely that he spoke of it at the time of their marriage, but fifteen years later, a letter from Alice to the Queen shows that in the aftermath of Prince Albert's death, he realised the precariousness of his own position.

> "Louis thought I would not hold to my engagement then anymore – for my heart was too filled with beloved adored Papa...to have room or wish for other thoughts."[151]

No matter how clearly he perceived the situation, he was left in the difficult position of being unable to change it; and for Alice, his apparent failure to empathise drove her to delve more deeply into her own inner world, seeking out answers to profound spiritual questions. She longed more than ever for a soul-mate who was capable of sharing the depths of her turmoil and, in 1868, such a man arrived in Darmstadt.

In an age of high infant mortality rates when the loss of a child was common even in royal families, it was quite remarkable that Alice had passed through childhood with little experience of death. Queen Victoria herself had not seen a dead body until the age of forty-one, when her mother's death marked a turning point for her, as it did for Alice: a banishing from the Eden of ignorance to the startling awareness of human mortality and the briefness of life.

From that point onwards, death surrounded Alice, not only through the all-consuming loss of her father, but also through various tragic incidents which occurred in the midst of her everyday life. Shortly after her arrival in Darmstadt, a young soldier collapsed while on duty in her home and died the same night. A couple of years later, while she and Louis were boating on the pond in Kranichstein, they heard a commotion and noticed a man floating face-down in the water. Rowing closer, they were able to pull him into their boat only to discover that his face was 'already blue and quite lifeless' and, as all attempts to revive him proved futile, it was realised that he had committed suicide.

"...It was very unpleasant for me," Alice wrote to the Queen, "to have that disfigured corpse next to me in the boat: and it haunts me now...for a violent death leaves frightful traces, so unlike anything else!...It brings death before one in its worst form...The indifference with which people treated it, and dragged him along was also revolting to one's feelings."[152]

Equally shocking, was the premature death of Louis' sister, twenty-one-year-old Anna. In the summer of 1864, Anna had married the Grand Duke of Mecklenburg-Schwerin and nine months later she gave birth to a little girl. Initially, the confinement appeared to have gone well and Anna was recovering quickly when she suddenly began to show symptoms of puerperal fever. Her death a week later came as a terrible blow to her family and particularly to Louis, to whom she had been very close.

For Alice, it served as a spur to devote herself still more diligently to her charities, as:

"...it makes one feel the uncertainty of life, and the necessity of labour, self-denial, charity, and all those virtues which we ought to strive after. Oh that I may I die having done my work and not having sinned with [neglecting my duty], the fault into which it is easiest to fall."[153]

Within a week of Anna's funeral, further sad news reached Darmstadt when Louis' cousin, Tsarevich Nicholas of Russia, died suddenly of spinal meningitis, at the age of twenty-one.

Two years later, in the summer of 1867, Alice and Louis attended a ball at India House in London, where they dined with the Turkish Ambassador, Constantine Musurus. During the meal, the Ambassador's wife became breathless and, as she retired from the table, she fainted. A doctor was called and a driver summoned to return her to the Embassy but she died in the carriage en route.

Hardly had Alice and Louis returned to Darmstadt when another sad event occurred within their own home. In 1863, Alice had taken an illiterate thirteen-year-old Malayan boy into her service and, within a short time, 'my good Willem' had become a constant companion for her children and a much-loved member of the household. His untimely death in August 1867 was yet another reminder of life's unpredictability; and when a second valued servant, a footman named Jäger, died of consumption that autumn, Alice wrote that 'a bit of my heart went with them.'

By the time that twenty-three-year-old Alice was working with the casualties of the Austro-Prussian War, she had already lived through the deaths of her grandmother, her father, her nephew, her sister-in-law and several members of the household. Those experiences combined with her concern for her brother Leopold's health, and her rising frustration with her life in Hesse, were spurring her to probe the mysteries of mortality and eternity.

Throughout her life, her Christian faith had been a firm anchor in times of sorrow and the inspiration behind many of her charitable works. Her letters frequently mentioned her trust in God and her absolute certainty of an afterlife in which she would see her father again. Her faith had served, too, as an outlet for her dissatisfaction, which she sought to dispel by constantly trying to 'improve' herself by painstakingly correcting her perceived faults. Even as an adolescent, her efforts to conquer her emotions and reactions had won the Queen's admiration, but the continual striving for perfection was exhausting, and her failure to live up to the high standards she set for herself invariably led to discouragement and a sense of her own inadequacy – particularly when she compared herself to the ideal of her father.

By the mid-1860s, this sense of inadequacy alongside the suffering and discord she saw all around her provoked in her a desire to make sense of the apparent disparity between her belief in a loving God, and the experience of her everyday life. Her mother's simple faith provided few answers to the questions that burned within her, and she began to read widely, becoming absorbed in the works of many modern thinkers who had not only shared the doubts which began to plague her – and which led the superficial Queen Augusta of Prussia to label her an atheist – but were also presenting a quite revolutionary interpretation of Christianity. She and Louis read together the writings of the evangelical preacher, Frederick William Robertson, whose doubts had taken him through various spiritual crises; and, in 1868 she became aware that the contentious Swabian philosopher and theologian, David Strauss, was living in Darmstadt.

Separated from his wife and renowned for his affairs, Strauss had provoked a storm of controversy thirty years earlier when he published his book: *The Life of Jesus Critically Examined,* which claimed that the New Testament could not be taken literally. Having dismissed their historical accuracy by pointing out the discrepancies between the Synoptic Gospels of Matthew, Mark and Luke, he systematically worked through the accounts of Christ's miracles to demonstrate that rather than being actual events they were myths, created to show that Jesus was the fulfilment of the Jewish Messianic prophecies.

At the time, such ideas were so unorthodox that many Christians viewed them as blasphemous, and when the book was translated into English by the equally scandalous George Eliot[r], it caused such furore that the Earl of Shaftesbury went so far as to describe it as 'the most pestilential book ever vomited out of the jaws of hell'. As the controversy raged, Strauss eventually withdrew from theology for twenty years, focussing instead on the lives of various philosophers.

In spite of his melancholic reputation and the debate surrounding his work, Alice was intrigued by Strauss' writings and, in the autumn of 1868, invited him to visit her at the New Palace. Although he was initially wary of accepting the invitation, when he finally arrived at the palace, he was pleasantly surprised by the welcome that he received.

> "I soon felt entirely at ease with this lady," he wrote. "Her simplicity, the kind manner in which she met me, and her keen bright intellect made me forget all differences of social position."[154]

Despite their twenty-five year age difference, Alice sensed that she had found a like-minded friend, and, according to the gossipy French Ambassador, Maurice

---

[r] George Eliot, the pen name of Mary Ann Evans, had caused a scandal by openly living with the married philosopher, George Lewes.

Paléologue, Strauss 'at once obtained a great influence over her'. He became a regular visitor to her home, where over the next few years they spent many hours discussing philosophy and religion. Their views were so compatible that when Strauss decided to write a biography of Voltaire, he asked if he might dedicate it to Alice. Soon afterwards, however, fearing that her reputation could be damaged by such an association, he considered withdrawing the dedication and was greatly moved when Alice replied that 'the fear of being misunderstood would never prevent her from doing what was right'.

By now, Strauss had also returned to his theological writings and, though some of his beliefs differed from Alice's, their discussions provided the stimulation she had craved and enabled her to clarify her own unorthodox opinions. Not since the evenings spent with her father had she been able to absorb herself in conversation with a man who thoroughly understood her and, while their meetings were perfectly innocent and took place with Louis' approval, she believed she had found the soul-mate for whom she had been seeking.

"But," wrote Maurice Paléologue, "the romance of their minds and hearts was still wrapped in a deep mystery, though it is impossible to doubt that he shook her faith to the depths and that she passed through a terrible crisis."[155]

The 'terrible crisis', in fact, owed more to a personal tragedy than to conversations with Strauss, for events would soon unfold which would plunge her into such despair that her only recourse was to abandon her spiritual seeking to cling to the faith of her childhood.

Chapter 17 – This Too Horrid War

At the height of Alice's involvement with Strauss, the Grand Duchy became embroiled in another bitter war. Since the triumph of 1866, Bismarck had been working towards creating a unified Germany, and his surest means of bringing the states together was to unite them against a common enemy. The antipathy between the French and the Prussians, which had continued since the days of Napoleon, made France the ideal foe, and, what was more, a war would provide Prussia with a chance to seize the disputed French territories of Alsace and Lorraine.

In order to gain support from the rest of Europe, Bismarck had to create the impression that the French were the aggressors, and so for four years he waited for an opportunity to provoke them into making the first move. That opportunity arose in the summer of 1870, when foreign princes were being put forward as candidates for the vacant Spanish throne.

Some years earlier, a revolution in Spain had led to the abdication of the unpopular Queen Isabella, and, as the Spaniards had grown disillusioned by the old regime, they hoped to establish a new dynasty. Various foreign princes were suggested but when the throne was offered to the German Prince Leopold of Hohenzollern-Sigmaringen, the French were horrified. A 'Prussian' king would not only put an end to French influence in Spain but would also pose a threat to France's southern border.

Already alarmed by Bismarck's designs on Alsace and Lorraine, Emperor Napoleon III sent an emissary to Vicky's father-in-law, King Wilhelm I of Prussia, at the spa town of Ems, demanding that Prince Leopold's name be withdrawn. On Bismarck's advice, the King agreed but, shortly afterwards, he was again approached by the French Ambassador who had been instructed to obtain an assurance that no other German candidate would be put forwards. The King, not wishing to provoke a war, responded politely and gave Bismarck permission to publish an account of the meeting. Seizing his chance, the Chancellor doctored the official record, creating the impression that King Wilhelm had refused to yield to French threats and had treated the Ambassador with contempt. As the account was circulated throughout Europe, the French were so incensed by the perceived insult that Napoleon III saw no alternative but to make a declaration of war.

Exactly as Bismarck had planned, the German states rose up in self-righteous unison against the French aggressors and, in the wave of indignation that followed, Vicky and Alice were caught up in the patriotic fervour. 'The conduct of the French was perfectly monstrous,'[156] Vicky told the Queen; and, as Louis departed with the army, Alice wrote:

"...The provocation of a war such as this is a crime that will have to be answered for, and for which there is no justification...there is a feeling of unity and standing by each other, forgetting all party quarrels, which makes one proud of the name of German."[157]

No matter how just the cause appeared to be, war once again placed a terrible strain upon Alice. Six months pregnant, and anxious that Louis' small division would be exposed to the fiercest fighting, she immediately set to work readying hospitals to receive the wounded. Fortunately, this time, she and Vicky were able to work together in organising medical relief. Moreover, Hesse-Darmstadt was better prepared than it had been in 1866, thanks largely to Alice's foresight in establishing the 'Ladies Union' to provide trained nurses of all classes, who would serve in short-staffed hospitals in peacetime, and be available to attend the wounded in time of war.

As the Ladies Union went into action, Alice established four base hospitals, which she visited daily, often taking her elder daughters with her to assist in rolling bandages and talking with the patients. When the hospitals became overcrowded, Alice personally nursed the soldiers within her own home, tending not only the wounded but also those suffering from disease. Typhoid was once again rife; and despite her advanced pregnancy, Alice was seen fearlessly lifting a soldier who was suffering from smallpox.

Being so close to 'the seat of war', there was a strong possibility that Darmstadt would be invaded, and several times Vicky pleaded with Alice to leave the Grand Duchy for the safety of Berlin, where the Prussian King had offered her the use of a palace. Committed to her work, however, she refused to abandon the Grand Duchy:

> "Now is a moment when a panic might overcome the people;" she told the Queen, "and I think it is my duty to remain at my post, as it gives the people courage and confidence."[158]

Unfortunately, rather than being encouraged by her presence, the people were sceptical of Alice's concern for the welfare of twelve hundred French prisoners-of-war who had been housed in the grounds of the New Palace; and, as German losses increased, rumours, fuelled by Vicky's archenemy, Bismarck, began to circulate that 'the English princesses' were secretly working for the enemy.[s]

Britain's neutrality and inaction had already sparked resentment in the German states. While pleading with her mother to send troops to support the Prussians, Vicky explained that:

> "The feeling is very general here that England would have had it in her power to prevent this

---

[s] Ironically, nearly half a century later, the same charges of being too concerned for the welfare of prisoners-of-war, and secretly working for the enemy would be levelled at two of Alice's daughters, Ella and Alix, with even more tragic consequences. See 'Most Beautiful Princess' by Christina Croft.

awful war, had she in concert with Russia, Austria and Italy, declared she would take arms against the aggressor, and that her neutrality afforded France advantages and us disadvantages. France can buy English horses as her ships can reach England, whereas ours cannot on account of the French fleet."[159]

When it was discovered that the British were profiting not only from the sale of horses but also by providing coal for French ships and shells for French guns, the reaction was so violent that the English were 'more hated than the French' and the brunt of the German anger was aimed at Vicky and Alice. Feelings ran so high that when Vicky attempted to improve the hospitals in Berlin and Potsdam, her help was 'contemptuously rejected' and word soon spread that she and Alice were passing military secrets to their mother, who was, in turn, warning the French in advance of the German plans.

Despite the criticism, exhaustion and her advanced pregnancy, Alice continued to work for the wounded, visiting up to four hospitals a day and spending hours at the bedside of the dying. As ever in war time, diseases spread rapidly, creating such an unhealthy environment that the prospect of her forthcoming confinement was frightening:

> "It is unhealthy at any time for one's confinement in a town full of hospitals with wounded..." she told the Queen, "and, should I be very ill, there is no authority to say anything about what should be done."[160]

It was hardly reassuring to hear from her trusted doctor, Weber, that his sister had just died of puerperal fever, which he feared he had given her 'from going to and fro to his wounded'; and by the end of September, Alice felt it necessary to forego her hospital visits.

On 7th October, her anxieties were alleviated when she gave birth to a premature baby, Frittie – a 'fat, pink' little boy with 'pretty features,' who appeared to be perfectly healthy. After only the briefest convalescence, she returned to her duties for a further six weeks before finally accepting Vicky's offer of a brief respite in Berlin at the beginning of December.

> "It is a great comfort to be with dear Vicky," she wrote to Queen Victoria. "We spend the evenings alone together, talking or writing letters."[161]

For three more months the war continued until the French Emperor was forced to flee in disgrace and the triumphant German armies marched on to Paris. Even at the moment of an imminent victory, antipathy towards the English princesses, and more particularly towards Vicky, resurfaced. As Fritz army approached the French capital it was widely hoped that he would avenge the German losses by completely destroying the city. To Vicky's relief, Fritz saw no need for such blatant aggression and refused to be swayed by the opinion of those 'gentlemen sitting at home in comfortable cosy rooms,' Nonetheless, Vicky took the blame for his hesitation, as he recorded in his diary:

> "In Berlin it is now the order of the day to vilify my wife as being mainly responsible for the postponement of the bombardment of Paris and to accuse her of acting under the direction of the Queen of England; all this exasperates me beyond measure."[162]

By March 1871, the war was over and, as Bismarck's plan reached fruition in the unification of Germany, Fritz's father was elevated from King of Prussia to German Emperor in a lavish ceremony in the Palace of Versailles.

The victorious armies returned home to a hero's welcome. Louis, whom Alice had not seen for seven months, and whose gallantry had earned him the Order *Pour la Mérite,* arrived in Darmstadt to find the streets decorated with lights and banners.

"Our house will also be illuminated," Alice told the Queen, "and I take the two eldest girls out with me to see it all. It is a thing for them never to forget, this great and glorious though too horrid war."[163]

In gratitude for his commitment and service, Louis' regiment presented him with a portrait of the victory at Gravelotte.

The conclusion of the Franco-Prussian War and the resultant German Unification heralded a forty-year period of peace and prosperity for the new nation. For Alice, too, life returned to a steadier pace, enabling her to concentrate on raising her growing family and furthering her charities. After all the stresses of the previous months, the spring and summer of 1871 brought a series of happy visits from her relations; and, in June, she and Louis participated in the great victory parade in Berlin, before taking their family on recuperative holiday to the seaside at Blankenberghe in Belgium.

In mid-September, reinvigorated by the sea air, they moved on to Balmoral where the Queen was suffering from rheumatic gout, and Alice was called upon to employ all her nursing skills to alleviate her pain. Two months later, her nursing skills would once again be called upon – this time on behalf of her favourite brother, Bertie.

In November 1871, the Hessians travelled from the remote wilds of Balmoral to the hub of the 'fast set' at Sandringham House – the Norfolk home of the Prince and Princess of Wales. The lack of 'Society' in Darmstadt made the visit more exciting for Alice, as the 'charming hosts' were renowned for their wonderful parties and the fascinating and varied characters they invited to their home.

Alice had always been close to her elder brother, but now they had something more than a shared childhood in common. Albeit for very different reasons, both had earned their mother's disapproval, and, just as had happened during their childhood, it frequently fell to Alice to plead Bertie's cause.

Still unable to forget the youthful misdemeanour which, she believed, had precipitated his father's death, Queen Victoria continued to view Bertie as too unreliable to be involved in affairs of state and consequently denied him any meaningful role whatsoever. In her lifetime and ever since, this intransigence earned her a good deal of criticism and earned her son a good deal of sympathy, but it cannot be denied that she had good reason for her obduracy.

In the years since the Prince Consort's death, Bertie had done little to regain her trust, and the contrast between his and his father's behaviour had become more glaring than ever. When, in the immediate months following their marriage, the Queen had denied Prince Albert any significant role, he had occupied his time fruitfully by reorganising the palaces and learning all he could about the system of government in England. Bertie, on the other hand, blaming his mother for his own lack of motivation, embarked on a sybaritic lifestyle of gluttonising, gambling and mixing with 'unsuitable' characters, with whom he spoke so freely that, even years later, Queen Victoria warned one of her granddaughters to be careful what she divulged to him since 'uncle can't keep anything to himself.' His beautiful wife could not satisfy his desire for the company of beautiful women, and, between his regular visits to the brothels of Paris, he indulged in numerous affairs so blatantly that Queen

Victoria confessed that she pitied Alexandra, who suffered his infidelities in silence.

His wife might have been prepared to accept Bertie's philandering but the public was not so forgiving. In 1867, Alexandra contracted rheumatic fever while recovering from the birth of her third child, but, while the public followed the accounts of progress with consternation, Bertie cheerfully remained at the Windsor Races, and even when he was finally pressurised into returning home, he continued to entertain his rowdy friends while his wife lay on her sickbed upstairs. Disgusted by his neglect of the popular Princess, audiences hissed him in the theatre and jeered at him in the street, but this was only the start of the decline in his reputation. Two years later his involvement in the infamous Mordaunt Case created a scandal which spread through the courts of Europe.

Bertie had been a regular visitor to the London home of the Conservative peer, Sir Charles Mordaunt, whose flirtatious young wife, Harriet, he had known since her childhood. She had been a regular guest at the Marlborough House parties, and, though Bertie always denied that they were lovers, he had written her a series of compromising letters and was known to have sent her gifts and visited her while her husband was away. On one occasion, Sir Charles returned unexpectedly from a fishing trip and was so incensed to find Harriet and Bertie together that he forced his wife to watch while he shot dead two beautiful white ponies, which she had purchased from the Sandringham estate.

In February 1869, Harriet gave birth to a daughter and, in the throes of post-natal depression, confessed to her husband that he was not the father of her baby before providing him with a list of her lovers, including the Prince of Wales. Sir Charles initiated divorce proceedings and, when the case went to court, Bertie was called as a witness. Under cross-examination, he acquitted himself well and firmly denied any impropriety so convincingly that even Queen Victoria was convinced of his innocence.

'His name ought never to have been dragged through the dirt or mixed up with such people,' she wrote, before adding, somewhat amusingly in the light of his well-documented relationships with other women, 'He did not know more of, or admire, the unfortunate, crazy Lady Mordaunt more than he does or did other ladies.'

Nonetheless, his reputation had been seriously damaged and, when Harriet's family declared her insane and had her committed to the Chiswick Asylum, it was widely believed that she had been silenced to protect the reputation of the Prince and the monarchy. Even as far away as Prussia, Bertie was viewed with contempt as a perjurer and adulterer, and, by the time of Alice's visit in autumn 1871, he had become so unpopular with the British public that it would take a near-fatal illness for him to regain their affection.

Shortly before Alice and her family arrived at Sandringham, Bertie had returned from Scarborough, where, while staying at the home of Lady Londesborough, he and several other guests had contracted typhoid. It would take several weeks for the symptoms to manifest and it was not until late November that he was diagnosed with a 'mild' fever. Although not unduly alarmed, Queen Victoria dispatched her doctors, William Jenner and William Gull, to Sandringham and over the next few days she was relieved to receive their favourable reports. By the end of the month, however, Bertie's symptoms had worsened, and even though the doctors assured the Queen that his life was not in danger, Alice, who was in constant attendance, feared the worst. To compound her anxieties, all her children and all their Wales cousins succumbed to a whooping cough epidemic and had to be quarantined in the nurseries of Buckingham Palace, while their mothers remained at Bertie's bedside in Norfolk.

As the tenth anniversary of her father's death approached, it appeared as though history were about to repeat itself, and Alice anxiously sent a telegram to the Queen, warning her that Bertie was seriously ill. Within days, the Queen arrived at Sandringham where, all past disagreements forgotten, she nervously sought to reassure herself that her 'beloved child' would recover.

Night and day, Alice remained with Alexandra at Bertie's side as he became increasingly delirious and short of breath, but her ministrations appeared to be of no avail. By 11th December the doctors were convinced that he was dying and reluctantly informed the Queen that the Prince of Wales was unlikely to survive the night.

"In those heart-rending moments," Queen Victoria wrote in her journal, "I scarcely knew how to pray aright, only asking God, if possible, to spare my beloved child."

By the 'terrible 14th' the end was imminent and the gloom which had filled Windsor Castle a decade earlier now seeped into the glittering world of Sandringham House. Alice, steeling herself for the inevitable, undoubtedly spent the day reliving the painful scenes at her father's deathbed, when suddenly, unexpectedly, the fever passed and towards evening Bertie began to revive.

Although his recovery was slow and debilitating, a surge of rejoicing swept through the country. Bertie's transgressions were forgotten and when he was finally well enough to appear in public, he was greeted by enthusiastic applause. The Queen emerged from her seclusion to attend a thanksgiving service at St. Paul's Cathedral, and later that day she appeared on the balcony of Buckingham Palace for the first time since the death of the Prince Consort.

Chapter 18 –
This Mad, Wicked Folly of Women's Rights

Revitalised by her travels and relieved by Bertie's recovery, Alice returned to Darmstadt in January 1872, filled with plans for further improvements to the standard of nursing in Hesse. Although pregnant with her sixth child, she was eager to make use of the experience she had gained in two wars and the studies she had made of English hospitals, where she had inspected every department from the wards to the kitchens.

Since the Austro-Prussian War, she had also maintained a correspondence with Florence Nightingale, whose impact on nurse training was still at its height, and whose designs for light, airy wards were providing the basis for the new infirmaries which were springing up across Britain. Alice hoped to apply the same designs to German hospitals and also recognised that it would be beneficial for her own nurses to undergo a period of training in England. Miss Nightingale readily agreed to this suggestion and, although she refused to shorten the length of the training as Alice had requested, a group of young German women were soon admitted to the School of Nursing at St Thomas' Hospital in London.

While the care of the sick was of major interest to Alice, her plans were not solely confined to improvements in nursing. In 1872, the welfare of orphans came to her attention, as many poor children were being neglected or abused by those who had been appointed to care for them. In Germany as in England it was often the case that poor children were taken in by unscrupulous factory owners, farmers or tradesmen, who received payment from the parish for their upkeep on the understanding that they would teach them a trade. In fact, many of the children were treated as nothing but unpaid workers, who were subjected to neglect and beatings from their masters.

Alice not only founded a new orphanage but also became involved in a scheme to inspect the homes to which these children had been sent to ensure that they were being well-treated and provided with an appropriate education. As ever, she was not content merely to administrate such a scheme without becoming actively involved. Theodore Martin described a cold winter night when she ventured into a house to find two little girls:

> "Hungry, chilled to the heart, they were sitting in an empty attic; their parents were dead, and they ate among strangers bread that was hard and grudgingly given, when that great lady appeared...From her, whose heart was ever yearning to the orphan's cry, they heard again, for the first time, gentle, loving words; by her provision was quickly made for their more kindly treatment."[164]

After Alice's death, those two little girls were seen placing small bunches of violets on her coffin.

As her schemes for social improvements expanded, she was keen to learn as much as possible from the pioneers who were already working in various fields. Corresponding regularly with some of the most forward-thinking philanthropists of the day, it occurred to her that the greatest good could be achieved if the different charitable institutions worked together in harmony. To facilitate this, in the summer of 1872, she organised a general assembly or 'Congress of Women', bringing together representative of all the charities in the region and beyond. Among the attendees were several prominent figures whose progressive ideas had earned the censure of governments and churches, but, just as Alice was happy to be associated with the controversial David Strauss, she had no qualms about making the acquaintance of these unorthodox women.

From Saxony came Marie Simon, who though less famous than Florence Nightingale, had made a major contribution to nursing in Germany. Having founded the Institution for Training Nurses in Dresden, she had played a major role in the Franco-Prussian War, directing the 'Women's Association for Relief in the Field.' In spite of strong opposition from government authorities, who believed that women were unsuited to work at the front, she gained the support of Saxony's Crown Princess Carola and, by her own strength of will, had not only succeeded in winning the hearts of the wounded but also had saved many lives.

> "...By persistent effort, she wearied her judges, and was allowed to proceed to the battlefield with a small staff of picked female nurses. The poor soldiers soon learned to know and bless her; for the fame of Madame Simon quickly spread through the armies; and where she was, the dying men still hoped for life. The smiles of 'Mother Simon,' as they familiarly called her, were more cheering to many of them than many of a thousand consolations or remedies offered by others."[165]

From England came Mary Carpenter, who had worked to improve the education of girls in India as well as in England, and had ventured into prisons to where she had 'done such good works for the reformation of convicts'.[166] Also present were Florence Hill, (the niece of the reformer, Rowland Hill, who had instituted the penny-postage), who advocated the admission of women workers into the Post Office; and Catherine Winkworth, who had made her name by translating German hymns into English and was a pioneer of female education.

Despite having adopted different branches of social improvements, these four women were united in pressing for the right of girls to enter Higher Education and were firm advocates of women's suffrage – a cause which Queen Victoria vehemently opposed.

Ironically, the Queen, who headed one of the most powerful empires in the world, considered the idea of women's involvement in politics anathema. 'Let women be what God intended, a helpmate for man, but with totally different duties and vocations,' she had said; and in 1870, reflecting her own dependence on strong male protectors, she proclaimed that she was:

> "…most anxious to enlist everyone who can speak or write to join in checking this mad, wicked folly of 'Women's Rights', with all its attendant horrors, on which her poor feeble sex is bent, forgetting every sense of womanly feelings and propriety. Feminists ought to get a good whipping. Were women to 'unsex' themselves by claiming equality with men, they would become the most hateful, heathen and disgusting of beings and would surely perish without male protection."

For Alice and her like-minded philanthropists, however, personal and political freedom was essential for women not only because their talents were being wasted and their minds stifled, but also to enable them to protect their children and families. Far from wishing to 'unsex' women by encouraging them to imitate men, the early women's rights campaigners sought to have women's unique abilities respected whether they chose to pursue a career or to devote themselves to motherhood. Those who had worked among the poor had frequently witnessed the effect of laws which failed to protect young girls from unprincipled employers and denied them the right to care for their own children.

Through her work with the orphans of Hesse, Alice would certainly have witnessed what the English Suffragette leader, Emmeline Pankhurst, would later recall from her experience as a Poor Law Guardian:

"I found there were many pregnant women in the workhouse, scrubbing floors, doing the hardest kind of work, almost until their babies came into the world. Many of them were unmarried women, very, very young...mere girls. These poor mothers were allowed to stay in the hospital after their confinement for a short two weeks. Then they had to make a choice of staying in the workhouse and earning their living by scrubbing and other work, in which case they were separated from their babies; or they could be discharged. They could stay and be paupers or they could leave – leave with a two-week old baby in their arms, without hope, without a home, without money, without anywhere to go..."[167]

Mrs. Pankhurst also observed that the greatest number of illegitimate babies were born to servant girls who, being unable to support their children, had no choice but to hand them over to 'baby farms' so that they could return to work. The baby-farms, in which children frequently suffered neglect even to the point of death, were not subject to inspection because:

"...if a man who ruins a girl pays down a sum of £20, the boarding home is immune from inspection. As long as the baby farmer takes only one child at a time, the house cannot be inspected. Of course the babies die with hideous promptness, often long before the twenty pounds has been spent, and then baby farmers are free to solicit another victim. For years, as I have said, women have tried to get that one reform of the Poor Law to reach and protect all illegitimate children, and to make it impossible for any rich scoundrel to escape future liability for his child because of the lump sum he has paid. Over and over again it has been tried, but it has always failed because the ones who really care about such things are women."[168]

Apart from the inherent injustice of denying women any say in how they were governed, it was for these reasons that the early suffragists demanded the vote. Alice, whose work with the poor had enabled her to see the effect of political inequality upon women and children, was willing to associate with these forward-thinking pioneers. Gladly, she listened to their speeches and, with the same disregard for public opinion with which she entertained Strauss, she unashamedly accompanied Mary Carpenter through the schools in Darmstadt.

Queen Victoria, somewhat alarmed by such associations, and probably searching for an ally, questioned whether Alice's mother-in-law supported her idea of bringing these women together.

"Of course, she does," Alice replied blithely. "We are so intimate together, that even where we differ in opinion we yet talk of everything freely, and her opinion is of the greatest value to me...She was much pleased and interested in the success of the meeting, but is of course as averse as myself to all extreme views on such subjects."[169]

A month later, Alice boldly sent the Queen an article about the rights of women.

Never failing to practise what she preached, Alice ensured that her daughters were raised in a spirit of independence, which recognised their individuality rather than treating them as mere appendages to husbands, brothers or fathers. It was common practice among German royalties to view young princesses as nothing more than future wives and to educate them accordingly, but to Alice such an idea was ludicrous, particularly in an age when a number of outstanding women were making an impact in the worlds of literature, art, social reform and medicine. Alongside her correspondence with Florence Nightingale, Alice had spoken in person to the housing reformer, Octavia Hill[t], and she was undoubtedly aware of the struggles of Elizabeth Garrett Anderson. She was also familiar with the works of Charlotte Bronte, whose eponymous heroine, Jane Eyre, struggling to maintain her individuality when contemplating marriage to Mr Rochester, expressed Alice's own views so succinctly:

"Women are supposed to be very calm generally: but women feel just as men feel; they need exercise for their faculties and a field for their efforts as much as their brothers do; they suffer from too rigid a restraint, too absolute a stagnation, precisely as men would suffer; and it is narrow-minded in their more privileged fellow-creatures to say that they ought to confine themselves to making puddings and knitting stockings, to playing on the piano and embroidering bags. It is thoughtless to condemn them, or laugh at them, if they seek to do more or learn more than custom has pronounced necessary for their sex."[170]

Thanks to her father's diligence, Alice's education had been beneficial and uplifting and she recognised the importance of ensuring her daughters received the same opportunity.

"The intellect of women is confined by an unjustifiable restriction of education," wrote the social theorist, Harriet Martineau. "As women have none of the objects in life for which an enlarged education is considered requisite, the education is not given. The choice is to be either ill-educated, passive, and subservient, or well-educated, vigorous, and free only upon sufferance…The sum and substance of female…is

---

[t] See Chapter 20

training women to consider marriage as the sole object in life."

It was a sentiment which Alice echoed when it came to raising her daughters:

"I want to strive to bring up the girls without *seeking* [marriage] as their sole object for the future – to feel they can fill up their lives so well otherwise," she told the Queen. "A marriage for the sake of marriage is surely the greatest mistake a woman can make."[171]

In this, she and her mother were, for once, in complete accord. Despite her own blissful years with beloved Albert, Queen Victoria had seen enough unhappy marriages to realise that for many women, marriage was more of a prison than a pleasure. 'A lottery', she called it, remarking that single people were often happier than those who were married, and if young girls knew in advance what awaited them, few would approach the altar.

Alice's views on women's independence did not, however, lead her to neglect her duties as a mother. On the contrary, she devoted much of her time to her children's upbringing and did her utmost to recreate for them the wonderful experiences of her own childhood.

Chapter 19 –
To Love One's Grief

On 25th November 1868, Alice gave birth to a son, Ernst Ludwig (Ernie) – another 'fat' baby who was too big for the clothes that had been prepared for him – and over the next six years, three more children – Frederick (Frittie), Alix and Mary (May) – were born.

Visitors to the New Palace commented on the joyful atmosphere of the house, which echoed with laughter and the noisy games of the boisterous children who were 'full of fun and mischief'. From his exile in the Netherlands after the First World War, Vicky's eldest son, Kaiser Wilhelm II, would look back nostalgically on his visits to Darmstadt, recalling the hospitality of 'Aunt Alice and Uncle Louis' and the happy times he had spent boating on the lake, riding through the grounds or playing tennis with his delightful Hessian cousins.

"On the same floor as the nurseries," wrote Baroness Buxhoeveden, "were [Princess Alice's] rooms, and there the little Princesses brought their toys and played while their mother wrote or read...Sometimes all the old boxes containing their mother's early wardrobe were brought out for dressing up. The children strutted down the long corridors in crinolines, and played at being great ladies, or characters from fairy tales, dressed in bright stuffs and Indian shawls, which their grandmother, Queen Victoria, could not have imagined being put to such a use..."[172]

In the picturesque gardens, the children learned to ride, swim and garden. All developed Alice's love of nature and continued the family tradition of caring for animals. The palace and grounds were filled with ponies, birds, cats, dogs and guinea pigs – which, according to Alice, turned the place into something of a menagerie. On one occasion, to the children's dismay, an owl escaped from a wooden cage and killed Alice's 'poor little bullfinch'.

There were regular family outings, holidays at the seaside in France and Belgium, visits to their numerous relatives, and the much-anticipated annual visit to Windsor, Osborne or Balmoral, where the children ran wild in noisy games of hide-and-seek, or gathered shells on the beach as their mother toured the hospitals, and the cottages of the poor fishermen at Eastbourne.

On their birthdays, parties were held for friends and local children; and, each Christmas, Alice sought to recreate her own happy experiences of the family festivities at Windsor.

> "A huge Christmas tree stood in the ballroom, its branches laden with candles, apples, gilt nuts, pink quince sausages, and all kinds of treasures. Round it were tables with gifts for all the members of the family. The servants came in and the Grand Duchess gave them their presents. Then followed a family Christmas dinner, at which the traditional German goose was followed by real English plum pudding and mince pies sent from England. The poor were not forgotten, and Princess Alice had gifts sent to all the hospitals."[173]

Alongside all the fun and laughter, Alice provided her children with a useful and comprehensive education. With Louis' full support, she prepared a curriculum, and a schoolroom was constructed within the New Palace, where from seven o'clock each morning both parents taught literature, history, geography and mathematics. Tutors were employed to instruct the children in religion and French; and, growing up in a bilingual household, they quickly became fluent in English and German. In order to foster their cultural awareness, opera singers and musicians were invited to perform at the palace; and

Alice, herself an accomplished musician, frequently played for the children and encouraged them in their musical endeavours. Like many other members of her family, she was also a gifted artist – a talent which several of her children inherited – and she was keen to nurture their appreciation of art, architecture and design.

Amid wars and the ever-present threat of revolution, Alice followed her father's example in preparing her children to live independently. From their earliest years, the girls were taught needlework and cookery while the boys learned woodwork and masonry, and all the children were taught how to grow vegetables and flowers. As Alice knew only too well, even royalties were sometimes compelled to live on a restricted budget, and so, drawing on her own experience, she introduced them to book-keeping and household management.

She recognised, too, the importance of a stable routine, and when the children were left in the care of their grandparents, she left detailed lists and instructions about their meal times, bed times and periods of study.

Above all, she wished to instil in them a sense of personal responsibility, dedication to duty and respect for other people. The young princes and princesses were fed on a simple diet ('indeed,' wrote Baroness Buxhoeveden, 'they kept all their lives hated memories of rice puddings and baked apples in endless succession') and were not permitted to ask the servants to do anything for them which they were capable of doing for themselves. Dressed in homemade and hand-me-down clothes, they made their own beds, cleaned their rooms, black-leaded the grates and lit fires.

"I strive to bring them up totally free from pride of position, which is nothing save what their personal worth can make it," Alice told the Queen. "I feel…how important it is for princes and princesses to know that they are nothing better or above others, save through their own merit; and that they have only the double duty of living for others and of being an example – good and modest. This I hope my children will grow up to do."[174]

To emphasise their responsibilities, Alice encouraged them to participate in her charities by creating and selling their own needlework and paintings and donating some of their toys to the poor.

'It is good to teach them early to be generous and kind to the poor,' she told her mother; and, so that they might learn by example, she took them with her on her hospital visits where they witnessed her willingness to carry out the most menial chores from scrubbing floors to emptying slop buckets.

Although she loved her children deeply and missed them terribly when they were apart, Alice was careful not to pamper them or to become 'one of those women who constantly speak of their children'. In an era where it was seen as unhelpful for children to be constantly in their parents' company, she excused the amount of time she spent with her own by claiming that it was more through necessity than choice.

"That they take a greater place in my life than is often the case in our families, comes from my not being able to have enough persons of a responsible sort to take charge of them always; certain things remain undone for that reason if I do not do them and they would be the losers."[175]

In reality, though, as her letters to the Queen reveal, she delighted in their company and missed them terribly when they were apart. 'They eat me up!' she wrote on one occasion, after being separated from them, and, 'My heart was full of joy and gratitude at being with them once more.' Each evening, she prayed with them and listened to their hymns; and she wrote in detail of their health, their progress and amusing things they had said or done. Unlike the Queen, who had no qualms about describing her children as plain, precocious or lazy, Alice wrote only of how pretty, how entertaining, how intelligent, how loving and how good her children were.

Victoria, the eldest and most dominant child, had inherited her mother's inquisitive nature and her grandfather's brilliant intellect. Throughout her life she was renowned for being a great 'chatterbox'; and as a child she was something of a tomboy, who was, in her mother's opinion, rather 'wild'. She was particularly close to her father, with whom she went for a walk before breakfast each morning, with her hands in her pockets, which greatly amused him.

> "Her adoration for Louis is touching," Alice wrote fondly to the Queen. "...She is a very dear little thing and gets on very fast, but equally in all things...She makes a face when she is not pleased and laughs so heartily when she is contented."[176]

Victoria was also inseparable from her younger sister, Ella, who preferred puppies and dolls to Victoria's more physical pursuits and was, according to Baroness Buxhoeveden, 'the personification of kindness'. Ella's interior beauty was matched by her physical appearance and she would soon earn the accolade of being 'the most beautiful princess in Europe.' Queen Victoria, who was ever quick to comment on an attractive face, noted that she was:

> "...sweet, sensible and also very intelligent and most lovely – indeed I rarely saw a more lovely girl and so loving and affectionate and with such charming manners."[177]

Unfortunately, the Queen was equally quick to comment on an unattractive appearance, and was less impressed by Alice's third daughter, Irène, whom she considered 'very plain'. Alice, on the other hand, thought

Irène was 'a pretty child and so very good', and, though she was a little overshadowed by her elder sisters, she was very close to her younger brother, Ernie, with whom she loved to sing and dance.

Of all her children, Alice felt the strongest bond with 'inexpressibly precious' Ernie, who shared her aesthetic passions and would soon become a connoisseur of art.

> "I fancy seldom a mother and child so understood each other, and loved each other as we two do," Alice wrote. "It requires no words; he reads in my eyes as I do what is in his little heart."[178]

Ernie was close, too, to his younger siblings, particularly his only brother, Frittie, with whom, despite his natural 'roughness', he was 'most tender and gentle and not jealous'. Since the country was at war at the time of Frittie's birth, Alice had feared that her exhaustion and work among the wounded could have an adverse effect upon his health, but in the event, he appeared to be perfectly healthy and thriving with 'fine, wide-awake and intelligent' features, and in his early months he thrived.

Before Frittie was two years old, a fourth daughter was born. Named Alix – because as her mother explained, the Hessians 'murdered; the name 'Alice' – she bore a physical resemblance to her elder sister, Ella, and had such a cheerful disposition and smile that she soon earned the family nickname 'Sunny'.

The youngest child, May, shared a birthday with her grandmother, Queen Victoria, who agreed to be her godmother. A 'sweet', 'pretty' and 'enchanting' child, her cheerfulness earned her the name 'Little Sunshine.'

By the time of May's birth, however, tragedy had struck the family and, much as Alice delighted in her sunny disposition, it could never fully alleviate the sorrow which would remain with her to the end of her life.

1873 dawned brightly for Alice, with the prospect of fulfilling a long-cherished dream to indulge her aesthetic passion for art and culture with a tour of Italy. For two months, leaving the children in the care of their father, she sated her senses on the masterpieces of the Renaissance, from Capri to Naples, and from Rome to Sorrento, recording each stage of her trip in her regular epistles to the Queen. The Sistine Chapel was dark, Alice noticed, and the frescoes were damaged by dust and smoke; the paintings of San Clemente were full of expression; the antique monuments were magnificent; and the terraces of the Via Doria Pamfili reminded her of Osborne. Far from the squalor of military base hospitals and Hessian slums, her thirtieth birthday was celebrated in Florence. Palm Sunday was spent in Rome, where Louis joined her to attend the opening of Mass in St. Peter's Basilica, and later they were given an audience with Pope Pius IX in his private apartments. Alongside asking Alice to convey his regards to Queen Victoria and all her family, the aged pontiff told Louis that he strongly opposed Bismarck's treatment of the German Catholics and he hoped that his sentiments would be conveyed to the appropriate quarters.

Returning refreshed to Darmstadt on 2nd May, Alice enjoyed a happy reunion the children, and looked forward to a peaceful summer with her family. It was not to be. Within a few weeks of her return from Italy, an accident occurred which would cast a shadow over the rest of her life.

Alice had long shared her mother's concern for her younger brother, Leopold, whose haemophilia had so blighted his childhood, but, while she regularly asked after Leopold's health, she had no idea that the condition was hereditary or that she might have passed it on to her children.

Haemophilia, which is carried by girls but manifests only in boys, was little understood in the 19th century, and, since Leopold was the only haemophiliac in the family, there was no reason for Alice to suspect that her own son could be similarly afflicted. In the summer of 1871, however, eight-month-old Frittie, became unwell with what Alice simply referred to as 'an illness'. 'I have been so anxious about him,' she told the Queen as he began to recover, and a week later, she remarked that he had had a 'slight return' of the condition.

By August, the colour had returned to his cheeks but over the next eight months Alice observed that he was often covered in bumps and bruises and she recognised the similarity of his symptoms to those of her brother, Leopold. Unwilling to consider the possibility that Frittie, too, was a haemophiliac, she accepted Dr Jenner's recommendation that he should take iron to strengthen his blood, and naively hoped that he would eventually outgrow the condition.

In February 1873, shortly before Alice left for Italy, a slight cut on Frittie's ear bled so profusely that for four days nothing could be done to staunch the flow. This time, Alice could no longer avoid the truth:

> "I own I was much upset when I saw that he had this tendency to bleed," she wrote to the Queen, "and the anxiety for the future, even if he gets well over this, will remain for years to come."[179]

Even then, she reassured herself that the colour in his cheeks was a sign that he had 'good blood and to spare' but, with the example of Leopold before her, she knew only too well that his life would be far from easy.

Four weeks after her return from Italy, while Louis was away inspecting the troops, Alice was lying in bed one morning, working through her papers while her two little boys ran playfully in and out. Eventually, at about eight forty-five, she left the room to call for the children's nurse, momentarily leaving Frittie alone. In that brief absence, he somehow climbed up to the open window and tumbled out onto the terrace below. Alice, returning in time to see him falling through the air, screamed in horror and rushed outside to where he lay on his side, unconscious but without any apparent sign of injury. There were no broken bones or obvious bleeding, but towards evening, the side of his head began to swell and the doctors suspected an internal haemorrhage. An aide was quickly dispatched to tell Louis of the accident, and telegrams flew back and forth between Darmstadt and Balmoral, where a shocked Queen Victoria waited for news. Alice, she was told, was calm and composed, aware of the danger that Frittie was in but clinging to a hope of his recovery.

At first Frittie's breathing was regular and he even managed to move his arm, but as the evening drew on his condition deteriorated and as night fell it was clear that he was dying. Alice, holding him in her arms, could only hope that Louis would return in time to say goodbye. It was a vain hope. At eleven o'clock that night, Frittie's breathing stopped and the doctors pronounced him dead. Alice burst into tears, finding solace only in the knowledge that his passing had been quite painless.

Three days later, little Frittie was laid to rest in a 'quiet spot amid trees and flowers', and, as Alice and Louis tried to come to terms with the shock, there was small comfort in Leopold's assurance that death was a blessing for the little boy who would otherwise have faced a lifetime of suffering. Queen Victoria commissioned a statue of Frittie, which remains to this day at Frogmore, and invited the family to Osborne to recuperate. The doyenne of mourners could not, though, be upstaged in grief, and shortly afterwards she somewhat coldly observed that the loss of a child was as nothing compared to the loss of a husband. Alice could only reply that the experiences were quite different, though equally painful.

Frittie's death had a profound effect upon Alice, and her natural grief was compounded by the thought that, had she not left him for that moment, the accident might have been avoided. Everywhere she saw reminders of him, particularly when she noticed flowers along the roadside, since he had been so fond of flowers; and, as soon as the first snowdrops appeared the following spring, she gathered them to place on his grave. The suddenness of his death reminded her again of the uncertainty of life and the necessity of doing all the good that she could while she still had time, but, while her charitable endeavours and commitment to her other children in no way diminished, in losing little Frittie, she lost much of her former drive and energy.

Seeking comfort, she abandoned her spiritual seeking to return to the security of her childhood faith, resigning herself to 'God's will' without question, and relying on the hope that one day she would see both Frittie and her father again. Her family was delighted by this 'return to the fold' but, with hindsight, her resignation appears to have sprung from deflation and the lack of energy to continue her quest for the truth, rather than from the realisation that her former efforts had been mistaken. Quite simply, she no longer had the will or the strength to go on searching. Ironically, at the same time, she, who had been so keen to shake her mother out of her excessive mourning, now mirrored the very attitude which she had once criticised.

"You understand," she told the Queen, "how long and deep my grief must be," she wrote. "And does not one grow to love one's grief, as having become part of the being one loved – as if through *this* one could still pay a tribute of love to them, to make up for the terrible loss, and missing of not being able to do anything for the beloved anymore?"[180]

Repeatedly in her mind she relived the last day of Frittie's life, torturing herself with thoughts of 'what might have been'. His birthday and the anniversary of his death were commemorated each year, and, in an exact replication of her mother's response to the death of the Duchess of Kent and Prince Albert, Alice now found every joyful occasion clouded by his absence. Even though she delighted in the birth of her youngest child, May, her christening at Jugenheim served only as a reminder that Frittie was no longer with them.

In the same way, too, as her mother had declared that earthly life held no meaning for her in the aftermath of Prince Albert's passing, eighteen months after Frittie's death, Alice wrote mournfully that 'much that was dearest, most precious…is in the grave; part of my heart is there, too.'

In a state of deepening depression, she had little inclination to make new friends, commenting that they could never replace old ones who were 'precious landmarks in the history of one's life'[u]; and suddenly events and places which had brought her pleasure in the past, no longer seemed so attractive. Three years earlier the 'heavenly' sea air, the long beach and the donkey rides at Blankenberghe had been sheer delight but now, as finances prevented the family from holidaying elsewhere, she wrote mournfully that they would have to make do with 'that dreadful Blankenberghe – without tree or bush, nothing but a beach and sand banks'. Music, which had long been her solace, became too painful, and it was weeks after Frittie's death before she could bring herself to play the piano again. Even thoughts of Osborne, which

---

[u] Among the friends she had lost was David Strauss, who had left Darmstadt in 1872 and died in February 1874.

had for so long been a haven for her and to which she would ever long to return, were shaded by the realisation that her childhood companions were no longer there, and even if the place remained the same, she could never relive the happy days of the past.

Throughout her life, Alice had struggled to overcome her tendency to be over-emotional but now the effort was too great.

> "People with strong feelings and of a nervous temperament, for which one is no more responsible than the colour of one's eyes, have things to fight against and to put up with, unknown to those of quiet equable dispositions, who are free from violent emotions and have consequently no feeling of nerves – still less of irritable nerves....One can overcome a great deal but *alter* oneself one cannot."[181]

Disappointed by her marriage, disillusioned by her spiritual seeking, and tired of struggling against her own nature, it was as though Frittie's death had led to a dam burst of all the feelings she had struggled so hard to overcome. The unspoken anguish she felt at the death of her father; the loneliness of realising that she and Louis were incompatible; the stress of financial struggles; and the strain of living through two wars – all were taking their toll, and, just as Prince Albert's repressed emotions had resulted in a myriad of apparently disconnected ailments, so, too, was Alice increasingly afflicted by various debilitating illnesses from which she would never fully recover.

Chapter 20 – How Far From Well I Am

Partial to puddings and pies, Queen Victoria's girth increased with age to the point where the waist of her drawers measured more than fifty inches[v]. At least three of her children shared her propensity to obesity, so it is unsurprising that Alice, who was slim, was frequently described as 'very thin'. This, combined with the Queen's regular references to Alice's health, has given the impression that there was a certain frailty about her, which has often been linked to her childhood episode of scarlet fever.

It must be remembered, though, that it was common practice for members of the Royal Family to comment on one another's appearance and, while for the Queen 'health' was often a euphemism for pregnancy, each minor ailment or the pallor of the skin was noted in letters and journals. Years later, Alice's daughter, Alix, recorded her children's temperatures and even the dates of her daughters' periods in letters to her husband, the Tsar. Alice herself informed the Queen of every childhood illness her children suffered – Ella had a 'violent cough'; Victoria had a cold; Ernie was pale; Irène had chicken pox – and she wrote often of the necessity of taking them to the seaside for its restorative effects.

This apparent obsession with health, which seems to verge on hypochondria, could well be explained by the fact that this was an age in which letter-writing was the sole means of communication, and consequently letters contained all kinds of minute details of everyday life. Moreover, Queen Victoria – herself a prolific letter-writer and avid reader of novels – expected to be kept informed of every incidental detail of her children's experience.

---

[v] Her appearance suggests that she might have been suffering from hypothyroidism, which could account for her obesity.

Far from viewing herself as frail, Alice considered herself to be particularly robust, and, apart from the 'typical family complaints' of rheumatism and colds – which were common at a time when central heating was unheard of, and the damp English climate was compounded by the smog of industrial cities – she commented that being ill was a nuisance since she was so unused to it. She had no misgivings about visiting disease-infected hospitals or having close contact with smallpox and typhus victims, and, until Frittie's death, she never felt so weak as to neglect her duties.

Nonetheless, throughout her married life, Alice had suffered from a number of symptoms which might be considered psychosomatic. In February 1868, while worrying about her brother, Leopold, who had been suffering from a serious haemorrhage, she was afflicted with such agonising neuralgia that she could barely open her eyes for over week.

"I have never felt so unwell, or suffered so much," she told the Queen, before going on to describe the intensity of the pain that affected one side of her head, leaving her so weak that she could not stand without fearing she would faint.

Trigeminal neuralgia, the symptoms of which, as Alice described, closely resemble those of migraine, is a recurrent condition caused by the compression or inflammation of the trigeminal nerve. While the cause of the inflammation remains open to debate, the fact that it is nerve-related is significant in Alice's case, since the Queen and Vicky had both mentioned that Alice was 'suffering from nerves', suggesting a link between the physical condition and the stresses of the recent war, concern for her brother and her unresolved issues around the death of her father.

In 1870, in the midst of the Franco-Prussian War, Alice had a recurrence of the condition, accompanied by an inflammation of her eyes which continued intermittently for several months. This episode was undoubtedly stress-related, coming at a time when she was simultaneously worrying about Louis and her forthcoming confinement, and paying daily visits to the military hospitals, where she sat at the bedside of the dying.

> "Though I have seen so many lately die hard deaths, and heard the grief of many heartbroken widows and mothers," she wrote, "it makes my heart bleed anew in each fresh case, and curse the wickedness of war again and again."[182]

It was almost to be expected that, surrounded by sights and sounds which were so distressing, Alice should suffer a physical reaction to her eyes and ears; and the tension of maintaining a dignified pose, restraining her tears in the midst of such sorrow, would certainly exacerbate the facial nerves which were already prone to inflammation.

When Alice's exhaustion and rheumatism became too much to endure, her faithful Dr Weber and members of the family usually recommended a cure at one of the popular spas, or a recuperative break in the countryside. Sometimes financial restraints and duties made this impossible but, when she could, Alice took the mineral waters at Wiesbaden and the salt waters at Blankenberghe, and escaped to breathe the 'good sea air' at every opportunity.

With Frittie's death, however, Alice seemed to lose the will to fight, and her health began a gradual decline which continued until her death. A simple cold left her feeling 'so weak and done up'; hot weather was oppressive and unbearable; cold weather brought on her rheumatism; and she was constantly tired. Mirroring her father's gradual decline, she thought and wrote often of death. When, in September 1876, her devoted Lady-in-

Waiting, Emily Hardinge, died, her 'tears would not cease'; and a few weeks later she told the Queen:

"I can do next to nothing of late, and must rest such much...Darling Mama, I don't think you know quite how far from well I am."

In the autumn of 1876, she made her annual visit to Balmoral, where, despite her exhaustion, she dragged herself to church to avoid shocking the locals by staying away. Revived by the Scottish air, she journeyed to London where she accompanied the housing reformer, Octavia Hill, through some of the worst slum districts, with a view to applying her ideas to the poorest parts of Hesse-Darmstadt.

Inspired by the visit and refreshed by the holiday, Alice began to feel a little better. The colour had returned to her cheeks, and she was convinced that she would be fully recovered in time for the winter. On returning to Hesse in late autumn, she resumed her spiritual reading, finding comfort once more in the sermons of Frederick William Robertson, and the work of the scholar Max Müller, whose fifteen-year-old daughter had recently died of meningitis, and who expressed so clearly Alice's own views:

"How mankind defers from day to day the best it can do, and the most beautiful things it can enjoy, without thinking that every day may be the last one, and that lost time is lost eternity!"

She was eager, too, to continue her philanthropic activities, visiting the slums of Mayence incognita, arranging to have Octavia Hill's writings translated into German, and watching the progress of her charities. The 'Alice Hospital' was prospering; the 'Alice Union for the Employment of Women' had extended its remit into the education of girls; the orphanage and asylum were functioning; and Alice was seeking ways to provide safe houses and rescue homes for the rehabilitation of prostitutes.

Although Frittie's death still hung like a cloud around her, her health was improving, when suddenly, in the spring of 1877 an event occurred to reopen old wounds and hurl her back into the now-familiar depressive exhaustion.

On 18th March, news reached Louis that his father, Prince Charles, was dangerously ill. He had developed a high fever and his skin had become red and inflamed. Erysipelas ('St Anthony's Fire') was diagnosed – a bacterial infection which affects the skin and lymphatic system, and which, in the days before antibiotics, often proved fatal. Throughout the day, Louis and Alice watched as Prince Charles' face became increasingly swollen, disfiguring his features.

Louis' mother and brothers did not leave his bedside as he drifted out of consciousness, and, though Louis and Alice briefly went home to snatch a few hours' sleep, they returned at dawn the following morning and remained with him for twelve hours until his death at six-thirty that evening.

The next day, when Prince Charles' body had been dressed in his uniform, Alice arranged the flowers around his bed and did all she could to comfort Louis and his mother. Preparations were soon underway for an interment in the Rosenhőhe – the family mausoleum in which Frittie was buried – and Alice was plunged again into the painful recollections of her son.

'My tears will not stop flowing,' she wrote, but, as with the death of her own father, there was little time to wallow in grief. Louis and his mother needed her emotional support and, on a practical level, there were numerous arrangements to make. Prince Charles' unexpected death meant that Louis was now the heir to

234

the seventy-one-year-old Grand Duke, whose views often conflicted with his own, and whose health was already precarious. Tired and lethargic, Alice dreaded the prospect of being forced into the position of Grand Duchess, particularly at a time when her frequent visits to England had made her unpopular and she feared she would not be welcomed by the people.

In the sweltering heat of summer, only three months after Prince Charles' death, Alice and Louis were summoned to Seeheim, where the Grand Duke lay dying. For a few days he fluctuated between deterioration and improvement until the 13th June, when Alice and Louis were urgently recalled to Seeheim, but by the time they arrived, 'Uncle' was already dead.

Now elevated to the position of Grand Duke, Louis set to work, trying to ensure the smooth running of the Grand Duchy but it soon became clear that his predecessor had left his affairs in disarray. With her husband preoccupied with matters of state, it was left to Alice to entertain the royalties who gathered in Darmstadt for the funeral. From Russia came the Tsar's younger brother, Pavel; Alice's brother-in-law, Fritz of Prussia, represented the Kaiser; and Queen Victoria dispatched Lenchen's husband, Christian – all of whom reported how frail and thin the new Grand Duchess appeared.

In the weeks following the funeral, an oppressive heat wave left Alice so exhausted and unwell that she feared she was dying. Even the optimistic Louis was so anxious about her that he urged her to leave Darmstadt for a recuperative holiday, and, despite her desire to support him in his new role, she agreed that her only hope of survival was to travel to the coast where she hoped the sea air would revive her.

In mid-July she arrived in Houlgate in Normandy where she was joined by the children in a small and rather dirty house by the sea. Notwithstanding the poor accommodation and the rainy weather, Alice delighted in the beautiful scenery, and, as she had hoped, regular sea-bathing revived her sufficiently to return Darmstadt in time for Louis' official inauguration on September 8th. The warmth of the crowds and the joyful atmosphere of the occasion exceeded her expectations and, by early autumn, she was ready to undertake her duties as Grand Duchess.

For the first time since her wedding, money was no longer an issue, and she immediately set to work expanding her charities, including new projects for providing adequate housing for the poor. Now, though, alongside her philanthropic works and her continued care of her family, she was expected to receive official guests, hold regular receptions and assist Louis in the day-to-day running of the Grand Duchy. As ever, she threw herself wholeheartedly into her duties but, in little over a month, she was once again exhausted to the point of collapse.

> "I have been doing too much lately," she told the Queen, "…and my nerves are beginning to feel the strain, for sleep and appetite are no longer good. Too much is demanded of one; and I have to do with so many things. It is more than my strength can stand in the long run…"[183]

As the year drew to a close, she surrendered all hope of a complete recovery, and, like her father before her, she sensed that she had not long to live. In December, she declined an invitation to Vicky's eldest daughter's wedding the following February, convinced that she would be too ill to attend; and, looking back at that time some months later, Vicky recalled sadly:

> "How anxious I have felt about her dear health I cannot tell you. It often tormented me to see her so frail, so white, and her nerves so unstrung, though it only added additional charm and grace to her dear person and seemed to envelop her with

something sad and touching that always drew me to her all the more, and made me feel a wish to help her and take care of her, poor dear!"[184]

The year 1878 began quietly for Alice. She maintained her interest in her charities, and her children's upbringing remained of paramount importance for her, but at the age of only thirty-four, she no longer felt capable of participating in social events or shunned public appearances as often as possible. As she had predicted, she did not feel strong enough to travel to Berlin for her niece's wedding but, in the spring, Louis decided to use his recently-acquired wealth to arrange a relaxing tour for the whole family.

Following a pleasant visit to Vicky and Fritz' home in Potsdam, the Hessians embarked on a Baltic cruise with Alice's old friend, Louise of Prussia, and her husband, the Grand Duke of Baden, before travelling on to the south coast of England, where they stayed for a week in a house on the seafront in Eastbourne. In July, they arrived at Windsor Castle, where Queen Victoria was delighted by the 'truly beautiful children', the eldest two of whom were already taller than their mother, but, she noted with consternation: 'dear Alice is looking dreadfully ill, so pale and thin.'[185]

With the Queen's encouragement, the Hessians returned by train to Eastbourne, where they stayed at the Duke of Devonshire's Jacobean house, Compton Place. As the Queen had expected, the sea air soon had a therapeutic effect on Alice, who, between visits to Osborne and Windsor, was able to enjoy excursions with Louis to Brighton, Hastings and St Leonards-on-Sea. Within a few weeks, she felt well enough to lend her support to local fund-raising events. In early August, she presented the prizes at a gala to raise money for local schools; and shortly afterwards attended a bazaar to raise money for a local church. She took her children to visit Sunday Schools and Day Schools; and, while they played on the beach, she toured the poor fishermen's cottages and listened to their stories of life on the sea. The holiday was proving so enjoyable and beneficial, that Alice and Louis decided to postpone their departure for a fortnight, remaining in the town until mid-September.

Although she was still frail, Alice used the opportunity of the stay on the south coast to further her knowledge about her most recent philanthropic interest – the rehabilitation of prostitutes. As with her interest in medicine and mental illness, she was venturing into an area which was largely taboo for women of her station. The vast migration into overcrowded cities over the past century had led to a significant rise in prostitution and, while many respectable men were happy to avail themselves of their services, the prostitutes themselves were treated as outcasts by society. Studies of the time demonstrated that the majority of the women had been driven to their trade by poverty and alcohol, and many had lost respectable positions after being abused by unscrupulous employers. Nonetheless, 'the Great Social Evil' was blamed on the women themselves and, while various religious institutions attempted to provide them with an alternative way of life, they were still viewed with contempt by governments and the majority of the population.

Throughout the 1860s and early 1870s, the plight of prostitutes had been highlighted in Britain by campaigners who sought to repeal the infamous Contagious Diseases Acts. Concerned by the number of soldiers and sailors suffering from venereal disease, the government had passed a series of laws by which women in the vicinity of military of naval bases could be forcibly detained and subjected to a medical examination. Apart from the inherent injustice of violating the human rights of the women while making no provision for similar examinations of their clients, not all of the women detained under the acts were prostitutes, and stories abounded of 'respectable' women being forcibly taken from the street as they went about their legitimate business. Women who were found to be suffering from venereal disease were labelled as 'dangerous', and confined in the so-called Lock Hospitals – a name stemming from the former leprosy hospitals when 'locks' or rags were used as bandages – where they underwent barbaric examinations and were treated more like prisoners than patients.

At the time of Alice's stay in Eastbourne, the 'purity campaigner', Ellice Hopkins had recently published a book entitled *Women's Mission to Women*, in which she described the various missions, providing safe homes for the euphemistically named 'female penitents' of Brighton. In a preface, Alice's long-time correspondent, Florence Nightingale, had 'entreated' the women of England to read the book, since:

"This is the cause, one would think, of every Englishwoman; for to every Englishwoman Home and Family, here imperilled, with or without her knowledge, have a sacred name; the cause of every wife and mother, for the happy wife and mother (as was truly said by one of these) has the strongest reason to do something to help those who have no home and no happiness; the cause of God, who is the Father of the poor outcasts as well as of the happy homes."[186]

Among the institutions mentioned by Ellice Hopkins was the Albion Hill Home, which had been taken over some years earlier by a devout young widow, Mrs Vicars, who had risked ridicule and physical injury during her tours of some of the worst brothels and 'dens' in the town, before agreeing to manage the refuge. Eager to meet her and to learn from her experience, Alice travelled incognita to Brighton to see the:

> "...pretty building...bright and pleasant to look at, set round with its glossy evergreens, and overlooking the valley below...A bright looking home...with no workhouse air about it, though indeed a house of cheerful work – with its warm red brick facings, its high gables and belfry, and its trim plot of garden round."[187]

During a tour of the home, Alice was shown how the institution was organised. No one applying for admission was ever turned away, and, in the event that the house was full, applicants would be boarded in the homes of local Christian women. The day ran to a strict routine, wherein the girls rose between five-thirty and six-thirty, and their days were taken up with acquiring various practical skills, with the option of attending lessons in basic mathematics and literacy. They were free to leave the home whenever they wished, or to remain until a suitable position was found for them, in which case they were given a gift of ten shilling to take to their new employment. By the time of Alice's visit, plans were underway to create a series of cottages within the grounds so that the women could be housed in groups, to make the refuge appear less institutional. Mrs Vicars' commitment and initiative inspired Alice with ideas for establishing similar houses in Hesse – her only objection would surely have been the somewhat overly religious atmosphere of the home – and, after some deliberation, she accepted Mrs Vicars' request that she should become the Patroness of Albion Hill.

Sadly, Alice's patronage would be very brief, for within two months of returning to Darmstadt, tragedy would strike her family, and within three months, Alice herself would be dead.

240

Chapter 21 – Dear Papa!

During the Hessians' stay at Eastbourne, a disaster occurred which, with hindsight, appears to be something of an omen. On a balmy, late-summer evening, the 3rd September 1878, a paddle-steamer, named *Princess Alice,* was returning to London from Gravesend, where the majority of the seven hundred and fifty passengers had enjoyed a day trip to the Rosherville Gardens.

The steamer was nearing Woolwich when it passed through a channel into which over seventy million gallons of raw sewage had been dumped earlier in the day; and, at the same time, a steam collier, the *Bywell Castle,* entered the same stretch of water. Due to a misunderstanding between the captains of the vessels, the *Bywell Castle* steamed directly into the starboard side of *Princess Alice,* cutting the boat in two and plunging all the passengers and crew into the filthy waters. Within four minutes the vessel had sunk and, despite desperate attempts at a rescue, over six hundred people died – many of them poisoned by ingesting the polluted water.

As the inquiry into the disaster continued, Alice and her family returned to Darmstadt, where the therapeutic benefits of the holiday quickly faded. In early November, she wrote to the Queen:

> "I am but very middling, and leading a very quiet life, which is an absolute necessity. It is so depressing to be like this."[188]

Two days later, a contagion entered the New Palace, and Alice's quiet life was thrown into turmoil.

On the evening of 7th November, her eldest daughter, Victoria, was reading *Alice in Wonderland* to her younger sisters when she became hoarse and complained of cold-like symptoms. The following morning, the symptoms were far worse and diphtheria was diagnosed.

One of the great killers of the era, the greatly feared and highly infectious disease, affects the throat and lymph nodes, causing the membranes to swell across the tonsils and, in extreme cases, across the airways, leading to suffocation. Known in Spain as 'the strangler', diphtheria leads to a very painful and unpleasant death, which is horrific to witness. Alongside the asphyxiating membranes, the toxins produced by the infection can lead to kidney, liver and nerve damage in victims whose immune system is already compromised or under-developed, which made it a particularly dangerous illness in children. The symptoms – a headache, sore throat and general malaise – do not usually manifest for five to ten days after the infection has been contracted, and so Alice's decision to isolate Victoria was of little avail. Within four days, her younger sister, Alix, displayed the same symptoms and, by the 13th November, Louis, Iréne and May had been diagnosed with the illness. For their own protection, Ella and Ernie were duly dispatched to their grandmother's home in Bessungen, but hardly had they arrived when Ernie, too, manifested the symptoms and was taken back home.

Alice, already in frail health, was suddenly faced with the stress of nursing her husband and five of her children, all of whom could easily die from the 'dreadful' illness. Night and day, with the help of eight nurses, she cared for them all. Adhering to the doctor's instructions, she refrained from hugging or kissing her patients, and arranged for the nurseries to be fumigated and many of their toys to be burned. Spraying herself regularly with disinfectant, she wore protective clothing when approaching their beds to administer the recommended treatment of a steam inhalation of chlorate of potash (potassium chloride) – a poisonous substance, intended to kill the infection.

Hastily written telegrams flew back and forth between Darmstadt, Berlin and England, where services were held throughout the country to pray for Alice and her family.

By May 15th, Victoria was out of danger, and her youngest sister, May, appeared to be recovering. Shortly after midnight, Alice left May's room to attend to her other patients when suddenly the little girl sat up and choked. Before Alice returned, she had died. Scribbling a pencilled note to Vicky, and dispatching a telegram to her mother, Alice waited until morning before breaking the news to Louis.

"The pain is beyond words," she told the Queen, "but God's will be done."[189]

To prevent the further spread of the contagion, it was necessary for the coffin to be closed and the interment to take place as soon as possible, and so, two days later, the funeral service was carried out within the palace. Since Louis was still too ill to rise from his bed, and Alice deemed it better not to tell her sick children what had happened, she undertook all the arrangements and attended the service alone. When the time came to remove the little coffin from the house, she could hardly bear to look, and, turning away, watched the mournful procession through a mirror.

"Thus do we learn humility," she murmured to a lady-in-waiting.

Keeping the news from her other children, was intensely difficult as she tried to maintain a cheerful appearance. When, almost a week after May's death, her favourite child, Ernie, whose own life still hung in the balance, asked her to give his little sister a book, she could barely restrain her tears.

"It made me almost sick to smile at the dear boy," she told the Queen. "But he must be spared yet awhile what to him will be such sorrow."[190]

On 22nd November, Queen Victoria received Alice's German librarian, Mr Sahl, who had recently arrived from Darmstadt.

> "He spoke with admiration of Alice's courage, calmness & resignation, but said she looked dreadful. He had seen the doctors several times, who said, all the cases were of the severest kind."[191]

The Queen was left in no doubt that if Alice were to contract the disease she would lack the strength to fight it.

By the end of the month, Ernie was out of danger and had begun to recover sufficiently for Alice to tell him the truth about May's death. So distressed was he, that her natural response was to take him in her arms and kiss him – perhaps, thereby contracting the illness herself.

By 6th December, the rest of the family was recovering, and Alice gained some relief from her vigils by taking a short carriage ride. The following afternoon she met her sister-in-law, Marie of Edinburgh, who happened to be passing through Darmstadt, but on Sunday 8th December, she woke with a sore throat and the unmistakable symptoms of diphtheria.

Over the next few days, despite the typical appearance of the membrane across her tonsils, she was able to eat, and gave instructions to the staff for the care of her children as well as asking about the progress of her charities. For five days, her condition, though painful and distressing, remained stable, and the Queen's doctor, William Jenner, who had been hastily dispatched to Darmstadt, held out hope of her eventual recovery.

Friday 13th December marked a turn for worse and, though Alice herself appeared more composed and relaxed, the doctors agreed that she was dying. Throughout that night, attended by her mother-in-law, she gradually drifted into unconsciousness and as the new day dawned – 14th December 1878, seventeen years to the day since the death of her father – she peacefully passed away. Her final words were a murmured,

"Dear Papa!"

The father whom she loved so deeply had come to take her home.

Three days after Alice's death, her body was taken from the New Palace to the Grand Ducal palace, where her closed coffin, covered in wreaths and flowers, was placed on a bier in the Great Hall. From every part of the Grand Duchy, from those who had benefitted from her charities, those who had met her personally, and those whose hearts went out to her grieving children, wreaths and bouquets flooded in until, according to Theodore Martin, the black velvet pall was invisible beneath the array of colour.

The following morning, a solemn crowd watched as her coffin, draped in the British flag, was carried through the silent streets of Darmstadt to the Rosenhöhe mausoleum. Her heartbroken children watched from an upstairs window, and among the mourners below were two of Alice's brothers – Leopold, who had himself been so close to death on so many occasions; and a devastated Bertie, who wrote sadly, 'we had gone through so much together.'

Noticeable for her absence at the funeral was Vicky, whose father-in-law had forbidden her from travelling to Darmstadt in case she should bring the infection back to Berlin.[w] Her grief, though, was intense, as she wrote to her mother:

> "Sweet darling Alice is she really gone? So good, and dear, so much admired. I cannot realise it, it is too awful, too cruel, too terrible."[192]

---

[w]In the event, the precautions proved futile. Within months, the epidemic had spread through Prussia, claiming Vicky's son, eleven-year-old Waldemar, among its victims.

Messages of condolence poured in from around the world, and nowhere was the grief felt more deeply than in Britain, where the people still remembered Alice's selfless devotion to her mother in the days after Prince Albert's death. Flags flew at half-mast across the Empire, public houses were closed, political engagements were cancelled and, as the curtains were drawn in the windows of Buckingham Palace, a bell tolled in Windsor. In his typically flamboyant fashion, Disraeli address the House of Lords:

> "A Princess, who loved us though she left us, and who always revisited her Fatherland with delight – one of those women the brightness of whose being adorns society and inspires the circle in which she lives – has been removed from this world, to the anguish of her family, her friends, and her subjects. The Princess Alice – for I will venture to call her by that name, though she wore a Crown – afforded one of the most striking instances that I can remember of richness of culture and rare intelligence combined with the most pure and refined domestic sentiments."[193]

But it was the Queen herself who paid Alice the compliment which she would have most appreciated:

> "She had darling Papa's nature, and much of his self-sacrificing character and fearlessness and entire devotion to duty!"[194]

Nothing would have pleased Alice more than being compared to 'dear Papa.'

Epilogue

For all their past disagreements, Queen Victoria was deeply affected by Alice's premature death, and her heart went out to her daughter's bereaved husband and children.

Louis, she decided would need help to raise his growing daughters, and her thoughts turned quickly to her own youngest daughter, Beatrice, who, she hoped would make an excellent replacement for Alice. Since neither Louis nor Beatrice was attracted to the other, and Beatrice was a mere six years older than her eldest Hessian niece, it was fortunate for them both that – to Queen Victoria's disgruntlement – the Church of England prohibited marriages between brothers- and sisters-in-law. In time, Louis consoled himself with instead with a Polish mistress, Alexandrine de Kolomine, whom, to the horror of his extended family, he surreptitiously married in 1884. Suspecting that the unsuitable Mme Kolomine was a gold-digger, Queen Victoria hastily enlisted the Prince of Wales to arrange an immediate annulment. Louis raised few objections and remained single to the end of his life. He died following a stroke, at the age of fifty-four in the spring of 1892.

On the same day as her father contracted his secret marriage, Alice's eldest daughter, Victoria, married the dashing Prince Louis of Battenberg, a son of her father's uncle, Prince Alexander of Hesse. Victoria would go on to become the grandmother of the present Duke of Edinburgh, husband of Queen Elizabeth II. She died in 1950 at the age of eighty-seven.

Two months after Victoria's wedding, her younger sister, Ella, having already rejected a proposal from her cousin, the future Kaiser Wilhelm II of Germany, married Grand Duke Serge Alexandrovich, a younger brother of Tsar Alexander III of Russia. Following her husband's assassination in 1905, Ella devoted her life to the care of the poor and sick, becoming the Abbess of a religious order which she founded in Moscow. Despite her saintly reputation, she was murdered by the Bolsheviks in 1918 and was subsequently canonised by the Russian Orthodox Church.

In 1888, Alice's third daughter, Irène, married her cousin, Henry of Prussia – the second son of 'Aunt Vicky'. Unfortunately, she had inherited the haemophilia gene and passed it on to two of her three sons, the youngest of whom died of the illness aged only four. Following the collapse of the German monarchy in 1918, Irène and Henry retired to their estate in Hemmelmarck, where Irène died at the age of eighty-seven in 1953, having outlived her husband, two of her sons and all of her siblings.

In 1892, Ernie succeeded his father as Grand Duke of Hesse and, two years later, through the machinations of Queen Victoria, married his cousin, Victoria Melita, daughter of the Duke of Edinburgh and Coburg. It was an unhappy marriage which ended in divorce following accusations of Ernie's homosexuality and the tragic death of the couple's only daughter, Elizabeth. In 1905, Ernie married Princess Eleanore of Solms-Hohensolms-Lich with whom he had two sons. Renowned as a patron of the arts, Ernie was horrified by the outbreak of the First World War but served in the headquarters of his cousin, Kaiser Wilhelm II. During the German Revolution of 1918, he refused to abdicate but, nonetheless, lost his title and authority. He died in the family's country schloss at Wolfsgarten in 1937.

While attending Ella's wedding in 1884, Alix met and fell in love with the Tsarevich Nicholas. Due to objections from both families, and Alix's scruples about having to convert to Orthodoxy, ten years passed before the couple were married, by which time Nicholas had inherited the throne. Tragically, Alix, too, had inherited the haemophilia gene and her only son, Alexei, suffered from the condition. Despite her deep love for Nicholas and her desire to do all she could to serve the Russian people, Alix was never fully accepted by the aristocracy, and, during the First World War, she and her elder sister, Ella, were falsely accused of being German spies. In the midst of the Russian Revolution, she and all her family were murdered by the Bolsheviks.

Alice's legacy, however, lived on through the hospitals founded in her honour, her charities, and the lives of her children who inherited her dedication to duty and her desire to serve the poor and the sick. As for Alice herself, as the first anniversary of her father's death approached, she had comforted herself and her mother with the belief that they would meet again 'in another home'. It would appear that, as she breathed her last breath, her father had come to take her to that home, where, she had always believed, she would be reunited with her children, Frittie and May, and with 'beloved Papa', Prince Albert, whom she had always loved so deeply.

By the same author:

Queen Victoria's Granddaughters 1860-1918

Most Beautiful Princess – A Novel Based on the Life of Grand Duchess Elizabeth of Russia

Shattered Crowns: The Scapegoats

Shattered Crowns: The Sacrifice

Shattered Crowns: The Betrayal

The Fields Laid Waste

The Counting House

Wonderful Walter

Notes

[1] Grey, Lieutenant-General, the Hon. C. *The Early Years of His Royal Highness, the Prince Consort*

[2] Martin, Theodore *The Life of the Prince Consort Vol 1* (D. Appleton & Co. 1875)

[3] Grey, Lieutenant-General, the Hon. C. *The Early Years of His Royal Highness, the Prince Consort*

[4] ibid

[5] Stockmar, Baron E. von, *Memoirs of Baron Stockmar Vol II* (Longman's, Green and Co. 1873)

[6] Stockmar, Baron E. von, *Memoirs of Baron Stockmar Vol II* (Longman's, Green and Co. 1873)

[7] Lancefield, Richard T. *Sixty Years a Queen* (G.M. Rose & Sons 1897)

[8] Garrett Fawcett, Millicent *Life of Her Majesty Queen Victoria* (Roberts Brothers 1895)

[9] Benson, Arthur Christopher, & Esher, Viscount (Edited by) *The Letters of Queen Victoria, Vol. II* (John Murray 1907) Memorandum by the Prince Albert 3rd March 1850

[10] Gordon Browne E. *Queen Victoria* (George G. Harrap & Company 1915)

[11] Benson, Arthur Christopher, & Esher, Viscount (Edited by) *The Letters of Queen Victoria, Vol. II* (John Murray 1907) Letter of Queen Victoria to the King of the Belgians 16th May 1843

[12] Benson, Arthur Christopher, & Esher, Viscount (Edited by) *The Letters of Queen Victoria, Vol. II* (John Murray 1907) Letter of Queen Victoria to the King of the Belgians, June 6th 1843

[13] Lyttelton, Baroness *Letters from Sarah, Lady Lyttelton* 1797-1870 (Spottiswoode & Co. 1873)

[14] Rusk, Rev. John *The Beautiful Life & Illustrious Reign of Queen Victoria* (Boland 1901)

[15] Stockmar, Baron von E. *Memoirs of Baron Stockmar Vol 2* (Longmans, Green & Co. 1897)

[16] Benson, Arthur Christopher, & Esher, Viscount (Edited by) *The Letters of Queen Victoria, Vol. II* (John Murray 1907) Letter of Queen Victoria to the King of the Belgians 4th June 1844

[17] ibid

[18] Lyttelton, Baroness *Letters from Sarah, Lady Lyttelton* 1797-1870 (Spottiswoode & Co. 1873)

[19] Benson, Arthur Christopher, & Esher, Viscount (Edited by) *The Letters of Queen Victoria, Vol. II* (John Murray 1907) Letter of Queen Victoria to Viscount Melbourne 3rd April 1845

[20] Lyttelton, Baroness *Letters from Sarah, Lady Lyttelton* 1797-1870 (Spottiswoode & Co. 1873)

[21] Ball, T. Frederick *Queen Victoria, Scenes and Incidents of Her Life and Reign* (Watson 1888)

[22] Garrett Fawcett, Millicent *Life of Her Majesty Queen Victoria* (Roberts Brothers 1895)

[23] *Marie, Queen of Roumania The Story of My Life* (Saturday Post 1931)

[24] Morris, Charles *The Life of Queen Victoria & The Story of Her Reign* (1901)

[25] Ball, T. Frederick *Queen Victoria, Scenes and Incidents of Her Life and Reign* (Watson 1888)

[26] Martin, Theodore *The Life of the Prince Consort* (D. Appleton & Co. 1877)

[27] Lyttelton, Baroness *Letters from Sarah, Lady Lyttelton* 1797-1870 (Spottiswoode & Co. 1873)

[28] Lyttelton, Baroness *Letters from Sarah, Lady Lyttelton* 1797-1870 (Spottiswoode & Co. 1873)

[29] Helena Victoria, Princess (editor) *Alice Grand Duchess of Hesse, Biographical Sketch and Letters* (John Murray 1884) ibid

[30] Lyttelton, Baroness *Letters from Sarah, Lady Lyttelton* 1797-1870 (Spottiswoode & Co. 1873)

[31] Louise, Duchess of Baden quoted in: Helena Victoria, Princess (editor) *Alice Grand Duchess of Hesse, Biographical Sketch and Letters* (John Murray 1884)

[32] Fulford, Roger (Editor) *Dearest Child – Letters Between Queen Victoria & The Princess Royal 1858-1861* (Evans Bros 1964)

[33] Knight, Alfred E. *Victoria, Her Life and Reign* (S.W. Partridge & Co. 1896)

[34] Packard, Jerrold *Victoria's Daughters*

[35] Helena Victoria, Princess (editor) *Alice Grand Duchess of Hesse, Biographical Sketch and Letters* (John Murray 1884)

[36] Hansard 17th December 1878

[37] Helena Victoria, Princess (editor) *Alice Grand Duchess of Hesse, Biographical Sketch and Letters* (John Murray 1884)

[38] Gordon Browne E. *Queen Victoria* (George G Harrap & Co 1915)

[39] ibid

[40] Benson, Arthur Christopher, & Esher, Viscount (Edited by) *The Letters of Queen Victoria, Vol. II* (John Murray 1907) Letter of Queen Victoria to the King of the Belgians 3rd May 1851

[41] Helena Victoria, Princess (editor) *Alice Grand Duchess of Hesse, Biographical Sketch and Letters* (John Murray 1884)

[42] Benson, Arthur Christopher, & Esher, Viscount (Edited by) *The Letters of Queen Victoria, Vol. II* (John Murray 1907) Letter of Queen Victoria to the King of the Belgians 2nd July 1850

[43] Jerrold, Clare *The Married Life of Queen Victoria* (G. Bell & Sons Ltd. 1913)

[44] Benson, Arthur Christopher, & Esher, Viscount (Edited by) The Letters of Queen Victoria, Vol. II (John Murray 1907)

[45] Benson, Arthur Christopher, & Esher, Viscount (Edited by) The Letters of Queen Victoria, Vol. II (John Murray 1907) Letter of Prince Albert to Lord John Russell 10th April 1848

[46] Parton, James *Eminent Women of the Age* (1868)

[47] Cook Edward Tyas *The Life of Florence Nightingale* (Macmillan & Co. 1913)

[48] Holmes, Richard R. Queen Victoria (Boussod, Valadon & Co. 1897)

[49] Benson, Arthur Christopher, & Esher, Viscount (Edited by) *The Letters of Queen Victoria, Vol. III* (John Murray 1907) Letter of Queen Victoria to Miss Nightingale January 1856

[50] Helena Victoria, Princess (editor) *Alice Grand Duchess of Hesse, Biographical Sketch and Letters* (John Murray 1884)

[51] Author unknown: *The Empress Frederick A Memoir* (Dodd, Mead & Company 1913)

[52] ibid

[53] ibid

[54] ibid

[55] Martin, Theodore *The Life of the Prince Consort* (D. Appleton & Co. 1877)

[56] ibid

[57] Fulford, Roger (Editor) *Dearest Child, Letters between Queen Victoria & the Princess Royal 1858-1861* (Evans Brothers 1964)

[58] ibid

[59] ibid

[60] Tytler, Sarah *The Life of Her Most Gracious Majesty the Queen Vol 2* (G. Virtue.

1885)

[61] Fulford, Roger (Editor) *Dearest Child, Letters between Queen Victoria & the Princess Royal 1858-1861* (Evans Brothers 1964)

[62] Gordon Browne E. *Queen Victoria* (George G Harrap & Co 1915)

[63] Benson, Arthur Christopher, & Esher, Viscount (Edited by) *The Letters of Queen Victoria, Vol. II* (John Murray 1907) Letter of Queen Victoria to the Duchess of Gloucester 12th December 1850

[64] Fulford, Roger (Editor) *Dearest Child, Letters between Queen Victoria & the Princess Royal 1858-1861* (Evans Brothers 1964)

[65] ibid

[66] Martin, Theodore *The Life of the Prince Consort* (D. Appleton & Co. 1877)

[67] ibid

[68] Fulford, Roger (Editor) *Dearest Child, Letters between Queen Victoria & the Princess Royal 1858-1861* (Evans Brothers 1964)

[69] ibid

[70] Fulford, Roger (Editor) *Dearest Child, Letters between Queen Victoria & the Princess Royal 1858-1861* (Evans Brothers 1964)

[71] ibid

[72] Martin, Theodore *The Life of the Prince Consort Vol 5* (D. Appleton & Co. 1880)

[73] Benson, Arthur Christopher, & Esher, Viscount (Edited by) *The Letters of Queen Victoria, Vol. III* (John Murray 1907) Letter from Queen Victoria to the King of the Belgians 25th April 1860

[74] Fulford, Roger (Editor) *Dearest Child, Letters between Queen Victoria & the Princess Royal 1858-1861* (Evans Brothers 1964)

[75] ibid

[76] Martin, Theodore *The Life of the Prince Consort Vol 5* (D. Appleton & Co. 1880)

[77] Bennet, Daphne *King Without A Crown* (William Heinemann Ltd. 1977)

[78] Fulford, Roger (Editor) *Dearest Child, Letters between Queen Victoria & the Princess Royal 1858-1861* (Evans Brothers 1964)

[79] Benson, Arthur Christopher, & Esher, Viscount (Edited by) *The Letters of Queen Victoria, Vol. III* (John Murray 1907) Letter from Queen Victoria to the King of the Belgians 31st July 1860

[80] Martin, Theodore *The Life of the Prince Consort Vol 5* (D. Appleton & Co. 1880)

[81] ibid

[82] Fulford, Roger (Editor) *Dearest Child, Letters between Queen Victoria & the Princess Royal 1858-1861* (Evans Brothers 1964)

[83] ibid

[84] Martin, Theodore *The Life of the Prince Consort Vol 5* (D. Appleton & Co. 1880)

[85] ibid

[86] Ball, T. Frederick *Queen Victoria, Scenes and Incidents of Her Life and Reign* (Watson 1888)

[87] Martin, Theodore *The Life of the Prince Consort Vol 4* (D. Appleton & Co. 1880)

[88] Fulford, Roger (Editor) *Dearest Child, Letters between Queen Victoria & the Princess Royal 1858-1861* (Evans Brothers 1964)

[89] Martin, Theodore *The Life of the Prince Consort Vol 5* (D. Appleton & Co. 1880)

[90] Martin, Theodore *The Life of the Prince Consort Vol 5* (D. Appleton & Co. 1880)

[91] Ball, T. Frederick *Queen Victoria, Scenes and Incidents of Her Life and Reign* (Watson 1888)

[92] Hansard 3rd May 1861

[93] Helena Victoria, Princess (editor) *Alice Grand Duchess of Hesse, Biographical Sketch and Letters* (John Murray 1884)

[94] Fulford, Roger (Editor) *Dearest Child, Letters between Queen Victoria & the Princess Royal 1858-1861* (Evans Brothers 1964)

[95] Martin, Theodore *The Life of the Prince Consort Vol 5* (D. Appleton & Co. 1880)
[96] Fulford, Roger (Editor) *Dearest Child, Letters between Queen Victoria & the Princess Royal 1858-1861* (Evans Brothers 1964)
[97] Martin, Theodore *The Life of the Prince Consort Vol 5* (D. Appleton & Co. 1880)
[98] Fulford, Roger (Editor) *Dearest Child, Letters between Queen Victoria & the Princess Royal 1858-1861* (Evans Brothers 1964)
[99] ibid
[100] ibid
[101] Martin, Theodore *The Life of the Prince Consort Vol 5* (D. Appleton & Co. 1880)
[102] Benson, Arthur Christopher, & Esher, Viscount (Edited by) *The Letters of Queen Victoria, Vol. III* (John Murray 1907) Letter from Queen Victoria to the King of the Belgians 11th December 1861
[103] Morris, Charles & Halstead, Morat *Life and reign of Queen Victoria including the lives of King Edward VII and Queen Alexandra* (1901)
[104] Benson, Arthur Christopher, & Esher, Viscount (Edited by) *The Letters of Queen Victoria, Vol. III* (John Murray 1907) Letter from Queen Victoria to the King of the Belgians 24th December 1861
[105] Argyll, John Douglas Sutherland Campbell, Duke of *The Life of Queen Victoria* (George Bell & Sons 1909)
[106] Helena Victoria, Princess (editor) *Alice Grand Duchess of Hesse, Biographical Sketch and Letters* (John Murray 1884)
[107] ibid
[108] ibid
[109] Knightley, Lady Louisa *The Journals of Lady Knightley of Fawsley 1856-1884* (John Murray 1924)
[110] RA VIC/MAIN/QVJ 12 July 1862 (Princess Beatrice's copies). Retrieved July 4th 2013
[111] Helena Victoria, Princess (editor) *Alice Grand Duchess of Hesse, Biographical Sketch and Letters* (John Murray 1884)
[112] ibid
[113] ibid
[114] Fulford, Roger (Editor) *Dearest Child, Letters between Queen Victoria & the Princess Royal 1858-1861* (Evans Brothers 1964)
[115] Knightley, Lady Louisa *The Journals of Lady Knightley of Fawsley 1856-1884* (John Murray 1924)
[116] Helena Victoria, Princess (editor) *Alice Grand Duchess of Hesse, Biographical Sketch and Letters* (John Murray 1884)
[117] ibid
[118] Argyll, John Douglas Sutherland Campbell, Duke of *The Life of Queen Victoria* (George Bell & Sons 1909)
[119] ibid
[120] Dickens, Charles *Martin Chuzzlewit* (1843)
[121] Helena Victoria, Princess (editor) *Alice Grand Duchess of Hesse, Biographical Sketch and Letters* (John Murray 1884)
[122] ibid
[123] ibid
[124] ibid
[125] ibid
[126] ibid
[127] Ponsonby, Frederick (editor) *The Letters of the Empress Frederick* (Macmillan & Co. 1928)
[128] ibid
[129] Helena Victoria, Princess (editor) *Alice Grand Duchess of Hesse, Biographical*

Sketch and Letters (John Murray 1884)
[130] Ponsonby, Frederick (editor) *The Letters of the Empress Frederick* (Macmillan & Co. 1928)
[131] Bolitho, Hector *The Reign of Queen Victoria* (Macmillan 1948)
[132] Helena Victoria, Princess (editor) *Alice Grand Duchess of Hesse, Biographical Sketch and Letters* (John Murray 1884)
[133] ibid
[134] Fulford, Roger (editor) *Your Dear Letter: Private Correspondence of Queen Victoria and the Crown Princess of Prussia 1865-1871* (Evans Bros. 1971)
[135] ibid
[136] ibid
[137] ibid
[138] Ball, T. Frederick *Queen Victoria, Scenes and Incidents of Her Life and Reign* (Watson 1888)
[139] Holmes, Richard R. *Queen Victoria* (Boussod, Valadon & Co. 1897)
[140] Helena Victoria, Princess (editor) *Alice Grand Duchess of Hesse, Biographical Sketch and Letters* (John Murray 1884)
[141] Fulford, Roger (editor) Your Dear Letter: Private Correspondence of Queen Victoria and the Crown Princess of Prussia 1865-1871 (Evans Bros. 1971)
[142] ibid
[143] ibid
[144] ibid
[145] ibid
[146] Helena Victoria, Princess (editor) *Alice Grand Duchess of Hesse, Biographical Sketch and Letters* (John Murray 1884)
[147] ibid
[148] ibid
[149] ibid
[150] ibid
[151] ibid
[152] ibid
[153] ibid
[154] ibid
[155] Paléologuc, Maurice *An Ambassador's Memoirs* (!923)
[156] Fulford, Roger (editor) *Your Dear Letter: Private Correspondence of Queen Victoria and the Crown Princess of Prussia 1865-1871* (Evans Bros. 1971)
[157] Helena Victoria, Princess (editor) *Alice Grand Duchess of Hesse, Biographical Sketch and Letters* (John Murray 1884)
[158] ibid
[159] Ponsonby, Frederick (editor) *The Letters of the Empress Frederick* (Macmillan & Co. 1928)
[160] *Alice, Grand Duchess of Hesse, Biographical Sketch and Letters* (John Murray 1884)
[161] ibid
[162] Ponsonby, Frederick (editor) *The Letters of the Empress Frederick* (Macmillan & Co. 1928)
[163] Helena Victoria, Princess (editor) *Alice Grand Duchess of Hesse, Biographical Sketch and Letters* (John Murray 1884)
[164] ibid
[165] *The Ladies' Repository* (1871)
[166] Helena Victoria, Princess (editor) *Alice Grand Duchess of Hesse, Biographical Sketch and Letters* (John Murray 1884)
[167] Pankhurst, Emmeline *My Own Story* (1914)

[168] ibid

[169] Helena Victoria, Princess (editor) *Alice Grand Duchess of Hesse, Biographical Sketch and Letters* (John Murray 1884)

[170] Bronte, Charlotte *Jane Eyre* (Smith, Elder & Co. 1847)

[171] Helena Victoria, Princess (editor) *Alice Grand Duchess of Hesse, Biographical Sketch and Letters* (John Murray 1884)

[172] Buxhoeveden, Baroness Sophie *The Life and Tragedy of Alexandra Feodorovna* (1928)

[173] ibid

[174] Helena Victoria, Princess (editor) Alice Grand Duchess of Hesse, Biographical Sketch and Letters (John Murray 1884)

[175] ibid

[176] ibid

[177] Fulford, Roger (editor) *Beloved Mama; Private Correspondence of Queen Victoria and the Crown Princess of Prussia, 1878-85* (Evans & Co. 1981)

[178] Helena Victoria, Princess (editor) Alice Grand Duchess of Hesse, Biographical Sketch and Letters (John Murray 1884)

[179] ibid

[180] ibid

[181] ibid

[182] ibid

[183] ibid

[184] Ponsonby, Frederick (editor) *The Letters of the Empress Frederick* (Macmillan & Co. 1928)

[185] RA VIC/MAIN/QVJ 16 August 1878 (Princess Beatrice's copies). Retrieved 24 July 2013

[186] Hopkins, Ellice *Women's Mission to Women* (1878)

[187] ibid

[188] Helena Victoria, Princess (editor) *Alice Grand Duchess of Hesse, Biographical Sketch and Letters* (John Murray 1884)

[189] ibid

[190] ibid

[191] RA VIC/MAIN/QVJ 22 November 1878 (Princess Beatrice's copies). Retrieved August 2nd 2013

[192] Ponsonby, Frederick (editor) *The Letters of the Empress Frederick* (Macmillan & Co. 1928)

[193] Hansard December 1878

[194] Fulford, Roger (editor) *Beloved Mama* (Evans 1981)